ESI™
INTERNATIONAL
an **informa** business

CBAP®EXAM

PRACTICE TEST AND STUDY GUIDE

SECOND EDITION

Glenn R. Brûlé, CBAP, CSM • ESI International • Arlington, Virginia

Published by

ESI International
901 North Glebe Road, Suite 200
Arlington, Virginia 22203

First Edition 2009
Second Edition 2011

Printed in the United States of America

ISBN 978-1-890367-54-1

CONTENTS

CONTENTS

ILLUSTRATIONS

FIGURES

TABLES

PREFACE

Since the launch of the Certified Business Analysis Professional™ (CBAP®) certification exam in November 2006, there has been a great deal of angst and questions throughout the business analysis community about the exam. With the profession only recently gaining its deserved recognition and International Institute of Business Analysis (IIBA®) only eight years new, the development and formalization of the profession is a new endeavor. In developing this guide, our goal at ESI International was to help the industry professional prepare for this challenging and exciting opportunity.

ESI paid careful attention to the development of this publication to ensure that (1) you are able to validate your knowledge and experience, (2) you orient and familiarize yourself with phrases and terminology, as well as question composition and rationale, and (3) the practice tests provide you with an opportunity for focused study and preparation for the exam that otherwise might prove to be overwhelming, considering the vast potential of extraneous resources available.

In alignment with policies outlined in IIBA's *Certified Business Analyst Handbook* (2011), this guide contains study hints, a list of exam topics, and multiple-choice questions for each of the six knowledge areas covered in the CBAP® exam. We have prepared 40 practice questions in each of these six areas. We also have included two 150-question representative practice tests with new questions. Many of our questions are scenario based, as are many on the CBAP® exam. We have purposely limited the number of definition-type questions, because they are not reflective of the work of business analysis.

As we did in the first edition of this study guide, as well as in our *PMP® Exam: Practice Test and Study Guide* and our *PgMP® Exam: Practice Test and Study Guide*, we have included a plainly written rationale for each correct answer along with a supporting reference list. References are provided at the end of this study guide for the six knowledge areas covered in the exam: Business Analysis Planning and Monitoring; Elicitation; Requirements Management and Communication; Enterprise Analysis; Requirements Analysis; and Solution Assessment and Validation.

Earning the CBAP® certification is a prestigious accomplishment. But studying for it should not be difficult when you use the tools available.

Good luck on the exam and in all future endeavors that the results may bring to you!

Glenn R. Brûlé
Courtice, Ontario, Canada

Certified Business Analysis Professional is a trademark owned by International Institute of Business Analysis.

CBAP is a registered certification mark owned by International Institute of Business Analysis.

PMP and PgMP are certification marks of the Project Management Institute, Inc., which are registered in the United States and other nations.

ABOUT THE AUTHOR

Glenn R. Brûlé, CBAP, CSM, Executive Director of Global Client Solutions at ESI International, brings more than two decades of focused business analysis experience to ESI client engagements. As an ESI subject matter expert, Mr. Brûlé works directly with clients to build and mature their business analysis capabilities by drawing from the broad range of learning resources that ESI offers.

A recognized expert in the creation and maturity of Business Analysis Centers of Excellence, Mr. Brûlé has helped numerous clients in the energy, financial services, manufacturing, pharmaceutical, insurance and automotive industries, as well as in government agencies across the world. His approach to maturing requirements management and development capabilities focuses on short-term reductions in costs, resources, and time to market, while at the same time also charting a path to long-term change that drives organizations competitively forward.

His extensive travels to speak at conferences, work with clients, and help build local chapters of International Institute of Business Analysis (IIBA®) affords Mr. Brûlé a rare global viewpoint on the state of business analysis (BA). Recent travels have brought him to six continents where he has addressed more than 10,000 business leaders. This on-the-ground experience provides ESI clients with a reality-based perspective of business analysis in diverse regions around the world and the proven guidance on how to overcome geographic, cultural, and language barriers.

In 2009, Mr. Brûlé published his first two books, the *CBAP® Exam: Practice Test and Study Guide* and *Business Analysis Terms: A Working Glossary*. He is also a regular contributor to Modern Analyst and BA Times, as well as other industry publications.

As a founding board member of IIBA® and former Vice President of Chapters, Mr. Brûlé fosters the advancement of the business analysis profession globally. His personal commitment and involvement has resulted in the founding of chapters in more than a dozen countries in the Americas, Europe, and Asia.

Prior to joining ESI in 2006, Mr. Brûlé was Director of Business Development and Learning Strategy with Nexient Learning. He attended Carleton University in Ottawa, Ontario.

Contributing Authors

Charles "Chip" Schwartz, CBAP, PMP, an instructor with ESI International, Inc., has more than 20 years of practical project management experience. He is the founder of Coresoft, LLC, a Maryland-based training and consulting practice. He works with organizations on project management, business analysis, leadership, communication skills, team building, group dynamics, strategic planning, process reengineering, iterative development, and effective organizational change.

Mr. Schwartz has extensive experience in all aspects of management, business analysis, leadership, business consulting, and education. His work with Coresoft involves both government and private organizations. Specializing in managing IT projects, team development, leadership, and process engineering, he has earned a reputation for dynamic classroom excellence.

Before he founded Coresoft in 2002, Mr. Schwartz led a successful career in the high-technology/aerospace sector with particular emphasis on software development. He led teams ranging in size from three to more than 250 members. He also served as a project manager and as a regional director of a highly successful consulting firm.

Mr. Schwartz holds a bachelor's degree from Central Michigan University and an master's degree from the University of Southern California. He is certified as a Project Management Professional (PMP®) by the Project Management Institute (PMI®) and is a Certified Business Analysis Professional™ (CBAP®) by International Institute of Business Analysis (IIBA®).

Nancy Y. Nee, CBAP, PMP, CSM, has more than 15 years of experience in the consulting industry, specializing in management consulting, project management, business analysis, information technology, continuous process improvement, and organizational change management for the private, public, and non-profit sectors. She has held positions at the management level, as an individual contributor, and as an educator.

Ms. Nee is skilled in aligning and defining the strategic enterprise architecture, developing project governance and selection frameworks, analyzing business processes to apply knowledge to improve organizational efficiency, and implementing automated solutions. She has provided project management and business analysis training and consulting services globally on project management and business analysis principles and practices to numerous Fortune 500 companies.

PMI is a service and trademark of the Project Management Institute, Inc., which is registered in the United States and other nations.

In addition to Ms. Nee's practitioner experience, she has been a speaker at professional association meetings and conferences around the world, including PMI® Global Congress, ProjectWorld/World Congress for Business Analysts and numerous IIBA® and PMI® events.

As ESI International's Executive Director of Product Strategy, Ms. Nee's primary role is to provide thought leadership in the field of project management and business analysis while incorporating the industry's best practices and professional advances into ESI's portfolio of project management and business analysis courses and services. She is a member of numerous professional associations, including the Project Management Institute (PMI®), International Institute of Business Analysis (IIBA®), and the Scrum Alliance. She is certified as a Project Management Professional (PMP®) from PMI®, a Certified Business Analysis Professional™ (CBAP®) from (IIBA®), and a Certified Scrum Master from the Scrum Alliance.

Mark Monteleone, CBAP, PMP, who contributed to the first edition of the *CBAP® Exam: Practice Test and Study Guide* (2009), has more than 30 years' experience in developing business application systems and managing infrastructure projects for the telecommunications, manufacturing, and oil industries. He is skilled in analyzing business processes to apply knowledge, improve organizational efficiency, and implement automated solutions. Mr. Monteleone holds a bachelor's degree in physics and a master's degree in computing science from Texas A&M University. He also has an Advanced Master's Certificate in Project Management and a business analyst certification (CBA®) from The George Washington University. He is a Certified Business Analysis Professional™ (CBAP®) and a certified Project Management Professional (PMP®).

ABOUT ESI

ESI International helps people around the world improve the way they manage projects, contracts, requirements and vendors through innovative learning. We specialize in programs for technical and specialized professionals in the areas of:

- ❖ Business Analysis
- ❖ Project Management
- ❖ Program Management
- ❖ Contract and Vendor Management
- ❖ Business Skills

In addition to thousands of instructor-led courses presented in-person and online each year, ESI delivers its learning through a broad range of modalities, from executive workshops to the latest micro-learning techniques. Our learning products and services are complemented by benchmarking, assessment and learning adoption support as well as consulting services. These products and services come together under ESI's Impact Model to ensure every program achieves its goals.

ESI's academic partner, The George Washington University (GW) in Washington, DC, provides additional assurance that our courses meet the highest standard of academic excellence. Through GW, ESI offers a range of certificate programs that serve as a recognized credential that enhances professional and organizational credibility.

Many of the world's best-known brands, as well as government agencies from the United States to Singapore, benefit from ESI's products and services. These clients represent a range of industries, including energy, information technology, telecommunications, financial services, manufacturing, healthcare, construction, and engineering, as well as civilian and defense government agencies.

ESI's programs have benefited more than one million professionals worldwide since 1981.

ESI has been involved with International Institute of Business Analysis (IIBA®) since its inception. We are a Founding Sponsor and an Endorsed Education Provider (EEP™).

Call ESI toll free at **+1 (888) ESI-8884** for a course catalog, or visit our website at **www.esi-intl.com** for more information.

ACKNOWLEDGMENTS

Conceiving and writing this book has indeed been a very challenging journey—without the support of a large circle of friends and colleagues I may not have seen the light at the end of the tunnel. Together, they have no doubt been my guiding light, and in their own way, they have been major contributors not only to this book but also toward the recognition of the Business Analysis profession.

Seven years ago, Bill Raspberry and Mona Mitchell took a chance on me and introduced me to ESI International, where we formally launched the Business Analysis program into the United States. For that I am ever grateful.

Four short years later, I formally joined the ESI family under the guidance and direction of J. LeRoy Ward, Executive Vice President of ESI International. As my coach, guide, and mentor, LeRoy challenged me to take on this project. His experience with writing exam preparation guides, plus his encouragement, understanding, and commitment to the success of this project, were truly inspiring.

Charles "Chip" Schwartz, CBAP— friend and colleague—was instrumental in assuring that the quality, integrity, and precision of all questions were as close to the CBAP® exam as possible. His commitment to the development of the profession has constantly challenged me to validate my findings.

It is with great appreciation that I acknowledge the tireless efforts of Nancy Y. Nee, CBAP, CSM, PMP. Not only did her great attention to detail facilitate the development of the first edition of this *CBAP® Exam: Practice Test and Study Guide*, but she has also contributed her business analysis expertise and personal insight into the knowledge areas and questions for this second edition.

Despite all the challenges and roadblocks that Myron Taylor, former Director of Production and Publications, faced, he has persevered and made certain that what I wrote was clear, concise, and communicated expertly. His keen eye for and attention to both editorial and production management details are held in high regard by myself and all of his colleagues. It is also with great appreciation that I acknowledge the contributions of ESI staff members Katie Wise for her superb layout and Jonathan Hurtarte for his attractive cover. Thank you!

The executive management team at ESI has been incredibly supportive and encouraging of this effort. It has been and will continue to be an honor to work for them. They are: John Elsey, President and CEO; Raed S. Haddad, Senior Vice President, Global Delivery Services; Patrice Collins, Vice President, Product Development; Laura Keyser Brunner, Senior Vice President, Global Client Services; Mary Simpkins, Vice President, Marketing, Communications and Open Enrollment; and Alan Garvey, Managing Director, EMEA and Asia.

Finally, I wish to send very special thanks to my loving wife, Carrie, who has unconditionally stood by me, supporting my late nights and early starts, hectic travel schedules, and our shortened vacations. Her faith and encouragement have been both inspirational and instrumental in the development of this book.

With my sincerest appreciation, I thank all of you!

INTRODUCTION

Congratulations on your commitment to pursue the International Institute of Business Analysis (IIBA®) Certified Business Analysis Professional™ (CBAP®) certification. The purpose of the study hints in this guide are to provide you some structure in your preparation approach and some direction on efficient and effective use of your time.

Someone once said, "It's the journey, not the destination." This is certainly true about achieving any certification. The fun and benefit are in the pursuit. The CBAP® journey will require you to blend your experiences with the guidelines stated in the IIBA® *Business Analysis Body of Knowledge® (BABOK® Guide)* Version 2.0, plus its cited references. However, it is important to realize that regardless of how many years you have as a business analyst (BA), your experience may be limited. As a result, when preparing for the exam, you will most likely need to brush up on topics, knowledge areas, and techniques from the *BABOK® Guide* V2.0.

The hints in this study guide concentrate on the *BABOK® Guide* V2.0. Depending on your experience level, you may need to read some of the *BABOK® Guide* V2.0 references. In addition, you will need to compare your lessons learned with the stated guidelines in the *BABOK® Guide* V2.0. Most of the time, your experiences will be confirmed by the *BABOK® Guide* V2.0, which will be a real confidence builder. However, there may be times when your lessons learned will not match the *BABOK® Guide* V2.0. If and when this happens, remember your objective: passing the exam. The first principle in this journey is: Know the IIBA® answer. This principle is true for any certification exam: Know the acceptable answers of the governing body that is offering the certification.

In preparing for this journey, it is highly recommended that you contact a local IIBA® chapter and ask for help. Join or start a study group. Besides taking a CBAP® exam prep course, working with a study group is the best approach. Suggested study group activities are:

❖ Conduct a walk-through of CBAP® applications before submission; ensure that experiences cited fall within the guidelines for exam qualification.

❖ Chart the processes of the six knowledge areas in the *BABOK® Guide* V2.0 and understand the natural sequence (parallel and iterative) of the flow.

❖ Create a group glossary of terms. In developing this glossary, make sure the definitions are derived from the *BABOK® Guide* V2.0, primarily to ensure that they are in line with IIBA®, and then use other *BABOK® Guide* V2.0 references as needed.

❖ Review and compare techniques cited in the *BABOK® Guide* V2.0. Know when and in which situations to use them (strengths, weaknesses, and alternative techniques).

As an individual, conduct a self-assessment on specific topics. Identify your weaknesses (lack of experience) and shore up your knowledge on those topics. In addition, familiarize yourself with the jargon used in each knowledge area. This preparation may take you one to three months of part-time study, depending on your study group schedule and level of experience.

REQUIREMENTS MANAGEMENT AND DEVELOPMENT ASSURANCE MODEL

The Requirements Management and Development Assurance Model (Figure 1) illustrates the series of critical activities that must be performed at all stages of a project life cycle to ultimately achieve business goals and objectives.

Requirements management activities, which consist of interaction, planning and management, are crucial because they ensure that each requirement can be traced back to the goals and objectives. These activities help to control, validate, and consistently align the scope of the desired solution.

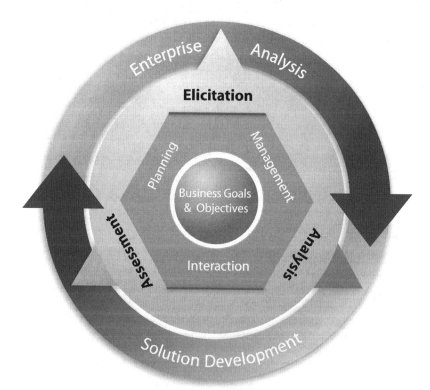

FIGURE 1. REQUIREMENTS MANAGEMENT AND DEVELOPMENT ASSURANCE MODEL

After the requirements management activities have been identified, the requirements development process begins. To ensure proper development, the requirements must be analyzed, elicited, and assessed. These three activities are performed iteratively during the entire process of definition and development of the solution.

Enterprise Analysis is the initial work that must be completed to meet the business goals and objectives. It provides a three-dimensional view of the organization so that the current and future states can be clearly articulated. As a result, Enterprise Analysis helps to determine solution scope, the feasibility of a proposed solution, and a business case to aid in quantifying the costs of the solution.

STUDY HINTS

The format of the study hints in this guide promotes the described approach by providing—

- ❖ A visual diagram on knowledge area processes and techniques
- ❖ Focus topics with *BABOK® Guide* V2.0 references
- ❖ An index of selective terms and phrases

You may need to augment these topics depending on your self-assessment. After studying the processes and techniques, use the sample exam questions to measure your progress.

Be aware that the composition of the CBAP® exam may change over time to reflect business analysis best practices in the industry. Currently, the exam is based on the *BABOK® Guide* V2.0, and the exam questions will fluctuate as IIBA® receives feedback.

The following are hints that may help you when studying for the exam:

- ❖ Most CBAP® exam questions will be in a multiple-choice format.
- ❖ Expect scenario and situation type questions to be the norm; straightforward or rote questions are rare.
- ❖ Be careful of negative questions that ask for the exception or an incorrect choice.
- ❖ Train yourself to read the last sentence of the scenario or situation first and then read the scenario or situation, as the last sentence is typically the actual question. This approach will help you to put the question in context on your initial reading.
- ❖ Attempt to answer the question before reviewing the choices and then read all the choices. In reading the choices, if you cannot immediately pick the correct answer, then eliminate as many choices as possible. This technique should leave you with two remaining choices to select the "best" answer. Mark any question about which you may still be undecided as how to answer.
- ❖ The CBAP® exam contains 150 questions; although you are given 3.5 hours to complete the exam, most individuals finish the exam within 2.5 hours. Take the entire 3.5 hours and review any undecided questions.

From all of us at ESI International, good luck and enjoy your CBAP® journey!

LIST OF ACRONYMS

AC – actual cost

ANSI – American National Standards Institute

AON – activity-on-node

BA – business analyst

BABOK® Guide – IIBA® *Business Analysis Body of Knowledge®*

BRD – business requirements document

CBAP® – Certified Business Analysis Professional™

CFO – chief financial officer

COTS – commercial off-the-shelf

CRM – customer relationship management

CRUD – create, read, update, delete

CTO – chief technology officer

DBA – database analyst

DFD – data flow diagram

EA – Enterprise Analysis

ERD – entity relationship diagram

GUI – graphical user interface

HR – human resources

IIBA® – International Institute of Business Analysis

IEEE – Institute of Electrical and Electronics Engineers

IT – information technology

JAD – joint application design

PLC – project life cycle

PM – project manager

PMBOK® Guide – A Guide to the Project Management Body of Knowledge

PMI® – Project Management Institute

PPMT – project portfolio management team

QA – quality assurance

RACI – responsible, accountable, consulted, informed

RFI – request for information

RFP – request for proposals

RFQ – request for quotation

ROI – return on investment

RTM – Requirements Trace Matrix

RUP – Rational Unified Process

SDLC – solution development life cycle

SME – subject matter expert

SRS – Software Requirements Specification

UAT – user acceptance testing

UI – user interface

UML – unified modeling language

WBS – work breakdown structure

PMBOK is a trademark of the Project Management Institute, Inc., which is registered in the United States and other nations.

BUSINESS ANALYSIS PLANNING AND MONITORING

STUDY HINTS

When studying the Business Analysis and Planning and Monitoring knowledge area, it is important to understand that its output is used as a foundation for the input to all other knowledge areas. Knowing this knowledge area in great detail will provide the basis from which you will study the remaining knowledge areas.

This knowledge area has five inputs, defines six tasks, and produces seven artifacts as a result of its output.

When studying this knowledge area be certain that you are comfortable with all the characteristics of plan-driven versus change-driven approaches for which business analysis activities might be conducted.

When studying Activity 2.2 Conduct Stakeholder Analysis, your grasp of the four elements cited is critical for exam success as well as your knowledge of techniques, specifically the RACI matrix, the two stakeholder maps cited (stakeholder matrix and the stakeholder onion diagram), and their respective categorization of stakeholders.

The best way to differentiate the Plan Business Analysis activities from Plan Requirements Management Process is to consider what needs to be done versus what is the protocol for accomplishing tasks. Plan Requirements Management Process activity focuses its efforts on approval of requirements and how to handle change requests that might lead to solution scope changes.

Note that the Plan Business Analysis Communication activity is highly dependent on the output from Plan the Business Analysis Approach. Also be aware that the degree of communication, level of formality, content, and to whom the content will be communicated will be largely dictated by the Approach and Stakeholder Analysis activities. The business analysis plans are likely to be updated or developed in parallel to this activity.

The entire knowledge area recognizes the use of 22 techniques ranging from Acceptance and Evaluation Criteria to Survey and Questionnaires. Be sure you understand the context for which each technique is applied as well as its respective technical elements.

The exam blueprint indicates that you can expect the highest percentage of questions for the Business Analysis Planning and Monitoring knowledge area; therefore, your understanding of this area must be thorough. There are approximately 29 questions on

Business Analysis Planning and Monitoring tasks on the CBAP® exam (that is, 19.33 percent of the exam). Figure 2 shows the Business Analysis Planning and Monitoring inputs, tasks and outputs. Each high-level task has an associated *BABOK® Guide* V2.0 section number and comprises many subtasks. The model provides a visual context; actual execution of some tasks may run in parallel and be iterative, meaning that they will continually evolve as other tasks are executed.

❖ *Start your learning process by reviewing the overall task flow of this knowledge area.* Even if you are very experienced in this area, context knowledge of the task and subtasks is a must.

❖ *Be familiar with Business Analysis Planning and Monitoring inputs, tasks, and output as well as their corresponding techniques by name and definition.*

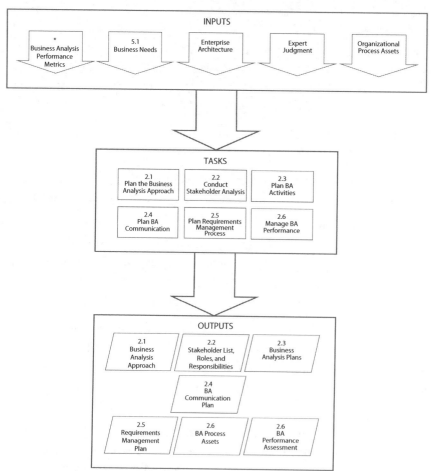

FIGURE 2. INPUTS, TASKS AND OUTPUTS, FOR BUSINESS ANALYSIS PLANNING AND MONITORING[1]

NOTES: 1. AN * INSIDE AN ICON IN THE ABOVE DIAGRAM INDICATES THAT THE ITEM IN QUESTION WAS LIKELY PRODUCED AS A RESULT OF MULTIPLE TASKS, 2. A NUMBER X.Y CITED IN AN ICON IN THE ABOVE DIAGRAM INDICATES THE KNOWLEDGE AREA AND TASKS THAT EITHER PRODUCED THE ARTIFACT OR WILL USE THE ARTIFACT AS AN INPUT. 3. AN ICON WITH NO * OR NUMBER WAS PRODUCED EXTERNALLY.

---

[1] Adapted from Figure 2-1, *BABOK® Guide* V2.0, 17.

FOCUS TOPICS FOR STUDY

After you understand the overall flow of the tasks for Business Analysis Planning and Monitoring Requirements (Figure 2), focus your attention on how to conduct each specific activity and its respective inputs, elements, techniques, stakeholders, and outputs.

- ❖ *Be especially familiar with plan-driven vs. change-driven approaches, including their respective characteristics.*

- ❖ *Stakeholder identification* should not be taken for granted. *BABOK® Guide* V2.0 reminds us to consider all elements associated with stakeholder management, including identification of stakeholders, complexity, attitude, and influence toward the project and the organization and, most importantly, their level of authority, particularly when it comes to requirements approval. A stakeholder may not necessarily have the authority to approve all requirements but may have the authority to approve a subset of requirements.

- ❖ *Plan Business Analysis activities should NOT be confused with the Plan Requirements Management Process, although both are very much dependent on one another.* Planning Business Analysis activities focus on identifying the necessary elements that are needed to completing the deliverables associated requirements development. These activities must consider such items as geographical distribution, approach to requirements development, and type of project. Be clear on how the *BABOK® Guide* V2.0 deconstructs the components of a work breakdown structure (WBS) into phases, deliverables into work packages, and work packages into activities, and how an activity may be produced.

- ❖ *Planning Business Analysis Communication is dependent on five critical elements:*
  - ◆ Approach and formality
  - ◆ Project type
  - ◆ Frequency
  - ◆ Geography
  - ◆ Culture

- ❖ *Types of projects will dictate the type of approach, activities, and processes involved in business analysis activities.* If you are clear on different project types, then you will realize this drives the approach (plan driven vs. change driven), which in turn drives the level of formality and consequently the frequency of communication. Pay particular attention to the cultural component of the Communication Plan Development activities as this will require some explicit understanding of the output created from stakeholder analysis. The *BABOK®* suggests that use of modeling techniques will likely mitigate some cultural challenges.

- ❖ *In the Plan Requirements Management Process, the primary focus of attention should be on both requirements attributes and traceability.* The *BABOK®* pays careful attention to define 10 requirements attributes and outlines derivation and allocation of requirements—where requirements evolved from and where they evolve to, respectively.

❖ *Although change management as an element for planning, the requirements management process is emphasized, it is very apparent that much of the change management effort will be crafted based on the previous four requirements planning and monitoring activities.* In this knowledge area, *BABOK®* defines the process for facilitating change requests that directly affect solution scope and the requirements supporting solution scope.

INDEX OF SELECTIVE TERMS AND PHRASES

Be able to explain the terms and phrases listed in Table 1. One caveat: The *BABOK® Guide* V2.0 page(s) shown provides a definition, a description, or a use of the term or phrase. The term or phrase may also appear on other pages.

TABLE 1. SELECTIVE TERMS AND PHRASES FOR BUSINESS ANALYSIS PLANNING AND MONITORING

Term or Phrase	BABOK® Guide V2.0 Page(s)
Agile	18, 20, 35, 40, 47
Business analyst	3, 17, 19
Business Need	18, 24
Change-driven methodology	20–22, 47–48
Change management	21–22, 46
Domain SME	11
Executive sponsor	18
Expert judgment	18
Implementation SME	11, 23, 31, 37, 41 48, 52
Iterative approach	20
Methodology	20
Onion diagram	23, 30
Organizational process assets	229
Plan-driven methodology	229
Project life cycle (PLC)	44
Project manager	18, 23, 31
Regulator	23, 31, 42
Business analysis planning and monitoring	17
Requirements prioritization	21, 45, 49
Sponsor	11, 13, 23, 31, 42, 49

Term or Phrase	BABOK® Guide V2.0 Page(s)
Stakeholder	10–11, 17, 22–24
Stakeholder map	29
Stakeholder matrix	29
Structured walkthrough	30
Subject matter expert (SME)	11
Supplier	11, 13, 23, 36, 41
Tester	11–12, 23, 31, 37, 42, 49, 52
Traceability	44
Waterfall approach	19–20

PRACTICE QUESTIONS

INSTRUCTIONS: Note the most suitable answer for each multiple-choice question in the appropriate space on the answer sheet.

1. Jonathan was recently assigned to a project that would implement a global supply chain management system, which would likely take between one and two years to complete. Which statement most accurately describes the type of project that Jonathan has inherited and the level of analysis required for this initiative?

    a. The solution will affect the core delivery of services and is directly related to key initiatives.

    b. The solution will affect a selected number of business units.

    c. The solution is readily achievable and easily understood.

    d. The solution is unclear or poses a challenge to complete.

2. When considering a business analysis approach, which of the following is considered a key input?

    a. Business need

    b. Stakeholder profiles

    c. Solution scope

    d. Scheduled resources

3. The primary objective of Business Analysis Planning and Monitoring can be best summarized as—

    a. Estimation of work effort to gather requirements

    b. Preparation of risk management plan to ensure effective development of requirements

    c. Evaluation of business architecture documentation to determine elicitation techniques

    d. Defining a business analysis approach, and defining roles, responsibilities, costs, deliverables, and metrics for the business analysis activities

4. You just hired a new business analyst and are ready to give the business analyst a first assignment. With Enterprise Analysis results already available, the first task at hand is to start planning an approach to develop requirements. Your advice to the new BA is to—

    a. Collaborate with the stakeholders to determine key roles, tasks, and estimated work effort

    b. Collaborate with the project manager to determine key roles, tasks, and estimated work effort

    c. Collaborate with the developers to clearly understand how the requirements will be implemented

    d. Evaluate the business architecture documents to determine roles and responsibilities to manage the requirements scope

5. Proper Business Analysis Planning and Monitoring ensures that—

    a. The solution is developed quickly
    b. The total number of iterations to create the deliverables are fully understood and realized
    c. The feasibility for the solution meets stakeholders' needs
    d. Changes are captured correctly and consistently

6. _____ and _____ are both considered output from the Business Analysis Planning and Monitoring activities.

    a. Create, Read, Update, Delete (CRUD) models; use diagrams
    b. Class diagrams; work breakdown structure
    c. Business analysis process assets; requirements management plan
    d. Requirements effort; brainstorming results

7. Nancy was assigned the task of working on a very large, high-profile project during the planning and management phase. She created a RACI chart to map out roles and responsibilities. What does "RACI" stand for?

    a. Responsible, accountable, consulted, and informed
    b. Responsible, accountable, created, and informed
    c. Responsible, authority, created, and involved
    d. Responsible, authority, consulted, and involved

8. A key source of information for identifying all possible stakeholders for a given project is—

    a. Use case diagrams
    b. Enterprise Architecture
    c. User profiles
    d. Workflow models

9. Because stakeholders refused to be interviewed for a stakeholder summary, Melanie decided to develop an online survey that she expected would take 10 to 15 minutes of her target audience's precious time to complete. Which of the following questions should Melanie NOT use in her survey?

    a. Who is directly affected by the project? (multiple choice)
    b. Which other business units might be affected by this implementation? (multiple choice)
    c. Are you responsible for initiating this change? (multiple choice)
    d. What are the roles of the stakeholders that you have identified in previous responses? (text box)

10. For the task of categorizing stakeholders, which of the following choices would be considered an appropriate stakeholder category?

    a. Performance review results
    b. Compensation package
    c. Tenure in the organization
    d. Influence on the project

11. The _____ is responsible for end-to-end project risks and is accountable for requirements risks.

    a. Business analyst
    b. Stakeholder
    c. Enterprise analyst
    d. Project manager

12. Requirements risks should be identified—

    a. At the beginning of the project
    b. At the end of the project
    c. Before stakeholder approval of project deliverables
    d. Throughout the requirements process

13. Lawson was asked to identify key inputs for his plan for the business analysis approach. His primary areas of focus should be—

    a. Organizational process assets
    b. Project risk
    c. Project expectations
    d. Project type

14. Requirements that are only gathered at the beginning of the project are often collected using which type of solution development life cycle?

    a. Iterative
    b. Waterfall or plan-driven
    c. Agile
    d. XTreme programming

15. What tool could you use to clearly understand stakeholder project responsibilities?

    a. Work breakdown structure
    b. Use case diagrams
    c. Context diagram
    d. RACI chart

16. Kaitlyn was preparing her list of the team roles that she wanted included in her business analysis activities. She was not clear on what was the difference between a domain subject matter expert and a business analyst. A domain subject matter expert can be best described as—

    a. The manager and developer of all functional requirements
    b. An individual who demonstrates a core expertise in the facilitation of requirements
    c. An individual whose core expertise for a particular functional area lends itself to the approval of functional requirements
    d. An expert on the development of high-level business requirements

17. Which of the following choices is NOT an activity that a business analyst would need to consider when planning the end-to-end requirements process?

    a. Enterprise Analysis
    b. Requirements Analysis
    c. Elicitation
    d. Requirements Management and Communication

18. What is the key deliverable when identifying the business analysis activities?

    a. Business analysis plan(s)
    b. Consensus from all stakeholders on what the solution should be
    c. Consensus from all the stakeholders and sign-off on the selected solution
    d. An itemized list of detailed diagramming activities and their respective techniques, including stakeholders

19. Bryan was asked to participate in and contribute to the Business Analysis Planning and Monitoring activities for an upcoming project. Sunnyside Corporation decided to develop its own intranet using internal resources. Using an iterative approach, the key stakeholders were concerned about their investment and were anxious to see the progress. Which approach is Bryan likely to have selected based on the context for this project?

    a. Analogous programming
    b. Data modeling
    c. Change-driven
    d. Workflow models

20. A major milestone can be defined as the completion of a group of activities or—

    a. Stakeholder sign-off
    b. Completion of user acceptance testing (UAT) on the final deliverable
    c. A significant point in the project life cycle
    d. A significant event marking the end of the project

21. The purpose of identifying requirements assumptions during the Business Analysis Planning and Monitoring phase can be best described by which of the following statements?

    a. Assumptions ensure that all stakeholders are clear on the potential cost overruns.
    b. Assumptions ensure the business analyst and project manager that all requirements are at risk regardless of planning and monitoring.
    c. Assumptions validate the need to identify necessary resources should the assigned resources not deliver on the assigned tasks.
    d. Assumptions are identified to assess their overall potential impact on requirements activities.

22. Which of the following choices is NOT considered a project metric?

    a. Risk
    b. Defects
    c. Performance
    d. Usability

23. When reporting project metrics, a business analyst would primarily focus on which type of criteria for success?
    a. Schedule
    b. Budget
    c. Defects
    d. Resources

24. True or false: Authority levels, including who is capable of signing off on requirements, should be included in the Requirements Management and Communication plan.
    a. True
    b. False

25. The most critical element when considering a requirements format is—
    a. Which language to use
    b. Appropriate level of detail
    c. No grammatical errors
    d. No punctuation errors

26. Which of the following is NOT an input required for the tasks and activities related to Business Analysis Planning and Monitoring?
    a. Business need
    b. Enterprise architecture
    c. Performance metrics
    d. Requirements management plan

27. Which of the following is NOT a task that is completed during Business Analysis Planning and Monitoring activities?
    a. Conduct stakeholder analysis
    b. Manage solution scope and requirements
    c. Plan business analysis communication
    d. Plan requirements management process

28. Estimating the effort required for business analysis tasks to be completed can be found in which knowledge area of the *BABOK® Guide*?
    a. Business Analysis Planning and Monitoring
    b. Enterprise Analysis
    c. Requirements Analysis
    d. Requirements Management and Communication

29. Which of the following choices is a key output produced during the Business Analysis Planning and Monitoring activities?
    a. Assessment of proposed solution
    b. Requirements structure
    c. Process assets
    d. Stakeholder concerns

30. Which of the following is considered a business analysis process improvement methodology?

    a. Agile
    b. Lean
    c. Spiral
    d. Waterfall

31. What must a business analyst consider before tailoring a predefined business analysis approach or method to satisfy the needs of a unique initiative?

    a. The impact on resources
    b. Organizational standards
    c. Consulting with the author of the approach or method
    d. The overall costs for changes to be made to the approach

32. Melanie worked late into the evening preparing for her meeting with key stakeholders to present to them the latest results of her business analysis scoping activities. She made certain to address such issues as the high-level overview of BA costs and estimates, her buy-versus-build approach, overall impact on other business units, and BA approach. She invited the business executive sponsor, business process owners, and the information technology (IT) management team. If Melanie could invite only one more party to this meeting, whom should she choose?

    a. Regulators
    b. Project manager
    c. Application developers
    d. End users

33. When considering a business analysis approach, which of the following is considered a key input?

    a. BA activities
    b. Expert judgment
    c. Prioritized requirements
    d. Solution scope

34. When considering a business analysis approach, which of the following is considered a key input?

    a. Business analysis activities
    b. Number of stakeholders
    c. Organizational process assets
    d. Stakeholder profiles

35. A _____ approach considers a low level of requirements risk within a project and that requirements are defined prior to their implementation.
    a. Change-driven
    b. Iterative
    c. Lean
    d. Plan-driven

36. A _____ approach is iterative in nature and is considered exploratory where the outcome of the solution is unclear upfront.
    a. Change-driven
    b. Big design upfront
    c. Lean
    d. Plan-driven

37. Business process re-engineering projects generally take on this type of business analysis approach.
    a. Change-driven approach
    b. Big design upfront approach
    c. Lean approach
    d. Plan-driven approach

38. The development of the proposed solution could only happen after the requirements had been defined in a plan-driven approach. Why did the business analyst select this approach?
    a. Exploration of a new nonexistent technology
    b. Financial constraints
    c. Requirement for quick delivery of a semi-functional solution
    d. Timing of business analysis work to be done

39. Which requirements attributes should Dale consider documenting as he captures his requirements?
    a. Source, value, and priority
    b. Risk, entities, and traceability
    c. Source, traceability, and verifiability
    d. Risk, priority, and profiles

40. Which technique is most likely to be used to Manage Business Analysis Performance?
    a. Brainstorming
    b. Requirements Workshops
    c. Scope Modeling
    d. Variance Analysis

ANSWER SHEET

1.	a	b	c	d
2.	a	b	c	d
3.	a	b	c	d
4.	a	b	c	d
5.	a	b	c	d
6.	a	b	c	d
7.	a	b	c	d
8.	a	b	c	d
9.	a	b	c	d
10.	a	b	c	d
11.	a	b	c	d
12.	a	b	c	d
13.	a	b	c	d
14.	a	b	c	d
15.	a	b	c	d
16.	a	b	c	d
17.	a	b	c	d
18.	a	b	c	d
19.	a	b	c	d
20.	a	b	c	d

21.	a	b	c	d
22.	a	b	c	d
23.	a	b	c	d
24.	a	b		
25.	a	b	c	d
26.	a	b	c	d
27.	a	b	c	d
28.	a	b	c	d
29.	a	b	c	d
30.	a	b	c	d
31.	a	b	c	d
32.	a	b	c	d
33.	a	b	c	d
34.	a	b	c	d
35.	a	b	c	d
36.	a	b	c	d
37.	a	b	c	d
38.	a	b	c	d
39.	a	b	c	d
40.	a	b	c	d

ANSWER KEY

1.   **a.**   **The solution will affect the core delivery of services and is directly related to key initiatives.**

Considering its potential size and impact on related projects, the project to which Jonathan has been assigned carries a high level of risk. Consideration for carefully planning and managing to Enterprise Analysis activities would clarify major organizational risks and constraints on this project and may in fact influence the selection of the final recommended solution. A plan-driven approach is most likely the proper course of action to follow in this case.

International Institute of Business Analysis (IIBA®), *Business Analysis Body of Knowledge® (BABOK® Guide)*, Version 2.0, 2009, 19–20

2.   **a.**   **Business need**

The business need will shape and help to determine what approach is best to use to implement a solution and will consider risk, time frame, and understanding of the business need.

IIBA®, *BABOK® Guide* V2.0, 2009, 18

3.   **d.**   **Defining a business analysis approach, and defining roles, responsibilities, costs, deliverables, and metrics for the business analysis activities**

Planning and Monitoring activities ensure that the right approach, the right stakeholders, activities, processes, and performance metrics are in place to ensure that the overall solution is realized in the most efficient manner possible.

IIBA®, *BABOK® Guide* V2.0, 2009, 17–18

4.   **b.**   **Collaborate with the project manager to determine key roles, tasks, and estimated work effort**

Because the project deliverables depend on clearly defined requirements, a business analyst must collaborate with the project manager to determine tasks, roles, responsibilities, risk, and communication plans that fit into the overall project planning and management activities.

IIBA®, *BABOK® Guide* V2.0, 2009, 31

5.   **d.**   **Changes are captured correctly and consistently**

During the planning and management phase of requirements, a business analyst needs to acknowledge the fact that requirements may change and, therefore, needs to consider any change control policies to evaluate the proper course of action.

IIBA®, *BABOK® Guide* V2.0, 2009, 42–43

6. **c.** **Business analysis process assets; requirements management plan**

There are seven artifacts that are produced as a result of Business Analysis Planning and Monitoring activities:

1. Business Analysis Approach; 2. Business Analysis Communication Plan; 3. Business Analysis Performance Assessment; 4. Business Analysis Plans; 5. Business Analysis Process Assets; 6. Requirements Management Plan; and 7. Stakeholder List, Roles and Responsibilities.

IIBA®, *BABOK® Guide* V2.0, 2009, 17

7. **d.** **Plan-driven approach**

Waterfall methods and business process re-engineering can be categorized as a plan-driven approach, as they generally tend to demonstrate characteristics that include but are not limited to a high degree of risk, solution definition before implementation begins, and the focus of efforts is to minimize uncertainty.

IIBA®, *BABOK® Guide* V2.0, 2009, 19-20

8. **b.** **Enterprise Architectrure**

In the early phases of EA, particularly around the development of the business architecture effort, key stakeholders are identified by their respective functional jurisdictions.

IIBA®, *BABOK® Guide* V2.0, 2009, 25

9. **d.** **What are the roles of the stakeholders that you have identified in previous responses? (text box)**

This is an open-ended question that would take longer for the stakeholders to answer. Multiple-choice questions are ideal for this type of survey because they can be answered much more quickly and can be more easily quantified into empirical data.

IIBA®, *BABOK® Guide* V2.0, 2009, 28, 214

10. **d.** **Influence on the project**

The IIBA® has identified four elements to consider when categorizing stakeholders: 1. identification; 2. complexity of stakeholder group; 3. attitude and influence; and 4. authority levels for business analysis work.

IIBA®, *BABOK® Guide* V2.0, 2009, 27

11.   **d.   Project manager**

The business analyst is responsible for end-to-end requirements management and is accountable for identifying requirement dependencies between overall project risks and requirements risks. The project manager, however, is ultimately responsible for end-to-end project risks and is accountable for requirements management, which is one element of scope management. Also refer to the RACI Matrix.

IIBA®, *BABOK® Guide* V2.0, 2009, 29, 31

12.   **d.   Throughout the requirements process**

Requirements need to be identified throughout the project life cycle to understand and allow for the proper evaluation of risks. Often, previously identified risks disappear and new ones appear.

IIBA®, *BABOK® Guide* V2.0, 2009, 44, 201

13.   **b.   Expert judgment**

Expert judgment is a key input required for determining the best solution approach, as well as any resources, including stakeholders, senior practitioners, and historical data or documentation.

IIBA®, *BABOK® Guide* V2.0, 2009, 18–19

14.   **b.   Waterfall or plan-driven**

Waterfall is the best known and oldest process, wherein developers follow a linear order to the execution of activities: state and analyze requirements; design a solution approach; design a software framework; develop, test, and deploy code; and follow up post-implementation.

IIBA®, *BABOK® Guide* V2.0, 2009, 19-20

15.   **d.   Plan-driven**

A plan-driven approach or waterfall method requires that requirements be defined at the beginning of a project and the project sponsor is the single approver of all requirements. This approach is intended to reduce risk where risk is high during implementation of a solution.

IIBA®, *BABOK® Guide* V2.0, 2009, 19–20

16.   **c.   An individual whose core expertise for a particular functional area lends itself to the approval of functional requirements**

A domain subject matter expert will most often work very closely with a business analyst and lend his or her expertise for a given functional area of the business. He or she works with a BA to define and approve solution requirements for a desired solution.

IIBA®, *BABOK® Guide* V2.0, 2009, 11

17. **a. Enterprise Analysis**

The business analyst is now basing all of his or her findings on the output of the Enterprise Analysis phase to determine how the planning and management of the requirements will proceed from this point forward. Considerations for requirements activities now include elicitation, analysis, design, communication, solution assessment, and validation.

IIBA®, *BABOK® Guide* V2.0, 2009, 43

18. **a. Business analysis plan(s)**

Through functional decomposition estimation and risk analysis activities, a business analysis plan is produced as an output to planning business analysis activities.

IIBA®, *BABOK® Guide* V2.0, 2009, 33

19. **c. Change-driven**

Given the nature of the project and the iterative development approach, Bryan will most likely select a change- driven approach so that he can demonstrate the semi-functional properties of the intranet to gain stakeholder consensus and approval throughout the life cycle of the project.

IIBA®, *BABOK® Guide* V2.0, 2009, 20

20. **c. A significant point in the project life cycle**

A significant point, or milestone, in the project life cycle can be used to benchmark the project's progress.

IIBA®, *BABOK® Guide* V2.0, 2009, 36

21. **d. Assumptions are identified to assess the overall potential impact on requirements activities.**

Identifying assumptions in Business Analysis Planning and Monitoring activities allows the business analyst, project manager, project sponsor, and stakeholders to understand the degree of risk, potential impacts, and potential costs associated with them.

IIBA®, *BABOK® Guide* V2.0, 2009, 6

22. **a. Risk**

Risk is not considered a project metric.

IIBA®, *BABOK® Guide* V2.0, 2009, 51, 182–183

23. **c.** **Defects**

A business analyst would be most concerned with defects as they relate to a product. Defects are easily traceable to poorly defined requirements from test cases, as well as poorly defined supplemental requirements and functional business requirements. A BA may be able to identify various quantifiable measures that demonstrate points of failure — for example, scope creep, poor solution development life cycle definition, poor estimation of effort, and other factors.

IIBA®, *BABOK® Guide* V2.0, 2009, 49–50

24. **a.** **True**

This is true, because part of Requirements Management and Communication output would include sign-off and approval. Identifying these signatories must be included in the Requirements Management and Communication plan.

IIBA®, *BABOK® Guide* V2.0, 2009, 38

25. **b.** **Appropriate level of detail**

To gain understanding and approval from stakeholders, a business analyst must carefully consider the stakeholders' levels of knowledge and their preferred modes of communication. The appropriate level of detail is the most critical element in the list.

IIBA®, *BABOK® Guide* V2.0, 2009, 44-45

26. **d.** **Requirements management plan**

The requirements management plan is a key deliverable and output in Business Analysis Planning and Monitoring activities

IIBA®, *BABOK® Guide* V2.0, 2009, 17

27. **b.** **Manage solution scope and requirements**

The management of solution scope and requirements is a task included in Requirements Management and Communication activities.

IIBA®, *BABOK® Guide* V2.0, 2009, 17, 63

28. **a.** **Business Analysis Planning and Monitoring**

During Task 2.3 Plan Business Analysis activities, it is expected that estimation of efforts for the defined activities is produced as an output as well as the measurement of progress of the defined activities.

IIBA®, *BABOK® Guide* V2.0, 2009, 17, 31

29.   **c.**   **Process assets**

The monitoring of business analysis activities are captured using process assets during Business Analysis Planning and Monitoring activities. Assessment of the proposed solution is an activity realized during the Solution Assessment and Validation activities, whereas requirements structure is an output of Requirements Analysis, and stakeholder concerns are realized during Requirements Elicitation activities.

IIBA®, *BABOK® Guide* V2.0, 2009, 17

30.   **b.**   **Lean**

Lean is a practice whose goal is to improve processes for which products are developed and intended to reduce waste by creating more value with less work.

IIBA®, *BABOK® Guide* V2.0, 2009, 18

31.   **b.**   **Organizational standards**

Organizational standards or governance is often put into place as a result of an acute understanding of all potential impacts and changes made to a business analysis practice.

IIBA®, *BABOK® Guide* V2.0, 2009, 18

32.   **b.**   **Project manager**

Based on the project manager's overall understanding of other ongoing projects, the team should be able to ascertain very quickly the proposed project's overall impact on any other existing projects, resources, and funding capabilities.

IIBA®, *BABOK® Guide* V2.0, 2009, 31

33.   **a.**   **Organizational process assets**

Organizational process assets may include such things as corporate standards, templates, methodologies or life cycles that may help determine how the entire requirements process is executed, which deliverables are produced, and when they are due. The project life cycle defines phases necessary to complete the project.

IIBA®, *BABOK® Guide* V2.0, 2009, 17, 19

34.   **c.**   **Organizational process assets**

Organizational process assets essentially refer to those tools, methods or approaches, and governance standards that already exist within an organization and which may be leveraged when considering an approach to developing a solution.

IIBA®, *BABOK® Guide* V2.0, 2009, 19

35. **d.** **RACI chart**

The RACI matrix is a tool used to illustrate the responsibilities of the stakeholders.

IIBA®, *BABOK® Guide* V2.0, 2009, 29

36. **a.** **Change-driven**

A change-driven approach is considered for solution deliverables where uncertainty is acceptable and the solution is created in an iterative and incremental fashion.

IIBA®, *BABOK® Guide* V2.0, 2009, 20

37. **a.** **Responsible, accountable, consulted, and informed**

A RACI chart/matrix is intended to match required roles with responsibilities of those individuals who will perform assigned tasks. Responsibilities include who is responsible, accountable, to be consulted, and to be informed. Consensus from the stakeholders on the results should be sought.

IIBA®, *BABOK® Guide* V2.0, 2009, 29

38. **d.** **Timing of business analysis work to be done**

Timing of the business analysis effort may require that stages of activities be performed prior to any subsequent work being done. This may also be an indication that executive sponsorship sign-off is necessary before proceeding with subsequent activities of the project.

IIBA®, *BABOK® Guide* V2.0, 2009, 20

39. **a.** **Source, value, and priority**

These requirements attributes will allow a business analyst to assess and validate requirements risks and stakeholder expectations to allow the requirements to be verified and traced.

IIBA®, *BABOK® Guide* V2.0, 2009, 44–45

40. **d.** **Variance analysis**

Variance analysis, when performed correctly, helps a business analyst understand the magnitude of what was expected versus what is actually occurring in terms of the performance of a solution. This is not a technique cited in Chapter 9 of the *BABOK® Guide* V2.0, but it is referenced in the knowledge area. Other techniques to assess and evaluate the performance of a solution might include Interviews, Lessons Learned Process, Metrics and Key Performance Indicators, Problem Tracking, Process Modeling, Root Cause Analysis and Survey/Questionnaire.

IIBA®, *BABOK® Guide* V2.0, 2009, 52

ELICITATION

STUDY HINTS

This area should be the most familiar to the business analyst. However, you may not be well versed in all the elicitation techniques cited in the *BABOK® Guide* V2.0. Conduct an inventory of your requirements-elicitation toolkit and add to it, as necessary. Your knowledge in this area must be thorough. You can expect approximately 21 questions on Elicitation tasks on the CBAP® exam (that is, 14 percent of the exam). There are 10 elicitation techniques that the *BABOK® Guide* V2.0 cites (Figure 4) for conducting Elicitation activities. Each technique has the associated *BABOK® Guide* V2.0 section number and is wrapped around planning, execution, documentation, and validation of requirements.

Although you should be well versed in each of these techniques, do not dismiss the critical importance of the elements associated with conducting Elicitation activities, as they essentially provide guidance on expected output of your efforts. Figure 3 provides a visual context of the Elicitation inputs, activities, and outputs; actual execution of some tasks may be serial and iterative. It is also important to understand that the Elicitation knowledge area represents activities that take place throughout the entire solution development life cycle. Understand that Elicitation is a requirement to complete Business Analysis Planning and Monitoring activities, much like Requirements Analysis is often completed using a combination of a variety of both elicitation techniques and modeling techniques.

❖ **Start your learning process by reviewing the overall inputs, tasks, elements, expected outputs, and techniques for this knowledge area.** Each technique has detailed steps, along with strengths and weaknesses.

FOCUS TOPICS FOR STUDY

After reviewing all the techniques, focus your attention on comparing them.

❖ **Be able to select a technique or set of techniques for various situations.** Highlight the group elicitation techniques: brainstorming, focus group, and requirements workshop. Facilitation skills are necessary for these group elicitation techniques.

❖ **Be familiar with Elicitation inputs, tasks, and outputs by name and definition.**

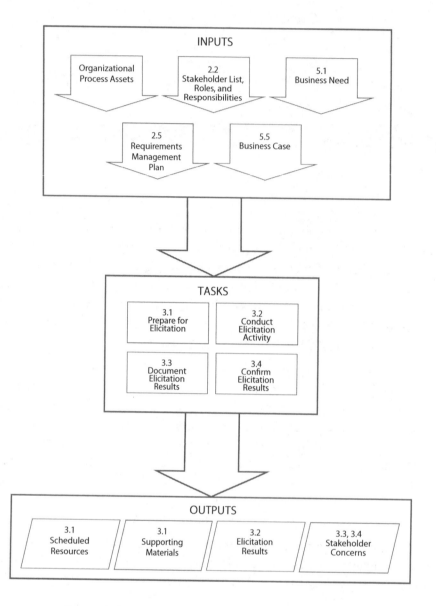

FIGURE 3: INPUTS, TASKS, AND OUTPUTS FOR ELICITATION[2]

NOTES: 1. AN * INSIDE AN ICON IN THE ABOVE DIAGRAM INDICATES THAT THE ITEM IN QUESTION WAS LIKELY PRODUCED AS A RESULT OF MULTIPLE TASKS, 2. A NUMBER X.Y CITED IN AN ICON IN THE ABOVE DIAGRAM INDICATES THE KNOWLEDGE AREA AND TASKS THAT EITHER PRODUCED THE ARTIFACT OR WILL USE THE ARTIFACT AS AN INPUT. 3. AN ICON WITH NO * OR NUMBER WAS PRODUCED EXTERNALLY.

---

²   Adapted from Figure 3-2, *BABOK® Guide* V2.0, 54.

Figure 4 represents the techniques that the *BABOK®* cites as those required to conduct elicitation activities.

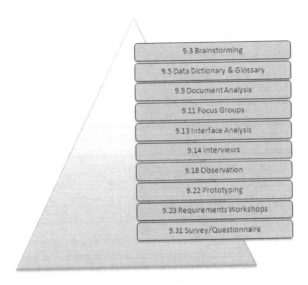

9.3 Brainstorming
9.5 Data Dictionary & Glossary
9.9 Document Analysis
9.11 Focus Groups
9.13 Interface Analysis
9.14 Interviews
9.18 Observation
9.22 Prototyping
9.23 Requirements Workshops
9.31 Survey/Questionnaire

FIGURE 4. TECHNIQUES FOR ELICITATION

INDEX OF SELECTIVE TERMS AND PHRASES

Be able to explain the terms and phrases listed in Table 2. One caveat: The *BABOK® Guide* V2.0 page(s) shown provides a definition, a description, or a use of the term or phrase. The term or phrase may also appear on other pages.

TABLE 2. SELECTIVE TERMS AND PHRASES FOR ELICITATION

Term or Phrase	BABOK® Guide V2.0 Page(s)
Brainstorming	223
Closed-ended questions	76, 179
Document analysis	226
Elicitation	53
Focus group	227
Heterogeneous	173
Homogeneous	173
Interface analysis	176
Interview	177
Observation	186

Term or Phrase	BABOK® Guide V2.0 Page(s)
Open-ended questions	178–179, 214
Problem tracking	59, 190
Prototyping	196
Requirements [stated]	9, 61
Requirements [stated, unconfirmed]	9, 61
Requirements attributes	58
Requirements elicitation	53
Requirements workshop	198
Stakeholders concerns [confirmed]	9, 61
Stakeholder concerns [unconfirmed]	9, 61
Supporting materials	56, 57
Survey/questionnaire	214

PRACTICE QUESTIONS

INSTRUCTIONS: Note the most suitable answer for each multiple-choice question in the appropriate space on the answer sheet.

1. After the observation session has concluded, it is good practice to—
   a. Provide immediate feedback to the shadowed user for validation
   b. Review all notes, document them carefully, and share them with the rest of the project management team
   c. Immediately prepare a semi-functional prototype so that the software development team has an opportunity to begin developing the new system
   d. Immediately transcribe all information to the business requirements document (BRD) and develop use case models based on the documented observation

2. The key output of the Business Analysis Planning and Monitoring activities that allows for successful Elicitation activities is—
   a. Overall scope of the problem or opportunity of the sponsoring organization
   b. Financial evaluation of the proposed solution to describe an accurate return on investment
   c. Identification of the appropriate techniques to be employed with the appropriate stakeholders
   d. Identification of the appropriate solution development life cycle and its relationship to the development of user requirements

3. Survey is to questionnaire as requirements workshop is to—
   a. Video analysis
   b. Interview
   c. Observation
   d. Focus groups

4. The primary objective of brainstorming is to—
   a. Allow a group of stakeholders to understand the AS-IS state and determine what is required to achieve the TO-BE state
   b. Allow a group of stakeholders to explore all possible ideas to generate a variety of solutions
   c. Refine an understanding of symptoms and to explore potential solutions
   d. Take a structured approach to understanding challenges, their impacts on one another, and the means by which they can be overcome

5. Bill was preparing for his first brainstorming session with the key stakeholders. He put together a list of guidelines that he knew to be critical success factors for this session. Which of the listed items would NOT be a success factor?
   a. Allow lively and creative debate
   b. Evaluate ideas at a later point
   c. Encourage building on others' ideas
   d. Encourage everyone to participate

6. A business analyst might consider interviews as an elicitation technique so that he or she might be able to—
   a. Interpret the results and create clear requirements
   b. Ask probing questions to confirm his or her understanding
   c. Gain stakeholder commitment to reach consensus on desired requirements
   d. Develop requirements to ensure the accurate development of a business case based on their interviewees' claims

7. Michael realized that, for his project at hand, not all subject matter experts (SMEs) would be available to help him to understand the business rules and how they might be affected by the proposed upgrade to the existing accounting system. Although it might prove to be a tedious process, which elicitation technique should Michael consider to gain insight into the AS-IS state of the accounting system?
   a. Focus groups
   b. Prototypes
   c. Interface analysis
   d. Document analysis

8. In addition to an experienced facilitator, who else needs to be involved in the delivery of a requirements workshop session?
   a. Scribe
   b. Project manager
   c. Customers
   d. Solutions delivery group

9. Which of the following is considered a non event based elicitation activity?
   a. Brainstorming
   b. Document analysis
   c. Focus groups
   d. Observation

10. Individuals in the group may self-censor if they are uncomfortable with their surroundings. While users perform their own tasks, you might consider—
    a. Spending a minimum of two days making your observations
    b. Offering the users multiple opportunities to take breaks to alleviate the stress of being observed
    c. Asking the users to talk about what they are doing so you can learn about the cognitive factors as well as the behavioral factors
    d. Videotaping the session so that you don't need to disrupt the users with questions

11. Typically, what is the recommended time to run a focus group?
    a. Two to four hours
    b. Four to eight hours
    c. One to two hours
    d. As long as it takes to solve the problem

12. True or false: Interface analysis is primarily concerned with the detailed requirements of graphical user interface (GUI) development.
    a. True
    b. False

13. A _____ is a recommended source of information that ensures a consistent perspective of requirements across all systems that may or may not be involved in the solution.
    a. Context diagram
    b. Glossary
    c. Business architecture plan
    d. Homogenous focus group

14. Vince needed to identify any inconsistencies in the BA team's recommendations during the planning and management phase. Which of the following statements might be a disadvantage to prototyping?
    a. It involves the customer.
    b. It quickly asserts the feasibility of a certain technology.
    c. It is a quick way to ascertain user interface requirements.
    d. It doesn't focus on the whats and whys.

15. True or false: An interview is a systematic approach to conversing with a person in a formal setting.
    a. True
    b. False

16. Which elicitation technique entails the examination of the AS-IS state using existing information such as business rules, entities, and attributes?
    a. Brainstorming
    b. Document analysis
    c. Interviews
    d. Focus groups

17. Which of the following choices would be considered a best practice when preparing for a requirements workshop?
    a. Focus on positions, not interest.
    b. Define the workshop agenda.
    c. Commit to workshop deliverables.
    d. Keep the workshop as informal as possible.

18. While working with a client to elicit requirements, Erin uncovered the need to ensure that the graphical user interface was clean, easy to navigate, and provided as much help functionality as possible. Erin documented this requirements under which category of requirements?

    a. Business
    b. Solution
    c. Stakeholder
    d. Transition

19. Observation is also referred to as—

    a. Watching someone from an undisclosed location using binoculars
    b. Structured walk-through
    c. Role modeling
    d. Job shadowing

20. Jake knew that he would need to be sensitive to the heterogeneous group of stakeholders during his focus group session. Why?

    a. Not all stakeholders would show up.
    b. He would have more attendees than the recommended number.
    c. The group would need to be focused on its own problem areas.
    d. Individuals in the group may self-censor if they are uncomfortable with their surroundings.

21. Elicitation can be best defined as—

    a. The means by which models can be validated
    b. The means by which information is drawn out of stakeholders
    c. A process defined by the output of Enterprise Analysis
    d. A process defined by the collaborative approach to uncovering a proposed business solution

22. The primary purpose of prototyping is to—

    a. Provide information on how the product works
    b. Set expectations on how the final product will look
    c. Provide information for visualizing interface requirements
    d. Evaluate the amount of resources required to develop the final product

23. Complete, clear, _____, and consistent. Which of the "4 Cs" is missing in this statement?

    a. Collaboration
    b. Concise
    c. Convenient
    d. Correct

24. Vince wanted to be certain that, as the project manager for the airline reservation system, he gave his team of business analysts plenty of time to conduct interface analysis. What is the primary reason for his concern?

    a. Vince wanted to ensure that if there were a collaborative effort among the projects, his project and the other projects would realize the full benefit of the collaboration.

    b. Vince wanted a clear view of what graphical user interfaces he needed to develop to ensure that he had allocated the right amount of time to each of these tasks.

    c. Vince needed to identify all stakeholders and constraints for this project to ensure that all business needs were clearly articulated.

25. _____ prototyping is eventually refined and developed in the final product.

    a. Horizontal
    b. Vertical
    c. Evolutionary
    d. Throwaway

26. Jim was under a lot of pressure from his project manager to complete the requirements definition phase of the solution development life cycle. Because of budgetary constraints, rather than conduct multiple interviews, Jim was forced to consider which type of elicitation technique?

    a. Prototypes
    b. Observation
    c. Survey/questionnaire
    d. Requirements workshop

27. What is the primary reason to send the documented results back to the interviewee?

    a. To justify the effort spent on interviews to project managers
    b. To validate the requirements necessary for the product deliverable
    c. To ensure the integrity of the overall communication plan as outlined by the project manager and the business analyst
    d. To ensure that the business analyst has accurately documented the results of the interview

28. There are many sources from which Stan could conduct document analysis. Stan is NOT likely to use which of the following documents in his analysis?

    a. Consultants' (SMEs') contracts
    b. Training guides
    c. Problem reports
    d. RFPs

29. Which of the following choices is a potential drawback to running a requirements workshop?

    a. The project scope might be redefined.
    b. Immediate facilitator feedback exists.
    c. Conflicting opinions could prevent consensus.
    d. The workshop's formality prevents flexibility.

30. When using _____, quantitative data are easy to obtain for statistical analysis.

    a. Open-ended questions
    b. Closed-ended questions
    c. Formal questions
    d. Informal questions

31. What is the "general rule of thumb" of the 4 Cs in Elicitation?

    a. Collaboration, compilation, consistent, correct
    b. Competent, complete, convenient, collaboration
    c. Complete, clear, correct and consistent
    d. Concise, complete, competent, convenient

32. Kelly was about to conduct her first prototyping session in hopes of gaining a better understanding of how a user interacts with the new online payment system. Her session would be focused on "checking out and payment and delivery methods" for her new online grocery store Web application. This is known as—

    a. Horizontal prototyping
    b. Vertical prototyping
    c. Throwaway prototyping
    d. Evolutionary prototyping

33. According to IIBA®, which phrase most accurately describes the word elicit and its objectives?

    a. Active interaction with stakeholders to define requirements
    b. Conducting facilitated sessions to define requirements
    c. Developing requirements from all resources available
    d. Drawing forth something that a stakeholder wants

34. When eliciting requirements, a business analyst is primarily concerned with developing what four categories of requirements; business, stakeholder, solution, and _____?

    a. Concise
    b. Functional
    c. Nonfunctional
    d. Transition

35. The observation elicitation technique is primarily focused on uncovering details about—
    a. Current processes
    b. Future state processes
    c. Unusual exceptions in current processes
    d. Critical situations in future processes

36. Job shadowing is the synonym for which elicitation technique?
    a. Brainstorming
    b. Document analysis
    c. Interviews
    d. Observation

37. In preparing for her Elicitation activities, Stacy made certain she had at hand which pieces of critical information?
    a. A risk management plan
    b. Documented information about the defined business solution
    c. A context diagram
    d. A RACI chart

38. If you find yourself considering the use of event based elicitation activities, you will likely consider what element when planning to conduct these activities—
    a. Ground rules
    b. Organizational process assets
    c. State machine diagrams
    d. Use case diagrams

39. Conducting a focus group session is an elicitation technique considered to be a form of—
    a. Quantitative research
    b. Qualitative research
    c. Diagnostic assessment
    d. Environmental assessment

40. The following describes a business analysts interpretation of requirements—
    a. [Requirements, Stated]
    b. [Requirements, Verified]
    c. [Stated, Confirmed]
    d. [Stated, Unconfirmed]

ANSWER SHEET

1.	a	b	c	d		21.	a	b	c	d
2.	a	b	c	d		22.	a	b	c	d
3.	a	b	c	d		23.	a	b	c	d
4.	a	b	c	d		24.	a	b	c	d
5.	a	b	c	d		25.	a	b	c	d
6.	a	b	c	d		26.	a	b	c	d
7.	a	b	c	d		27.	a	b	c	d
8.	a	b	c	d		28.	a	b	c	d
9.	a	b	c	d		29.	a	b	c	d
10.	a	b	c	d		30.	a	b	c	d
11.	a	b	c	d		31.	a	b	c	d
12.	a	b				32.	a	b	c	d
13.	a	b	c	d		33.	a	b	c	d
14.	a	b	c	d		34.	a	b	c	d
15.	a	b				35.	a	b	c	d
16.	a	b	c	d		36.	a	b	c	d
17.	a	b	c	d		37.	a	b	c	d
18.	a	b	c	d		38.	a	b	c	d
19.	a	b	c	d		39.	a	b	c	d
20.	a	b	c	d		40.	a	b	c	d

ANSWER KEY

1. **a. Provide immediate feedback to the shadowed user for validation**

    If you confirm your observations immediately after your session, the information is still fresh in everyone's mind. In this way, you can determine whether some tasks require additional observation or allow for the development of the appropriate models.

    IIBA®, *BABOK® Guide* V2.0, 2009, 187–188

2. **c. Identification of the appropriate techniques to be employed with the appropriate stakeholders**

    The IIBA® *BABOK® Guide* V2.0 has identified six pieces of output from Business Analysis Planning and Monitoring that are key to developing Elicitation activities. These key pieces include the identification of elicitation techniques, stakeholders, traceability strategy, requirements attributes, and output necessary to support the analysis and documentation phase.

    IIBA®, *BABOK® Guide* V2.0, 2009, 32–33

3. **d. Focus groups**

    Like requirements workshops, focus groups are intended to bring groups of individuals together to explore, and capture requirements. Because participants are carefully selected to provide their insight and feedback, both sessions require an objective and neutral facilitator to guide conversations and activities.

    IIBA®, *BABOK® Guide* V2.0, 2009, 172, 198

4. **b. Allow a group of stakeholders to explore all possible ideas to generate a variety of solutions**

    Brainstorming is intended to allow a group of stakeholders to explore, without biases, all possible creative solutions.

    IIBA®, *BABOK® Guide* V2.0, 2009, 58, 157

5. **a. Allow lively and creative debate**

    The idea for brainstorming is to encourage creative thinking and to generate ideas quickly. Lively debate risks diverting the focus from the key purpose and may discourage participants from contributing.

    IIBA®, *BABOK® Guide* V2.0, 2009, 157

6. **b. Ask probing questions to confirm his or her understanding**

   After reviewing documentation from both the Enterprise Analysis phase and the Business Analysis Planning and Monitoring phase, a business analyst may very well consider interviewing stakeholders to ensure that he or she is clear on what the overall business goals and strategies and product scope are.

   IIBA®, *BABOK® Guide* V2.0, 2009, 179

7. **d. Document analysis**

   Although reviewing the existing documentation may prove to be both tedious and out-of-date, it would certainly give Michael a starting point from which to understand the AS-IS state of the accounting system.

   IIBA®, *BABOK® Guide* V2.0, 2009, 169

8. **a. Scribe**

   A scribe's role is to document the business requirements as they are uncovered during the workshop. He or she should be prepared to review the requirements with the team during the workshop for confirmation.

   IIBA®, *BABOK® Guide* V2.0, 2009, 198–199

9. **b. Document Analysis**

   Event based elicitation techniques involve direct interaction with stakeholders and would include their participation in defining requirements. The BABOK identifies the following as event based activities; brainstorming, focus groups, interviews, observation, prototyping, & requirements workshops. Non event based activities would include; document analysis, & interface analysis

   IIBA®, *BABOK® Guide* V2.0, 2009, 55

10. **c. Asking the users to talk about what they are doing so you can learn about the cognitive factors as well as the behavioral factors**

    By asking users to discuss what they're doing, you can encourage them to speak about those activities that might otherwise be done intuitively or without thinking. They might also be able to articulate challenges and point out shortcuts.

    IIBA®, *BABOK® Guide* V2.0, 2009, 187

11. **c. One to two hours**

    If a business analyst is well prepared and flexible, if the right group is selected, if a scribe is assigned, and if goals and objectives are defined, then one to two hours should be sufficient time for six to 12 attendees to address five or six questions.

    IIBA®, *BABOK® Guide* V2.0, 2009, 174

12. **b.** **False**

Interface analysis focuses primarily on what interfaces are needed, addressing such issues as connectivity to and from internal and external systems and hardware systems.

IIBA® BABOK® Guide V2.0, 2009, 176

13. **b.** **Glossary**

Ensuring that an up-to-date glossary is available during interface analysis will help to determine whether two or more systems depend on the same data.

IIBA® BABOK® Guide V2.0, 2009, 160

14. **d.** **It doesn't focus on the whats and whys.**

A business analyst must carefully adjust the expectations of the group involved in the prototyping of any interface or system. Users should focus on what is necessary to complete to task (the how questions). The what and why questions will be answered at a later point, during the elicitation and analysis process.

IIBA®, BABOK® Guide V2.0, 2009, 198

15. **b.** **False**

Interviews may also consider groups of people and be an informal process.

IIBA®, BABOK® Guide V2.0, 2009, 177

16. **b.** **Document analysis**

Document analysis is a way to examine the AS-IS state using existing documentation and to identify relevant information by considering such issues as business rules, entities, and attributes.

IIBA®, BABOK® Guide V2.0, 2009, 169

17. **b.** **Define the workshop agenda.**

An agenda will ensure that all participants are clear on the direction, points of discussion, and time frames to execute to the activities.

IIBA®, BABOK® Guide V2.0, 2009, 199

18. **b.** **Solution**

Solution requirements can be broken down into two subsequent categories: functional and nonfunctional requirements. Non-functional requirements provide "support" to further define functional requirements in that they describe required capabilities including usability and performance characteristics.

IIBA®, BABOK® Guide V2.0, 2009, 6, 184

19. **d.** **Job shadowing**

   Job shadowing is an alternative name or technique for observing the behavior of a user on the job.

   IIBA®, *BABOK® Guide* V2.0, 2009, 186

20. **d.** **Individuals in the group may self-censor if they are uncomfortable with their surroundings.**

   A heterogeneous audience is a group of individuals with a broad set of backgrounds, skills, talents, perspectives, and fears.

   IIBA®, *BABOK® Guide* V2.0, 2009, 173

21. **b.** **The means by which information is drawn out of stakeholders**

   The IIBA® definition of elicitation is to draw forth or bring out (something latent), to call forth or draw out as information or response. Models are validated during Requirements Analysis and Solution Assessment and Validation. Elicitation is done during Enterprise Analysis activities to realize the development of identified business solutions and business requirements and to address business problems and opportunities.

   IIBA®, *BABOK® Guide* V2.0, 2009, 53

22. **c.** **Provide information for visualizing interface requirements**

   The primary purpose of prototyping is visualization. The visual, tangible aspect of prototyping provides a means to communicate clearly with the stakeholders and developers, reduces abstraction (which could lead to confusion), and determines the feasibility of a solution in development.

   IIBA®, *BABOK® Guide* V2.0, 2009, 196

23. **d.** **Correct**

   Correct refers to the accuracy with which a requirement is captured, and accuracy may be dictated by organizational process assets and consequently may define the syntax with which requirements must be captured.

   IIBA®, *BABOK® Guide* V2.0, 2009, 53

24. **a.** **Vince wanted to ensure that if there were a collaborative effort among the projects, his project and the other projects would realize the full benefit of the collaboration.**

    A collaborative effort required for other projects would certainly affect Vince's project, although the effect might be a negative one: Requirements on his project might not be realized until the other projects were completed. On the other hand, requirements uncovered from another project could expedite the elicitation technique of interface analysis.

    IIBA®, *BABOK® Guide* V2.0, 2009, 176

25. **c.** **Evolutionary**

    While there are many different types of prototypes including; throw-away, vertical and horizontal prototypes, the evolutionary prototype is intended to work continuously with both input from developers and users in order to adapt the solution to system requirements

    IIBA®, *BABOK® Guide* V2.0, 2009, 198

26. **d.** **Requirements workshop**

    Because a requirements workshop depends on consensus from a carefully selected group of stakeholders, this technique generally proves to be the most cost-effective.

    IIBA®, *BABOK® Guide* V2.0, 2009, 198

27. **d.** **To ensure that the business analyst has accurately documented the results of the interview**

    While the interview is still fresh in the stakeholder's mind, it is recommended that a business analyst have the interviewee review the documentation to ensure that he or she conveyed what was intended to be conveyed.

    IIBA®, *BABOK® Guide* V2.0, 2009, 180

28. **a.** **Consultants' (SMEs') contracts**

    A consultant's contract would not likely reveal much about the AS-IS state of an existing system.

    IIBA®, *BABOK® Guide* V2.0, 2009, 170

29. **c.** **Conflicting opinions could prevent consensus.**

    A strong facilitator is necessary to work with a group to ensure consensus. He or she should be fully aware of the group dynamics before conducting the session to avoid unnecessary conflicts.

    IIBA®, *BABOK® Guide* V2.0, 2009, 200

30. **b.** **Closed-ended questions**

Closed-ended questions, which provide a respondent with a choice of answers, are much easier to analyze than are open-ended questions, particularly when validation of issues is required.

IIBA®, *BABOK® Guide* V2.0, 2009, 214

31. **c.** **Complete, clear, correct, and consistent**

When eliciting requirements, it should be the business analyst's goal to ensure that all requirements captured are complete, clear, correct, and consistent.

IIBA®, *BABOK® Guide* V2.0, 2009, 53

32. **b.** **Vertical prototyping**

Vertical prototyping focuses on understanding the feasibility of a specific area of the application in question—that is, how that specific area will function.

IIBA®, *BABOK® Guide* V2.0, 2009, 198

33. **a.** **Active interaction with stakeholders to define requirements**

Elicitation is the practice by which a business analyst interacts with stakeholders to draw forth something latent or potential, such as information or a response to an existing business need. Facilitated sessions and other techniques are activities employed to engage stakeholders or other available resources. What a stakeholder wants versus what the business needs often can be two very different sets of requirements, and as such, a business analyst must remain objective in his or her Elicitation approach.

IIBA®, *BABOK® Guide* V2.0, 2009, 53

34. **d.** **Transition**

The *BABOK® Guide* V2.0 defines four categories of requirements: business, stakeholder, solution, and transition requirements. Transition requirements are needed to describe how a proposed solution will migrate from an organization's current state to the desired state. They are considered temporary requirements and are often developed during solution assessment and validation activities. Transition requirements also describe needs such as data conversion and organizational and individual competencies.

IIBA®, *BABOK® Guide* V2.0, 2009, 6, 53

35. **a.** **Current processes**

These processes allow a business analyst to understand how users and stakeholders operate in the context of their environment, if it seemed that explanations from previous interviews were not accurate.

IIBA®, *BABOK® Guide* V2.0, 2009, 186

36.   **d.   Observation**

Observation, whose synonym is job shadowing, is one of many generally accepted elicitation techniques. This technique allows a business analyst to observe a stakeholder's work environment in order to help provide insight into the current environmental state or conditions.

IIBA®, *BABOK® Guide* V2.0, 2009, 53, 186

37.   **d.   A RACI chart**

The most critical piece of information at this point for Stacy would be a RACI chart, which would give her insight into the stakeholders' respective roles. Supporting documentation to the RACI chart would address such issues as stakeholders' willingness to participate and a group's ability to reach consensus. A RACI chart is likely to be part of the stakeholders list, roles and responsibilities produced during the planning and monitoring activities, specifically stakeholder analysis.

IIBA®, *BABOK® Guide* V2.0, 2009, 29, 54-55

38.   **a.   Ground Rules**

Ground rules will ensure that bringing stakeholders to consensus in an orderly fashion, timing of feedback, and a means to ensure that information elicited during the session is verified and acceptable to all stakeholders for signoff.

IIBA®, *BABOK® Guide* V2.0, 2009, 55

39.   **b.   Qualitative research**

Focus groups are a method of qualitative research used to identify themes, perspectives, attributes, and experiences.

IIBA®, *BABOK® Guide* V2.0, 2009, 172

40.   **d.   [Stated, Unconfirmed]**

Requirements [stated, unconfirmed] are those requirements that have been captured during an event based requirements elicitation activity and documented by a business analyst. Until such a point in time that a business analyst can confirm the elicitation results requirements in this state are produced as a result of a business analysts understanding of what stakeholders intentions are.

IIBA®, *BABOK® Guide* V2.0, 2009, 61

REQUIREMENTS MANAGEMENT AND COMMUNICATION

STUDY HINTS

The primary purpose of the Requirements Management and Communication knowledge area is to ensure that all stakeholders affected by the solution in question are aware of the supporting activities and outcomes that support the desired outcome. This knowledge area consists of five major activities that focus on bringing a group of stakeholders to a collective understanding. The Requirements Management and Communication knowledge area entails the whos, whats, whys, whens, wheres, and hows of developing and maintaining a requirements baseline, communicating business analysis progress, and obtaining sign-offs. As a result, it is necessary to ask yourself, "What is the best way to communicate deliverables? Are there different formats? Do different types of audiences require different levels of detailed information and is the timing of delivery of the information influenced by the type of stakeholder to whom you are delivering the message? You can expect approximately 24 questions on Requirements Management and Communication tasks (that is, 16 percent of the exam). Figure 5 depicts the five major tasks of Requirements Management and Communication, as well as the inputs and outputs of those tasks. Each high-level task has an associated *BABOK® Guide* V2.0 section number and comprises many subtasks. The model provides a visual context; actual execution of some tasks may be parallel and iterative.

❖ **Start your learning process by reviewing the overall task flow of this knowledge area.** Keep in mind that this knowledge area interfaces with all the other knowledge areas. Communication is iterative and conducted in parallel with other activities.

FOCUS TOPICS FOR STUDY

After you understand the overall flow, focus your attention on the following deliverables: the requirements communication plan, requirements issue log, and the requirements package.

❖ **When studying this knowledge area you will quickly realize that requirements traceability is not simply understanding the differences between derivation and allocation.**[3] Your understanding of the different types of relationships amongst requirements will prove to be equally important. They include necessity, effort, subset, cover, and value.

---

[3]   IIBA®, *BABOK® Guide* V2.0, 2009, 68.

❖ **The distinction between a configuration management system and a coverage matrix will provide insight into the number of requirements captured and stored by either method.**[4]

❖ **Know the components of the requirements package, including the differences between a work product and a deliverable.**[5] Various formats for presenting requirements are provided, depending on the purpose and audience.

❖ **Know the purpose and definition of maintaining requirements for reuse.**[6]

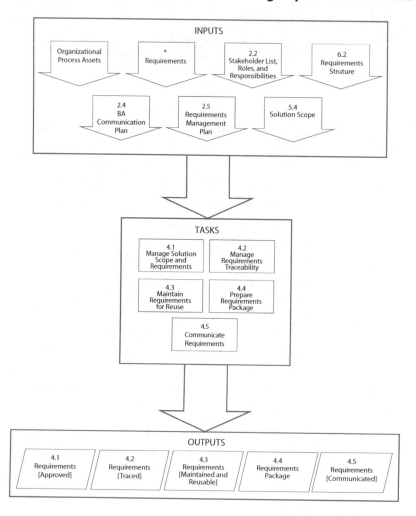

FIGURE 5. INPUTS, TASKS, AND OUTPUTS FOR REQUIREMENTS MANAGEMENT AND COMMUNICATION[7]

NOTES: 1. AN * INSIDE AN ICON IN THE ABOVE DIAGRAM INDICATES THAT THE ITEM IN QUESTION WAS LIKELY PRODUCED AS A RESULT OF MULTIPLE TASKS, 2. A NUMBER X.Y CITED IN AN ICON IN THE ABOVE DIAGRAM INDICATES THE KNOWLEDGE AREA AND TASKS THAT EITHER PRODUCED THE ARTIFACT OR WILL USE THE ARTIFACT AS AN INPUT. 3. AN ICON WITH NO * OR NUMBER WAS PRODUCED EXTERNALLY.

---

4   IIBA®, *BABOK® Guide* V2.0, 2009, 70.

5   IIBA®, *BABOK® Guide* V2.0, 2009, 74–75.

6   IIBA®, *BABOK® Guide* V2.0, 2009, 75–76.

7   Adapted from Figure 4-1, *BABOK® Guide* V2.0, 63.

INDEX OF SELECTIVE TERMS AND PHRASES

Be able to explain the terms and phrases listed in Table 3. One caveat: The *BABOK® Guide* V2.0 page(s) shown provides a definition, a description, or a use of the term or phrase. The term or phrase may also appear on other pages.

TABLE 3. SELECTIVE TERMS AND PHRASES FOR REQUIREMENTS MANAGEMENT AND COMMUNICATION

Term or Phrase	BABOK® Guide V2.0 Page(s)
Allocation	69
Baseline	64, 66
Baselining	66
Configuration management system	70
Conflict and issue management	65
Coverage	69
Coverage matrix	70
Deliverables	75
Derivation	69
Domain SME	67
Effort	69
Facilitation	150
Impact analysis	69
Implementation SME	67
Necessity	69
Ongoing requirements	71
Problem Tracking	190
Request for Information	76
Request for Proposal	76
Request for Quote	76
Requirements [maintained and reusable]	72
Requirements communication	63
Requirements coverage	69
Requirements package	77
Requirements presentation	79

Term or Phrase	BABOK® Guide V2.0 Page(s)
Requirements review	66
Requirements signoff	66
Requirements traceability	67
Requirements workshop	198
Satisfied requirements	72
Solution requirements [communicated or traced]	64
Solution scope	64, 125
Stakeholder requirements [communicated or traced]	64
Structured walkthrough	211
Subset	69
Transition requirements [communicated or traced]	64
Value	69
Vendor selection	76
Requirements [approved]	67
Requirements [communicated]	64, 80
Requirements [maintained and reusable]	72
Requirements [traced]	64, 70
Requirements package	72

PRACTICE QUESTIONS

INSTRUCTIONS: Note the most suitable answer for each multiple-choice question in the appropriate space on the answer sheet.

1. What is the primary purpose for establishing a requirements baseline?
    a. To ensure that requirements satisfy stakeholder needs
    b. To ensure that the solution passes user acceptance testing
    c. To ensure that a reference point is established to identify scope changes and to track actual project progress
    d. To ensure that a reference point at the beginning of the project is maintained so that no changes to the requirements are allowed

2. It prevents unnecessary change requests. It is mandatory during a requirements review that the _____ be present.
    a. Scribe
    b. Project manager
    c. Moderator
    d. Author

3. A traceability/coverage matrix can identify predecessors and successors. It can also show the linkage between high-level product descriptions and requirements. What is wrong with this traceability matrix?

	REQUIREMENT 1	REQUIREMENT 2	REQUIREMENT 3
PRODUCT 1_DESCRIPTION 1	•	•	
PRODUCT 2_DESCRIPTION 2	•	•	•
PRODUCT 3_DESCRIPTION 3	•		•
PRODUCT 4_DESCRIPTION 4	•		•
PRODUCT 5_DESCRIPTION 5	•		•

    a. Requirement 2 cannot be traced back to product descriptions 3, 4, and 5.
    b. Product 1_Description 1 is not traceable to Requirement 3.
    c. Product 2_Description 2 has too many requirements.
    d. Requirement 1 is listed in too many product descriptions and could be decomposed further.

4. Most presentations will likely be based on a certain component of the business requirements document. The _____ must be carefully considered to help the business analyst determine the level of detail and objectives in order to get sign-off.
    a. Solution recommendation
    b. Audience
    c. Duration
    d. Location

5. Which of the following choices is NOT considered a Requirements Management and Communication activity?

    a. Manage solution scope and requirements
    b. Ensure usability of the solution
    c. Manage requirements traceability
    d. Prepare requirements package

6. _____ are considered as input to the Communicate Requirements task.

    a. Requirements [communicated]
    b. BA communication plan
    c. Requirements [stated]
    d. Requirements packages

7. Who is the primary communicator of requirements in a project?

    a. Business analyst
    b. Project manager
    c. Stakeholders
    d. Business project sponsor

8. A best practice for managing requirements conflicts would be to—

    a. Host a pep rally to encourage team participation
    b. Hire a mediator to negotiate the issues
    c. Allow stakeholders enough time to figure it out for themselves
    d. Facilitate communication with the stakeholders to resolve the conflict

9. Which facilitation technique are you most likely to use in the case of a requirements conflict?

    a. Prototyping
    b. Brainstorming
    c. Formal meetings
    d. Visioning

10. When planning to conduct a requirements presentation, a business analyst should be sure to include critical information. If the BA creates an outline, which of the following items should NOT be included in the outline?

    a. Project background
    b. Introductions
    c. Presentation objectives
    d. Summary and review of Gantt chart activities

11. You are about to present your requirements to the software development team. Which of the following choices would you likely include in the presentation?

    a. High-level requirements

    b. Assumptions

    c. All requirements

    d. Goals and objectives

12. Company ABC is considering purchasing new software that will help with its supply chain management challenges. As the principal business analyst creating a Requirements Management and Communication plan, you want to be sure that your review includes a—

    a. Review of detailed functional requirements

    b. Technical review of the differences between the existing system and the new system

    c. Review of processes, data modes, and business rules

    d. Review of business and user requirements, as well as constraints and possibly a structured walk-through

13. What is the purpose of a formal requirements review?

    a. To obtain sign-off from all stakeholders involved in the project

    b. To conduct a focus group session to determine which requirements are good

    c. To validate the time and effort required to continue collecting requirements

    d. To give stakeholders an opportunity to verify the completeness of the requirements

14. Not every work product needs to be included in a—

    a. Database

    b. Deliverable

    c. Online collaboration tool

    d. Formal presentation

15. What would be a recommended component of an introduction to your Requirements Management and Communication plan for any given audience?

    a. Steps and deliverables in the review process

    b. Risk management plan

    c. Overview of costs and schedules

    d. Detailed description of the proposed solution

16. Status reports to convey progress on requirements development are integral to which type of presentation?

    a. Informal presentation

    b. Formal presentation

    c. Mandatory presentation

    d. Structured walk-through

17. Requirements sign-off is completed only when—
    a. The stakeholder has signed off
    b. All stakeholders have signed off
    c. The project manager and business analyst have signed off
    d. The IT architects have signed off

18. It is important to let participants know that, during a requirements review, they are NOT there to—
    a. Solve problems
    b. Review project background
    c. Review deliverable status
    d. Agree to a course of action

19. Susan was very particular about ensuring that all her documentation was accurate and up-to-date. The project in question involved 86 stakeholders. To make certain that all stakeholders were clear on the requirements that were specific to them, Susan decided to—
    a. Create different versions of the package for each group of stakeholders
    b. Present the entire package to all stakeholders at the same time
    c. Create a single requirements package with a table of contents that directed stakeholders to their individual areas of interest
    d. Create subpackages containing information specific to each stakeholder

20. Requirements reviews may also be referred to as—
    a. Edits
    b. Walk-throughs
    c. Constructive criticism
    d. Validation sessions

21. The expected outcome for the creation of a requirements package is a—
    a. Comprehensive review of all requirements
    b. Sign-off
    c. Verification of all the requirements
    d. Validation of all the requirements

22. For Harry to successfully create and manage the appropriate communications plan, he should have a clear understanding of—
    a. Project stakeholders
    b. Desired solution outcome
    c. Contents of the communication plan template
    d. How to create a presentation using presentation software

23. A likely outcome from your requirements presentation is—
    a. Clear understanding of business strategy
    b. Development of user profiles
    c. Actions for business users
    d. Definition of work division strategies

24. Kendall finally completed the last of her analysis and documentation activities, and the executive team was anxious to hear her results. What information should Kendall selectively present to the executive team?
    a. The entire business requirements document
    b. User and system requirements
    c. Regulatory and business requirements
    d. Goals, objectives, impact, and risks

25. According to the *BABOK® Guide* V2.0, a _____ is a formal collection of supporting documentation to organize and analyze requirements.
    a. Database
    b. Online collaborative tool
    c. Work product
    d. Requirements management tool

26. Fran was preparing for a requirements review. One stipulation that she made for participation in the review was that—
    a. Attendees at the session must have reviewed the requirements before the group session
    b. Attendees must have actively participated in the analysis and documentation activities
    c. All documentation to be reviewed needed to be signed off on by all stakeholders before the review
    d. All documentation needed to be complete, accurate, and within the project scope

27. Which kind of requirements presentation involves obtaining acceptance and sign-off, as well as prioritizing a set of requirements?
    a. Informal presentation
    b. Formal presentation
    c. Mandatory presentation
    d. Structured walk-through

28. When considering the development of your Requirements Management and Communication template, which of the following items would you include?
    a. Version number, WBS, approach, and schedule
    b. Version number, approach, schedule, and QA process
    c. WBS, QA process, assumptions, and risks
    d. Approach, schedule, assumptions, and risks

29. Kate was preparing to have several of her requirements packages reviewed. She intended to send the first package out to the business unit managers for a preview. It is likely that Kate asked them to review the—

    a. Entity relationship diagrams
    b. Process decomposition diagrams
    c. Quality assurance and government regulations documentation
    d. Results from black-box re-engineering activities

30. Each requirements package should include a(n)—

    a. Appendix
    b. Stakeholder profiles
    c. Table of contents
    d. Section for diagrams

31. Ideally, Mark would like to conclude his requirements session with a—

    a. List of grammatical and punctuation errors
    b. List of agreed-upon issues
    c. Stakeholder sign-off
    d. Clearly defined project scope

32. How does traceability aid in scope management?

    a. It ensures clarity of customers' needs by tracing functional requirements back to business requirements.
    b. It provides an understanding of how specifications will pass user acceptance testing.
    c. It helps to better understand how design function impacts project scope.

33. Formal sign-off of requirements acknowledges that stakeholders—

    a. Agree with the proposed solution
    b. Are clear about the proposed budget
    c. Agree that the requirements are accurate and complete
    d. Agree that it is time to build the proposed solution

34. True or false: More than one requirements package may be created for a project.

    a. True
    b. False

35. The primary goal of Requirements Management and Communication is to—

    a. Define with clarity the approach a business analyst will take to deliver requirements
    b. Ensure that all stakeholders are clear about the deliverables of a proposed solution
    c. Identify all stakeholders and their explicit needs for communication
    d. Identify metrics to be considered for the management of requirements

36. Where communication activities are concerned, part of the responsibility of the business analyst is to—
    a. Communicate as often as possible to all stakeholders
    b. Determine relevancy of requirements to a diverse group of stakeholders
    c. Ensure that all stakeholders are aware of all requirements necessary to develop the solution
    d. Provide the stakeholders with a status update on all project activities

37. Ensuring that the development of requirements maps back to _____ is part of the requirements management activities and responsibility of the BA.
    a. Business objectives
    b. Communicated requirements
    c. Functional requirements
    d. Nonfunctional requirements

38. Reviewers are encouraged to comment on _____ and not the _____.
    a. Processes; language used
    b. Modeling notation; stakeholders
    c. Content; author
    d. Typos; contributor

39. Why should a business analyst be involved in the RFP and RFI process?
    a. To ensure that the RFP or RFI is essentially a means for prospective vendors to map their solutions to the described business requirements
    b. To accurately understand all stakeholders needs
    c. To determine exactly what solution is appropriate for the stakeholders
    d. To gain insight into what the desired deliverables are and how the business requirements could be met by a possible vendor

40. The primary goal of requirements traceability is to—
    a. Ensure that a risk response plan is properly managed and maintained.
    b. Provide insight into scope and change management issues
    c. Demonstrate lineage to originally stated business goals and objectives
    d. Ensure that all sibling requirements have a parent(s) requirement

Answer Sheet

1.	a	b	c	d
2.	a	b	c	d
3.	a	b	c	d
4.	a	b	c	d
5.	a	b	c	d
6.	a	b	c	d
7.	a	b	c	d
8.	a	b	c	d
9.	a	b	c	d
10.	a	b	c	d
11.	a	b	c	d
12.	a	b	c	d
13.	a	b	c	d
14.	a	b	c	d
15.	a	b	c	d
16.	a	b	c	d
17.	a	b	c	d
18.	a	b	c	d
19.	a	b	c	d
20.	a	b	c	d

21.	a	b	c	d
22.	a	b	c	d
23.	a	b	c	d
24.	a	b	c	d
25.	a	b	c	d
26.	a	b	c	d
27.	a	b	c	d
28.	a	b	c	d
29.	a	b	c	d
30.	a	b	c	d
31.	a	b	c	d
32.	a	b	c	d
33.	a	b	c	d
34.	a	b		
35.	a	b	c	d
36.	a	b	c	d
37.	a	b	c	d
38.	a	b	c	d
39.	a	b	c	d
40.	a	b	c	d

ANSWER KEY

1. **c.** **To ensure that a reference point is established to identify scope changes and to track actual project progress**

    A baseline is established to ensure that the validity of both the requirements and the developed solution do not deviate from the stakeholders' originally proposed business solution.

    IIBA®, *BABOK® Guide* V2.0, 2009, 66

2. **d.** **Author**

    The author must be present so that reviewers can have their questions answered about content. Thus the author receives firsthand any comments or suggestions and can make changes accordingly. Yet, although it is desirable for a moderator to be present, budget constraints often prevent using a moderator.

    IIBA®, *BABOK® Guide* V2.0, 2009, 212

3. **d.** **Requirement 1 is listed in too many product descriptions and could be decomposed further.**

    Because Requirement 1 is listed in too many product descriptions, it may prove very difficult to apply test strategies. Requirement 1 should probably be decomposed further, as it is too broad in its definition.

    IIBA®, *BABOK® Guide* V2.0, 2009, 70

4. **b.** **Audience**

    The audience must be carefully considered for determining content and objectives. Sharing a detailed overview of system requirements will not likely be very productive. The executive sponsor of the project is probably more interested in such issues as assumptions, constraints, and business requirements.

    IIBA®, *BABOK® Guide* V2.0, 2009, 63, 73

5. **b.** **Ensure usability of the solution**

    "Ensure usability of the solution" falls under the Solution Assessment and Validation activities.

    IIBA®, *BABOK® Guide* V2.0, 2009, 63

6. **d.** **Requirements packages**

    The level of formality selected during planning and monitoring activities, determines how the requirements package is articulated and to whom the information contained within the requirements packages is best articulated to.

    IIBA®, *BABOK® Guide* V2.0, 2009, 78-79

7. **a. Business analyst**

For all things requirements-related, the BA is responsible for developing and managing communication to all stakeholders. If the project is of significant size, the BA may choose to appoint representatives to communicate with the lead BA's directives.

IIBA®, *BABOK® Guide* V2.0, 2009, 63

8. **d. Facilitate communication with the stakeholder to resolve the conflict**

More often than not, especially within complex projects with a large representation of stakeholders, conflicts and disagreement about requirements will come to surface. It is a business analyst's responsibility to facilitate conflict to resolution where possible. This can be done in a formal or informal setting or through a third-party arbitrator. There are a number of techniques, including voting, that may help to resolve conflict. Conflict regarding requirements must be resolved in order to gain formal and final approval of said requirements.

IIBA®, *BABOK® Guide* V2.0, 2009, 65

9. **c. Formal meetings**

Where conflict cannot be resolved in a requirements workshop setting, a formal meeting may be convened where a third-party facilitator or arbitrator may be present to employ whatever methods are appropriate to resolve the conflict.

IIBA®, *BABOK® Guide* V2.0, 2009, 65

10. **d. Summary and review of Gantt chart activities**

This task is likely to be the responsibility of a project manager.

IIBA®, *BABOK® Guide* V2.0, 2009, 79–80

11. **c. All requirements**

Developers are the creators of the solution. As such, they should intimately know all requirements: AS-IS and TO-BE states, goals, objectives, assumptions, constraints, and so forth.

IIBA®, *BABOK® Guide* V2.0, 2009, 80

12. **d.** **Review of business and user requirements, as well as constraints and possibly a structured walk-through**

In a situation where the solution has been purchased (COTS), detailed functional requirements are likely to pre-exist within the product itself. In the situation where an upgrade to existing systems is at hand, reviewing the difference between the two systems is critically important. If changes to an existing business process are the solution, then examining the requirements that support process, data, and business rules plays a critical role. Reviewing the constraints, as well as the business and user requirements, is the best course of action considering a COTS-based solution. The constraints review is especially important.

IIBA®, *BABOK® Guide* V2.0, 2009, 80

13. **d.** **To give stakeholders an opportunity to verify the completeness of the requirements**

Requirements reviews, which can be done iteratively, seek to verify the accuracy, feasibility, clarity, correctness, and scope of requirements.

IIBA®, *BABOK® Guide* V2.0, 2009, 79

14. **b.** **Deliverable**

Deliverables are documents required to demonstrate work that has been completed. Deliverables play a critical role in the Requirements Management and Communication plan by helping a business analyst to determine who shall receive what information and when it will be received.

IIBA®, *BABOK® Guide* V2.0, 2009, 75

15. **a.** **Steps and deliverables in the review process**

Steps and deliverables in the review process are critical for setting stakeholders' expectations of the requirements about to be communicated and for achieving the desired outcome for the session. Other components include executive summary of the package, frequency of review sessions, list of other reviews, and so forth.

IIBA®, *BABOK® Guide* V2.0, 2009, 79

16. **a.** **Informal presentation**

Generally speaking, if no stakeholder sign-off, prioritization, scope impact, or consensus are required, a presentation could be deemed informal. Usually, informal presentations are done as a "one-way" communication. Status reports fall into this category.

IIBA®, *BABOK® Guide* V2.0, 2009, 80

REQUIREMENTS MANAGEMENT AND COMMUNICATION

17. **b.** **All stakeholders have signed off**

If the opportunity exists, all stakeholders should sign off on their respective requirements packages. All stakeholders should have been identified during Requirements Planning and Management activities and further clarified during Requirements Communication planning.

IIBA®, *BABOK® Guide* V2.0, 2009, 67

18. **a.** **Solve problems**

The idea behind a review is to verify the requirements' accuracy rather than to find the perfect solution. If a solution can be found within a relatively short time without losing the focus of the review, then it needs to be included.

IIBA®, *BABOK® Guide* V2.0, 2009, 80, 211

19. **d.** **Create subpackages containing information specific to each stakeholder**

Creating different versions would make it challenging to keep documents up-to-date. Subpackages allow a more structured approach to distributing requirements and to ensuring that individual stakeholders' needs are addressed for purposes of clarity and sign-off.

IIBA®, *BABOK® Guide* V2.0, 2009, 77

20. **b.** **Walk throughs**

Requirements reviews are also referred to as walk throughs, peer reviews, or inspections.

IIBA®, *BABOK® Guide* V2.0, 2009, 80, 211

21. **b.** **Sign-off**

Sign-off from stakeholders for continuous development of requirements or the completion of requirements is expected as a result of the creation of the requirements package.

IIBA®, *BABOK® Guide* V2.0, 2009, 79

22. **a.** **Project stakeholders**

Knowing all the project stakeholders gives a business analyst a greater chance of success of correctly tailoring the communication format.

IIBA®, *BABOK® Guide* V2.0, 2009, 78

23. **c.** **Actions for business users**

All these items, with the exception of choice c, result from facilitated sessions, whether during the Enterprise Analysis phase or the Business Analysis Planning and Monitoring phase. The purpose of presentations is to ensure that all stakeholders understand clearly what the requirements are in their current state. This will allow the group to reach consensus or sign-off. If consensus has not been achieved, then there may be an opportunity for business users to clarify a business analyst's findings with additional activities, which may result in additional facilitated sessions.

IIBA®, *BABOK® Guide* V2.0, 2009, 79–80

24. **d.** **Goals, objectives, impact, and risks**

It is not likely that the executive team will be interested in or will read the entire business requirements document. User and system requirements should be presented to the user of the product. Customers are most interested in adherence to regulatory requirements and in how the regulations fit the customers' business needs. Executives, on the other hand, are most interested in how the proposed requirements would align with their organizational goals and objectives and in what risks and effects (positive or negative) the requirements may have on their business.

IIBA®, *BABOK® Guide* V2.0, 2009, 73

25. **c.** **Work product**

At any point during a project, a business analyst may be called upon to share his or her work products. Examples include meeting minutes, an issues log, a work plan, and status reports.

IIBA®, *BABOK® Guide* V2.0, 2009, 74

26. **a.** **Attendees at the session must have reviewed the requirements before the group session**

It is desirable that attendees read the assigned package or deliverable, so that they arrive at the session prepared to discuss any inconsistencies in the requirements package.

IIBA®, *BABOK® Guide* V2.0, 2009, 80

27. **b.** **Formal presentation**

Formal presentations of a requirements package are most often conducted to gain approval for developing a solution or for moving to the next iteration of requirements development (based on the prioritization of requirements).

IIBA®, *BABOK® Guide* V2.0, 2009, 66–67

28. **d.** **Approach, schedule, assumptions, and risks**

How and to whom you deliver your communication, the frequency of your communication, assumptions (whether all meetings are allowed or are not), and the associated risks are all necessary components of Requirements Communication. Version number would also be considered an essential element.

IIBA®, *BABOK® Guide* V2.0, 2009, 78

29. **b.** **Process decomposition diagrams**

A process decomposition diagram would show the business unit manager a high-level breakdown and hierarchy of his or her business process descriptions.

IIBA®, *BABOK® Guide* V2.0, 2009, 77

30. **c.** **Table of contents**

A clearly defined table of contents allows a business analyst to categorize his or her requirements according to the audience's needs, as well as for ease of navigation.

IIBA®, *BABOK® Guide* V2.0, 2009, 75

31. **b.** **List of agreed-upon issues**

All issues—including ambiguities, redundancy, feasibility, and priority of requirements—need to be documented and acted upon according to an agreed-upon plan of action.

IIBA®, *BABOK® Guide* V2.0, 2009, 66

32. **a.** **It ensures clarity of customers' needs by tracing functional requirements back to business requirements.**

Functional requirements are a by-product of what has been defined during the Enterprise Analysis phase. The EA phase proposes to uncover the overarching business need as such. Dependencies of functional requirements to the business must be clearly understood to prevent scope creep.

IIBA®, *BABOK® Guide* V2.0, 2009, 68–69

33. **c.** **Agree that the requirements are accurate and complete**

Formal agreement on accuracy of requirements by stakeholders ensures that the project scope has been clearly defined, and it may help to avoid developing new requirements while working on the solution.

IIBA®, *BABOK® Guide* V2.0, 2009, 66–67

34. **a.** **True**

Although requirements packages can be created at any point during a project, they can also be tailored to meet certain audience expectations or needs.

IIBA®, *BABOK® Guide* V2.0, 2009, 74

35. **b.** **Ensure that all stakeholders are clear about the deliverables of a proposed solution**

Requirements Management and Communication activities serve to ensure that all stakeholders are clear in their understanding of the proposed solution and in agreement with the requirements serving to deliver the solution.

IIBA®, *BABOK® Guide* V2.0, 2009, 63

36. **b.** **Determine relevancy of requirements to a diverse group of stakeholders**

It is critical that the business analyst understand what requirements, what level of formality, what degree of frequency, and that he or she delivers requirements communication with the highest possible level of clarity and conciseness.

IIBA®, *BABOK® Guide* V2.0, 2009, 78

37. **a.** **Business objectives**

The role of the BA in the management of requirements is to ensure that business goals and objectives are mapped directly into the solution through the development of requirements.

IIBA®, *BABOK® Guide* V2.0, 2009, 63

38. **c.** **Content; author**

It is important that the reviewers focus on content. Any potentially ambiguous requirements, omissions, or lack of clarity in the requirements are the session's focus—not the author or the author's ability. It is crucial that stakeholders maintain a level of objectivity. With that in mind, a checklist for them to use may be invaluable.

IIBA®, *BABOK® Guide* V2.0, 2009, 80, 211–212

39. **a.** **To ensure that the RFP or RFI is essentially a means for prospective vendors to map their solutions to the described business requirements**

A business analyst needs to be involved in capturing the requirements necessary, likely as an RFP or RFI, to solve a business problem or opportunity. Because these requirements must be met by external vendors, the business analyst should be involved in assessing and evaluating all responses from vendors.

IIBA®, *BABOK® Guide* V2.0, 2009, 76

40. **c.** **Demonstrate lineage to the originally stated business goals and objectives.**

While all responses in this question are correct, the *BABOK®* suggests that the primary reason to demonstrate requirements traceability is to ensure that all requirements, demonstrate traceability back to the originally stated goals and objectives.

IIBA®, *BABOK® Guide* V2.0, 2009, 68

ENTERPRISE ANALYSIS

STUDY HINTS

Enterprise Analysis (EA) forms the foundation from which all subsequent requirements evolve. The activities in this knowledge area collectively demonstrate the purpose for undertaking the development of a solution and ensure that what is being developed is in alignment with the overall goals and objectives of the sponsoring organization. You can expect approximately 21 questions on EA tasks on the CBAP® exam (that is, 15.33 percent of the exam). Figure 6 shows the EA tasks, including inputs required and expected outputs. Each task has the associated Business Analysis Body of Knowledge® (*BABOK® Guide* V2.0) section number. The model provides a visual context; actual execution of some tasks may be parallel and iterative. The application of Elicitation, Requirements Analysis, and Solution Assessment and Validation activities are all guided by both Business Analysis Planning and Monitoring and Requirements Management and Communication.

> ❖ ***Start your learning process by reviewing the overall task flow of this knowledge area.*** The review starts with the establishment of a strategic plan. According to this plan, the heart of the area is the selection of a program of projects that supports the plan. Note that the effort does not end with the selection; rather, it continues with the monitoring of project successes through the use of metrics. The EA work is never complete. Strategic plans continue to evolve; new projects are identified in response; and past business cases should be monitored to ensure that investment is still warranted and that business value is finally realized. Benefit tracking may continue past the project's completion.

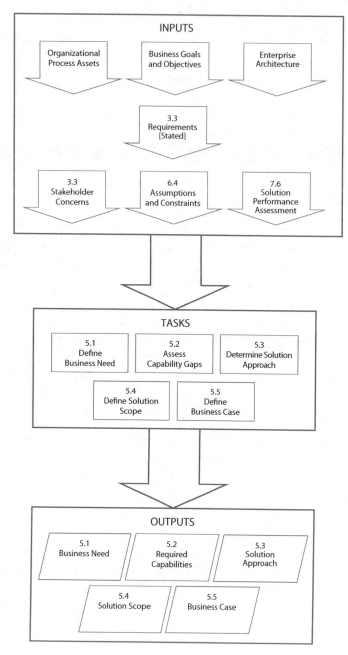

FIGURE 6. INPUTS, TASKS, AND OUTPUTS FOR ENTERPRISE ANALYSIS[8]

NOTES: 1. AN * INSIDE AN ICON IN THE ABOVE DIAGRAM INDICATES THAT THE ITEM IN QUESTION WAS LIKELY PRODUCED AS A RESULT OF MULTIPLE TASKS, 2. A NUMBER X.Y CITED IN AN ICON IN THE ABOVE DIAGRAM INDICATES THE KNOWLEDGE AREA AND TASKS THAT EITHER PRODUCED THE ARTIFACT OR WILL USE THE ARTIFACT AS AN INPUT. 3. AN ICON WITH NO * OR NUMBER WAS PRODUCED EXTERNALLY.

---

[8]   Adapted from Figure 5-1, *BABOK® Guide* V2.0, 81.

FOCUS TOPICS FOR STUDY

After you understand the overall flow, focus your attention on how project selection is accomplished. First, note the need for a business architecture framework to provide context for a proposed project.

❖ *Understand how to use the methods for conducting feasibility studies and analyzing alternatives.*[9] The outcome is a recommended proposal that needs to be scoped and examined using a supporting business case, and a risk assessment.

❖ *Know the means by which a business need can be generated, including the four different approaches.* This is only possible if you have an understanding of the business' goals and objectives, the business need or opportunity, and finally the desired outcome. Of course, a desired outcome can only be achieved by ensuring that an organization and its resources are competent enough to accomplish its goals or that it acquires said competencies either by working with a vendor or developing them internally.

❖ *Developing solution scope ensures that direction is given to what will be involved and how the conceptualized solution will be realized.*

❖ *Understand how to craft a problem or vision statement using the four elements cited in the BABOK® Guide V2.0 (p. 94).*

❖ *Many of the tasks and techniques in this knowledge area deal with decision, root cause analysis, SWOT (strengths-weaknesses-opportunities-threats) analysis, functional decomposition, estimation, and benchmarking. Be clear on your understanding of these critical techniques*. Furthermore, do not dismiss process modeling techniques to help you understand the scope of activities that will be explored to realize a solution.

❖ *Have a good comprehension of the project selection and priority process.*[10] After the decision package is approved, an assigned project manager (PM) develops a project charter.

INDEX OF SELECTIVE TERMS AND PHRASES

Be able to explain the terms and phrases listed in Table 4. One caveat: The *BABOK® Guide* V2.0 page(s) shown provides a definition, a description, or a use of the term or phrase. The term or phrase may also appear on other pages.

---

[9]   IIBA®, *BABOK® Guide* V2.0, 2009, 90.

[10]   IIBA®, *BABOK® Guide* V2.0, 2009, 96–97.

TABLE 4. SELECTIVE TERMS AND PHRASES FOR ENTERPRISE ANALYSIS

Term or Phrase	BABOK® Guide V2.0 Page(s)
Analogous estimation	170
Assumptions	87, 90, 92, 95
Average rate of return	167
Benchmarking	85, 156
Bottom-up estimation	171
Business analysis	3
Business architecture	224
Business case	94, 224
Business goals and objectives	83
Business need	81, 224
Business problem or opportunity	84
Capability gap	85
Cause-and-effect diagram	202
Commercial off-the-shelf (COTS) packages	225
Constraints	90, 92, 224
Context diagram	207
Cost benefit analysis	225
Data flow diagrams (DFD)	161
Decision analysis	166
Desired outcome	84
Delphi estimation	171
Discounted cash flow	167
Domain modeling	224
Enterprise analysis	81
Enterprise architecture	86
Estimation	171
Feasibility study	90, 227
Feature	227
Functional decomposition	174

Term or Phrase	BABOK® Guide V2.0 Page(s)
Historic analysis	171
Internal rate of return	167
Net present value	167
Parametric estimation	170
Requirements [stated]	83
Risk assessment	96
Rolling wave estimation	171
Root cause analysis	202
Six Sigma	195
SMART	83–84
Solution approach	88
Solution scope	91, 232
Strategic planning	217
SWOT (strengths-weaknesses-opportunities-threats) analysis	88, 90, 97, 217
System interface analysis	176
Three-point estimation	171
Work breakdown structure	97, 175, 235

PRACTICE QUESTIONS

INSTRUCTIONS: Note the most suitable answer for each multiple-choice question in the appropriate space on the answer sheet.

1. Which of the following choices is not a prescribed technique for the development of solution scope?

   a. Functional decomposition
   b. Interface analysis
   c. Root cause analysis
   d. User stories

2. Select the one word that best describes a business case:

   a. Accurate
   b. Quantitative
   c. Qualitative
   d. Practical

3. Which of the following activities is NOT part of the Enterprise Analysis process?

   a. Definition of assumptions and constraints
   b. Determination of solution approach
   c. Development of the business case
   d. Prioritization of requirements

4. Who is ultimately responsible for ensuring that the defined business needs are met as defined by Enterprise Analysis activities?

   a. Business analyst
   b. Business sponsor
   c. Project manager
   d. Quality assurance manager

5. A business process model is something that can be described as a(n)—

   a. Broad look at the people, processes, and technologies based on their business units, functions, or locations
   b. Activity model that reflects on the horizontal view of the enterprise, regardless of business units or functions
   c. Activity to describe the relationships between unchanging information
   d. Actor's involvement in business process or system functions

6. According to *BABOK® Guide* V2.0, risk is an—

   a. Uncertain event that, if it occurs, has a negative effect on the project constraints
   b. Event, the probability of the event, the impact, and the planned response
   c. Assessment of organizational readiness
   d. Uncertain event that, if it occurs, has a negative or positive effect on the project constraints

7. Ron has been assigned the task of conducting a feasibility study for his company Creative Solutions Inc. All market trends indicate that service-oriented architecture integration software is very much in demand. Which documentation or activities should Ron consider to begin the task of conducting his feasibility study?

    a. Strategic plans and goals
    b. Business case report
    c. Risk response plan
    d. Root cause analysis

8. Which technique is most likely to be used to define and development solution scope?

    a. Context diagrams
    b. Business case
    c. Prototyping
    d. Requirements workshop

9. The Pollination Company, an online flower-ordering company, hired Art as an external consultant to determine the best solutions for increasing its overall profitability from 53 to 61 percent in an 18-month period. He examined all aspects of the business and came up with three possible alternatives. Which technique would be best suited for Art to help communicate the logic behind the selection of a recommended solution?

    a. Use case model
    b. Feasibility study
    c. Decision analysis
    d. POLDAT framework

10. During what Enterprise Analysis activity did Melanie determine that her organization would provide resources to develop an additional module to their current CRM application that would allow them to generate data on clients behavior patterns while exploring their Website?

    a. Business case development
    b. Business need definition
    c. Gap analysis
    d. Solution approach

11. What are the five tasks necessary to complete Enterprise Analysis activities?

    a. Business needs articulation; solution scope definition; requirements definition; define assumptions and constraints; and development of business case
    b. Business needs articulation; assess capability gaps; determine solution approach; solution scope definition; and development of business case
    c. Define business goals and objectives; solution scope definition; assess capability gaps; define assumptions and constraints; and development of the business case
    d. Define business goals and objectives; assess capability gaps; develop enterprise architecture; determine solution approach; and development of the business case

12. Scope definition and decomposition activities in the early stages of Enterprise Architecture are the responsibility of the—
    a. Customer and business executive sponsor
    b. Project manager and business process owner
    c. Business analyst and senior project manager
    d. Business analyst and supplier

13. Becky has decided to use a context diagram to demonstrate a high-level overview of her proposed solution. Which other diagramming technique might she have considered as an alternate to help clarify behavioral goals and interactions with a system?
    a. Storyboard
    b. Swim lane diagram
    c. Use case diagram
    d. User stories

14. Lewis is a new business analyst who is eager to please his clients and stakeholders. He has just completed his initial risk assessment and is preparing for an executive briefing. What are the critical documents that he will need to present in order to convince the decision makers to move forward?
    a. Business case, recommendations, proposed risk response, funding requirements, and gap analysis results
    b. Business artifacts, feasibility study, root cause analysis, strategic alignment, and risk responses
    c. Business case, business need, required capabilities, solution approach, and solution scope
    d. Base case, return on investment, risk management plan, the solution, and work breakdown structure

15. Of the items that follow, which choice would NOT likely be used to help develop a business case?
    a. Credit report
    b. Future view of costs and benefits converted to today's value
    c. Interests rates with a net present value of zero
    d. Payback period

16. Project manager Determination and definition of an organization's intention to satisfy a business opportunity or resolve a problem is commonly referred to as—
    a. Defining a business need
    b. Project scope
    c. Solution assessment
    d. Solutioning

17. This documentation is required as an input for Enterprise Analysis activities:
    a. Business case documentation
    b. Capabilities documentation
    c. Solution scope documentation
    d. Requirements [stated]

18. Which of the following phrases accurately describes cost-benefit analysis?
    a. Demonstration of strengths and weakness related to the proposed solution, including both positive and negative results
    b. Determination of total cost of ownership including development costs, operation costs, and the time to recover these costs
    c. You get what you pay for!
    d. Comparison of the solution's implementation costs with the actual value realized by the implemented solution

19. The purpose of a feasibility study is to—
    a. Uncover nonfunctional requirements
    b. Test the feasibility of a proposed single solution to a problem
    c. Identify business problems or opportunities and their interrelated technical, economic, or operational feasibility
    d. Identify business opportunities with multiple solutions and their financial viability

20. Mark recently inherited a project that needs some initial risk assessment before the decision package is presented to the stakeholders. The matter is urgent, and he does not have the luxury of reviewing all the materials related to this project. Which of the following information is NOT critical to Mark to help him prepare the initial risk assessment?
    a. Current state of business architecture
    b. Feasibility study
    c. Scope definition
    d. Business case report

21. Which of the following choices does NOT accurately describe the business case?
    a. To predict the overall impact of proposed changes on business operations
    b. To describe methods and the rationale used to arrive at a proposed solution
    c. To make budgetary estimates, including potential return on investment (ROI)
    d. To define processes concerned with overall risk management plans

22. Enterprise Analysis depends on which of the following documents as input?
    a. Business case
    b. Business need
    c. Enterprise architecture
    d. Required capabilities

23. Justification of value to the business in both qualitative and quantitative terms, and the rational used to demonstrate business objectives, can be found in what output created during Enterprise Analysis activities?

    a. Business architecture
    b. Business need
    c. Business case
    d. Business process model

24. A business requirement is best described as statements that describe—

    a. The goals, objectives, and needs of an enterprise, as well as the desired measurable outcome
    b. The goals, vision, mission, and financial status of an organization
    c. How a stakeholder will interact with a system
    d. Conversion from one system to another and are often temporary in nature

25. Why would Sarah use a scope model during the Enterprise Analysis phase?

    a. Sarah would use this technique to justify the next steps that would need to be taken for the new opportunity to officially become an active project.
    b. Sarah would use this technique to help her to clarify and determine how an organization will maximize its strengths and minimize its weaknesses, given a proposed solution set.
    c. Sarah would use this as a technique to help her to clarify and determine project objectives and boundaries to provide enough high-level, detailed information to begin building a business case.
    d. Sarah would use this technique for a preliminary analysis to determine whether a proposed solution could be successfully completed and would be financially profitable for the sponsoring organization.

26. Which of the following choices would NOT be considered a technique for preparation of the business case?

    a. SWOT
    b. Financial valuation
    c. Cost-benefit analysis
    d. Activity-based collaboration

27. What types of requirements generally provide the platform from which all other requirements are derived?

    a. Business requirements
    b. Functional requirements
    c. Nonfunctional requirements
    d. Stakeholder requirements

28. Which phrase most accurately describes a primary need for conducting Enterprise Analysis?

    a. A means by which organizational business units are identified
    b. A structured approach to conduct organizational capability assessment
    c. A means to measure the gradual improvement of an organization's progress
    d. To extract or draw forth something latent

29. That which defines the capabilities of a solution is often referred to as—
    a. Functional requirements
    b. Nonfunctional requirements
    c. Project scope
    d. Solution scope

30. Which phrase best describes the purpose of determining the solution scope task in Enterprise Analysis?
    a. The financial evaluation of a proposed solution
    b. The determination of boundaries and high-level capabilities of a solution
    c. The determination of how best to allocate requirements to obtain maximum financial benefit to the organization
    d. The prioritization of requirements based on immediate stakeholder needs

31. Most Enterprise Analysis activities are—
    a. By definition limited to only one iteration or phase of a project
    b. Followed according to defined business analysis plans
    c. Dependent upon the development of a solution that meets the business needs as an output
    d. The platform upon which all other business analysis activities are measured

32. Which input to the Enterprise Analysis activities defines how an organization functions in its current state?

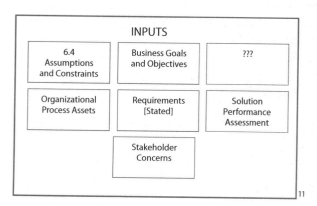

    a. Business case
    b. Business need
    c. Enterprise architecture
    d. Executive Summary

---

11 Adapted from Figure 5-1, *BABOK ®Guide* V2.0, 81.

33. Ravi understood that the definition of the business needs during Enterprise Analysis activities was critical to the development of which dependent task?

    a. Development of a stakeholder analysis
    b. Development of business goals and objectives
    c. Development of stated requirements
    d. Development of a work breakdown structure

34. Which of the following choices is NOT a task conducted during Enterprise Analysis efforts?

    a. Assess capability gap
    b. Define business need
    c. Determine solution approach
    d. Prepare requirements package

35. Which element is considered an output to Enterprise Analysis activities?

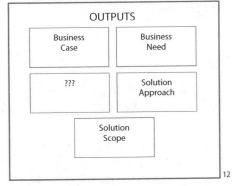

    a. Assumptions and constraints
    b. Required capabilities
    c. Requirements [Prioritized]
    d. Stakeholder requirements

36. Jerome planned a presentation to showcase the results of his business case. He invited the business executive sponsor, business process owners, and the IT management team. If Jerome could invite only one more party to this meeting, whom should he choose?

    a. Application developers
    b. End users
    c. Implementation subject matter expert
    d. Project manager

---

12   Adapted from Figure 5-1, *BABOK® Guide* V2.0, 81.

37. What is a key input in driving the development of a business need?

   a. Organizational goals and objectives
   b. Prioritized requirements
   c. Solution approach
   d. Stakeholder concerns

38. _____ and business goals and objectives are required as input for the defining of a business need.

   a. Assumptions
   b. Constraints
   c. Requirements [stated]
   d. Stakeholder concerns

39. A cargo container logistics company was consistently receiving customer complaints that shipments were not arriving at their destination on time. This prompted the organization to begin exploring the root cause of the problem. To resolve this problem Kelly suggested that—

   a. Business needs should be defined
   b. More ships be added to the fleet
   c. Requirements analysis would quickly reveal a lack of corporate capabilities
   d. Solution scope be defined to develop a tracking device for each cargo container

40. Calculation of currency exchange rates by the expense management spreadsheet was often done with inconsistent and outdated data and costing the ACME company a 0.1 percent decrease in overall profitability. The initiative to explore a resolution to this matter is commonly referred to as a _____ initiative.

   a. Bottom-up
   b. Externally driven
   c. Management-driven
   d. Top-down

ANSWER SHEET

1.	a	b	c	d	
2.	a	b	c	d	
3.	a	b	c	d	
4.	a	b	c	d	
5.	a	b	c	d	
6.	a	b	c	d	
7.	a	b	c	d	
8.	a	b	c	d	
9.	a	b	c	d	
10.	a	b	c	d	
11.	a	b	c	d	
12.	a	b	c	d	
13.	a	b	c	d	
14.	a	b	c	d	
15.	a	b	c	d	
16.	a	b	c	d	
17.	a	b	c	d	
18.	a	b	c	d	
19.	a	b	c	d	
20.	a	b	c	d	

21.	a	b	c	d
22.	a	b	c	d
23.	a	b	c	d
24.	a	b	c	d
25.	a	b	c	d
26.	a	b	c	d
27.	a	b	c	d
28.	a	b	c	d
29.	a	b	c	d
30.	a	b	c	d
31.	a	b	c	d
32.	a	b	c	d
33.	a	b	c	d
34.	a	b	c	d
35.	a	b	c	d
36.	a	b	c	d
37.	a	b	c	d
38.	a	b	c	d
39.	a	b	c	d
40.	a	b	c	d

ANSWER KEY

1.   **c.**   **Root cause analysis**

Root cause analysis is used to identify problems and opportunities and is cited as a technique for usage consideration in the Business Analysis Planning and Monitoring Knowledge area, definition of business needs, and in the Solution Assessment and Validation knowledge area.

IIBA®, *BABOK® Guide* V2.0, 2009, 202

2.   **b.**   **Quantitative**

All costs and benefits must be quantified as a result of the output of the business case. This task allows the stakeholders to make accurate financial decisions on the proposed solution(s). Quantifying other requirements also allows for a decision based on the merits of output. For example, "the system shall improve overall processing time of a client's application by 15 percent in the next 18 months."

IIBA®, *BABOK® Guide* V2.0, 2009, 95

3.   **d.**   **Prioritization of requirements**

This is something that is done as a Requirements Analysis activity. Although a stakeholder analysis is certainly an activity that a business analyst would undertake, identifying all team roles and responsibilities is an activity that would be clearly articulated in the planning and management phase of a solution development life cycle (SDLC).

IIBA®, *BABOK® Guide* V2.0, 2009, 81

4.   **b.**   **Business sponsor**

The business sponsor is responsible for crafting a vision, mission, and organizational goals so that the rest of the business has direction to manage and maintain its overall goods and services responsibilities.

IIBA®, *BABOK® Guide* V2.0, 2009, 85

5.   **b.**   **Activity model that reflects on the horizontal view of the enterprise, regardless of business units or functions**

Process models are a depiction of how an organization shares business-relevant information and the systematic means by which this activity is accomplished.

IIBA®, *BABOK® Guide* V2.0, 2009, 206

6. **d.** **Uncertain event that, if it occurs, has a negative or positive effect on the project constraints**

This factor should be included in risk management planning as part of the planned response to a risk-based event. It is also a means by which requirements can be prioritized and sequenced into the deployment of the solution.

IIBA®, *BABOK® Guide* V2.0, 2009, 201

7. **a.** **Strategic plans and goals**

By considering an organization's strategic plans and goals, Ron might be able to realize very quickly that developing a common platform of product goods and services supporting all lines of business is in line with the organization's desired direction.

IIBA®, *BABOK® Guide* V2.0, 2009, 83

8. **a.** **Context diagrams**

Techniques identified by the *BABOK® Guide* V2.0 for the definition of solution scope include: functional decomposition, interface analysis, scope modeling (context diagrams), and user stories.

IIBA®, *BABOK® Guide* V2.0, 2009, 93, 207

9. **c.** **Decision analysis**

A business analyst uses a decision table to help the stakeholders assess each option's feasibility by laying out, in a matrix format, the logic of a recommended solution. Many variables may be used to assess the solution's feasibility to map them out in a decision table. A BA is likely to use force field analysis and gap analysis to arrive at the decision table results.

IIBA®, *BABOK® Guide* V2.0, 2009, 96, 166

10. **d.** **Solution approach**

Solution approach is an activity that provides insight into the best possible means for addressing how an organization will achieve its goals and objectives and the delivery of a solution(s) that meets those needs.

IIBA®, *BABOK® Guide* V2.0, 2009, 81, 88

11. **b.** **Business needs articulation; assess capability gaps; determine solution approach; solution scope definition; and development of business case**

Opportunities may include everything from improving existing processes, deploying new goods and services, and updating existing goods and services. Building a business architecture framework would demonstrate the means by which the goods and services are delivered and supported, and determining optimum project investment would allow all stakeholders involved in developing the solution to realize rates of ROI, as well as the present and future value of the goods and services. These costs might also include support costs involved in the ongoing use of the goods and services. Service-level agreements might be required.

IIBA®, *BABOK® Guide* V2.0, 2009, 81

12. **c.** **Business analyst and senior project manager**

By conducting activities around scope definition and decomposition, a business analyst and senior project manager are better prepared to begin planning and management activities, as well as developing a WBS, which may facilitate the refinement of solution scope.

IIBA®, *BABOK® Guide* V2.0, 2009, 94

13. **c.** **Use case diagram**

A use case diagram is a technique used to demonstrate a high level of interaction between a person/actor and an organization or another system to show how the interaction will occur. There should be no need to decompose a use case diagram.

IIBA®, *BABOK® Guide* V2.0, 2009, 105–106, 204

14. **c.** **Business case, business need, required capabilities, solution approach, and solution scope**

All items listed in the response are considered outputs derived from Enterprise Analysis activities, and they would very likely contain some or part of the elements listed in the incorrect responses. For example, return on investment, funding, and risks are likely to be considered components of the business case.

IIBA®, *BABOK® Guide* V2.0, 2009, 81

15. **a.** **Credit report**

A credit report is not generally used to evaluate the financial feasibility of a solution. Typically, a vendor who has been selected to implement the proposed solution uses the credit report to ensure that the client is able to finance the project, after an RFP has been awarded post-solution assessment and evaluation.

IIBA®, *BABOK® Guide* V2.0, 2009, 90–91, 167

16. **a.** **Defining a business need**

Articulating a problem or opportunity that must be overcome or implemented is the objective of defining a business need.

IIBA®, *BABOK® Guide* V2.0, 2009, 81

17. **d.** **Requirements [stated]**

Stated requirements: are the perceived needs articulated by stakeholders. This may often represent the starting point for a business analyst for diagnosing problems or opportunities.

IIBA®, *BABOK® Guide* V2.0, 2009, 82–83

18. **d.** **Comparison of the solution's implementation costs with the actual value realized by the implemented solution**

Cost-benefit analysis would allow a business analyst to quantify and demonstrate the costs to implement a solution and the savings realized by implementing the proposed solution. This is only one factor considered in the overall selection of a group of recommended solutions, but it often carries the most weight. Answer "a." refers to the SWOT analysis activities, whereas answer "b." refers to activity-based costing.

IIBA®, *BABOK® Guide* V2.0, 2009, 96, 167

19. **c.** **Identify business problems or opportunities and their interrelated technical, economic, or operational feasibility**

A feasibility study, through a series of planned activities studies to collect objective data and statistical information, helps an organization to realize the likelihood that a potential solution or solutions will meet its overall business need or resolve a business problem.

IIBA®, *BABOK® Guide* V2.0, 2009, 90, 227

20. **a.** **Current state of business architecture**

The current state of business architecture would not likely help to accurately define initial risks for the project more than the proposed recommendations based on the feasibility study, scope definition, and business case report. Current infrastructure may pose challenges in implementing the recommended solution.

IIBA®, *BABOK® Guide* V2.0, 2009, 96

21. **d.** **To define processes concerned with overall risk management plans**

Risk management plans are developed after the business case has been defined and depend on the output of the business case.

IIBA®, *BABOK® Guide* V2.0, 2009, 95

22. c. **Enterprise architecture**

The enterprise architecture documentation contains information that includes the current and future state of an organization's business process, IT architecture, operations, and their respective relationships.

IIBA®, *BABOK® Guide* V2.0, 2009, 81

23. c. **Business case**

A business case is produced iteratively and contributions made to it during the Enterprise Analysis activities serve to justify and quantify business value as it relates to overall business objectives. The business case includes information not limited to the following: estimates of time and cost to deploy the solution, profitability, break-even costs, expected cash flow, and benefits realization.

IIBA®, *BABOK® Guide* V2.0, 2009, 94–95

24. a. **The goals, objectives, and needs of an enterprise, as well as the desired measurable outcome**

A business requirement may address many things and is usually captured using a variety of methodologies, including the Zachman framework, POLDAT, or even the IBM component model. Business requirements must be unambiguously written and form the foundation from which all other requirements are derived.

IIBA®, *BABOK® Guide* V2.0, 2009, 5

25. c. **Sarah would use this as a technique to help her to clarify and determine project objectives and boundaries to provide enough high-level, detailed information to begin building a business case.**

A context/business domain model would help Sarah depict a high-level view of the business solution and its interactions with other internal and external actors.

IIBA®, *BABOK® Guide* V2.0, 2009, 93, 206

26. d. **Activity-based collaboration**

Activity-based collaboration measures the performance and cost of activities to develop the proposed solution.

IIBA®, *BABOK® Guide* V2.0, 2009, 95

27. a. **Business requirements**

Business requirements are developed during Enterprise Analysis activities. They are developed to ensure that clarity of business goals and needs, solution scope, a business case, and feasibility of solution options can be further defined and clarified.

IIBA®, *BABOK® Guide* V2.0, 2009, 5, 81, 224

28. **b. A structured approach to conduct organizational capability assessment**

All items listed as possible answers are techniques that a business analyst would use to understand an organization's ability to reach its goals and objectives. Understanding business problems or opportunities, assessing an organization's capability, determining what solution best meets organizational goals and objectives, solution scope, business case, and defining business requirements are all tasks conducted during Enterprise Analysis activities.

IIBA®, *BABOK® Guide* V2.0, 2009, 81

29. **d. Solution scope**

Defining solution scope is an activity conducted during Enterprise Analysis activities that defines what the desired output of a solution is expected to accomplish in relationship to its business needs.

IIBA®, *BABOK® Guide* V2.0, 2009, 81, 232

30. **b. The determination of boundaries and high-level capabilities of a solution**

Solution scope evolves from a number of artifacts that serve as the input for business needs and solution approach. It is important that at this point in solution development stakeholders have just enough informaton so they can begin to visualize the proposed solution.

IIBA®, *BABOK® Guide* V2.0, 2009, 91–92

31. **b. Followed according to defined business analysis plans**

Most business analysis activities are to be followed by a defined set of business analysis plans. Enterprise Analysis may even be considered an entire project unto itself and may require a completely separate set of plans to facilitate its activities.

IIBA®, *BABOK® Guide* V2.0, 2009, 81

32. **c. Enterprise Architecture**

Enterprise architecture is one of seven inputs required to support Enterprise Analysis activities. It defines the organization's current capabilities across all functional business units and most often includes references to both internal and external systems.

IIBA®, *BABOK® Guide* V2.0, 2009, 81, 86

33. **a. Development of a stakeholder analysis**

Development of stakeholder analysis is a task that is dependent on the output of the development and definition of business needs. Conducting a stakeholder analysis is part of Business Analysis Planning and Monitoring in the *BABOK® Guide*.

IIBA®, *BABOK® Guide* V2.0, 2009, 82

34. **d. Prepare requirements package**

Preparation of the requirements package, a task typically conducted during Requirements Management and Communication activities, serves to ensure that all stakeholders are clear in their understanding of the proposed solution and are in agreement with the requirements to deliver the solution.

IIBA®, *BABOK® Guide* V2.0, 2009, 72, 81

35. **b. Required capabilities**

The current and desired future capabilities of an enterprise are produced as outputs of Enterprise Analysis activities.

IIBA®, *BABOK® Guide* V2.0, 2009, 81, 88

36. **c. Implementation subject matter expert**

Based on the project portfolio management team's understanding of other ongoing projects, the team should be able to very quickly ascertain the proposed project's overall impact on any other existing projects, resources, and funding capabilities.

IIBA®, *BABOK® Guide* V2.0, 2009, 97

37. **a. Organizational goals and objectives**

Organizational goals and objectives as well as requirements [stated] are required as key inputs for the defining of a business need.

IIBA®, *BABOK® Guide* V2.0, 2009, 83

38. **c. Requirements [stated]**

Requirements stated and business goals and objectives are required input for activities that would allow a business analyst to define business needs.

IIBA®, *BABOK® Guide* V2.0, 2009, 83

39. **a. Business needs should be defined**

In this case, the external drivers (customers) are prompting this organization to take stock of a potential resolution by examining what problem actually needs to be resolved.

IIBA®, *BABOK® Guide* V2.0, 2009, 83–84

40. **a. Bottom-up**

Bottom-up initiatives that prompt an organization to begin Enterprise Analysis activities and specifically define business needs evolve out of a need to increase efficiencies with existing processes or systems or to replace them with new or updated processes.

IIBA®, *BABOK® Guide* V2.0, 2009, 83

REQUIREMENTS ANALYSIS

STUDY HINTS

The primary goal for this knowledge area is to articulate stakeholder requirements so as to craft solution requirements based on the analysis of the current state of business. Prioritizing, organizing, specifying and modeling requirements, verifying and validating requirements, as well as the iterative development of assumptions and constraints, are all activities executed to in this knowledge area. You can expect approximately 29 questions on Requirements Analysis tasks (that is, 19.33 percent of the exam). Figure 7 illustrates the Requirements Analysis tasks, plus their inputs and outputs. *BABOK® Guide* V2.0 Requirements Analysis considers three elements: text, matrixes, and models. There are 16 modeling techniques. As requirements and their respective models and notation are developed, the ability to capture requirements attributes and identify potential opportunities for improvement increases respectively.

❖ ***Start your learning process by reviewing the overall task flow of this knowledge area and the models used.*** Your comparative analysis, as stated above, will lead you to the tasks and models that need further study. Input to this area comes as a result Elicitation and very often is done during Elicitation activities. This knowledge area addresses the tasks of structuring, analyzing (via models), documenting, and finally validating or verifying requirements. Three analysis techniques are cited: business process analysis, object-oriented analysis, and structured analysis.

❖ ***Be familiar with requirements analysis inputs, tasks, and outputs by name and definition.***

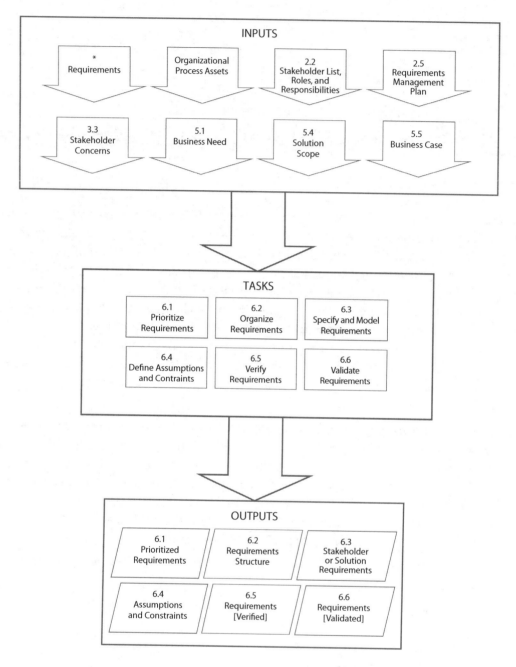

FIGURE 7. INPUTS, TASKS, AND OUTPUTS FOR REQUIREMENTS ANALYSIS[13]

NOTES: 1. AN * INSIDE AN ICON IN THE ABOVE DIAGRAM INDICATES THAT THE ITEM IN QUESTION WAS LIKELY PRODUCED AS A RESULT OF MULTIPLE TASKS, 2. A NUMBER X.Y CITED IN AN ICON IN THE ABOVE DIAGRAM INDICATES THE KNOWLEDGE AREA AND TASKS THAT EITHER PRODUCED THE ARTIFACT OR WILL USE THE ARTIFACT AS AN INPUT. 3. AN ICON WITH NO * OR NUMBER WAS PRODUCED EXTERNALLY.

---

[13]   Adapted from Figure 4-1, *BABOK® Guide* V2.0, 99.

FOCUS TOPICS FOR STUDY

After you understand the overall flow, focus your attention on knowing the terms, types of requirements, and how analysis and documentation is accomplished.

❖ *Be familiar with tools and techniques for requirements prioritization.*

❖ *Be familiar with the assumptions and constraints and their respective characteristics.*

❖ *Be familiar with the eight characteristics of requirements quality: cohesive, complete, consistent, correct, feasible, modifiable, unambiguous, and testable.*

❖ *Be able to state the purpose and application of each model along with its complementary and alternative techniques.*

❖ *Be familiar with all elements that influence activities and stakeholders involved in this knowledge area.*

❖ *Be able to differentiate requirements validation from requirements verification.*

❖ *Be able to identify all 10 elements considered during requirements prioritization process.*

❖ *There are two elements to consider when organizing requirements;* be clear in your understanding of model selection for the purposes of requirements articulation.

❖ *There are a total of 16 techniques that the* **BABOK**® *prescribes for specifying and modeling requirements.* Your clear understanding of when and how to use each technique is critical for your success in writing the exam.

❖ *Define and be able to differentiate assumptions from constraints.*

INDEX OF SELECTIVE TERMS AND PHRASES

Be able to explain the terms and phrases listed in Table 5. One caveat: The *BABOK® Guide* V2.0 page(s) shown provides a definition, a description, or a use of the term or phrase. The term or phrase may also appear on other pages.

TABLE 5. SELECTIVE TERMS AND PHRASES FOR REQUIREMENTS ANALYSIS

Term or Phrase	BABOK® Guide V2.0 Page(s)
Activity diagram	194
All in	102
All out	102
Abstraction	105
Assumption	111, 223
Budgeting	102, 105
Business and technical constraints	112
Business case	100, 224

Term or Phrase	BABOK® Guide V2.0 Page(s)
Business domain model	224
Business need	100, 224
Business rules	106, 158
Business rules analysis	106
Business value	101
Checklists	117
Class model	163, 225
Cohesive	115
Complete	115
Consistent	115
Constraint	112
Correct	115
Data dictionary	160
Data flow diagram	106
Data modeling	106
Define assumptions and constraints	112
Entity relationship diagrams	163, 226
Feasible	116
Feature list decomposition	8
Flowchart	193
Functional decomposition	106
Functional requirements	227
Matrix documentation	109
Metadata definition	165, 228
Metrics and key performance indicators	228, 192
Modeling formats	109
Modeling notation	110
Models	109
Modifiable	116
MoSCow analysis	156, 102

Term or Phrase	BABOK® Guide V2.0 Page(s)
Nonfunctional requirements analysis	184
Object-oriented modeling	228
Opportunity cost	119
Organization modeling	106, 188
Organize requirements	103
Prioritization	229
Prioritize requirements	99
Process modeling	106
Processes	192
Quality of service requirements	106, 184
Request for proposals/request for quotation (RFP/RFQ)	230
Requirements	4, 9
Requirements [prioritized]	103
Requirements [stated]	103
Requirements [validated]	120
Requirements [verified]	114, 117
Requirements analysis and documentation	117, 120
Requirements attributes	110
Requirements management plan	231
Requirements structure	108
Risk analysis	201
Rules	106
Scenario and use cases	107
Scope modeling	107
Selective	102
Sequence diagram	208
Solution scope	104, 232
Specify and model requirements	107
Stakeholder list, roles, and responsibilities	233
Stakeholder or solution requirements	232–233

Term or Phrase	*BABOK® Guide* V2.0 Page(s)
State machine diagram	210, 233
Storyboard/screen flow	197, 233
Structured analysis	162
Structured walk through	117, 120, 211, 233
Testable	116, 155
Timeboxing	102, 234
Unambiguous	116
Use case description	107, 204
Use case diagram	107, 204
User classes	105
User classes, profiles, or roles	105
User story	106, 219, 234
Validate requirements	117, 234
Validation	117, 234
Verification	114, 234
Verify requirements	114, 234
Voting	102

PRACTICE QUESTIONS

INSTRUCTIONS: Note the most suitable answer for each multiple-choice question in the appropriate space on the answer sheet.

1. Business needs are best described as—
    a. The vision that an organization is trying to create
    b. A system trigger initiated by humans
    c. Functional requirements
    d. Business objectives

2. Stated requirements are an input to Requirements Analysis activities. They are defined by—
    a. Elicitation activities
    b. Feasibility studies
    c. Completion of the Enterprise Analysis phase
    d. Solution Assessment and Validation

3. Under which circumstances should Requirements Analysis occur?
    a. After Elicitation, but not before Solution Assessment and Validation
    b. Upon completing the Enterprise Analysis phase, where the stakeholders' needs have been identified and a potential solution and its capabilities need to be defined
    c. After Business Analysis Planning and Monitoring, but not before Solution Assessment and Validation
    d. Upon completing Business Analysis Planning and Monitoring, after Elicitation, and during Solution Assessment and Validation

4. What input is required for Requirements Analysis activities?
    a. Assumptions and constraints
    b. Business goals and objectives
    c. Solution options
    d. Stakeholder list, roles, and responsibilities

5. Requirements Analysis activities are NOT considered completed until—
    a. Requirements are verified and validated, and constraints are understood
    b. Requirements are verified and validated, and assumptions are understood
    c. Requirements are verified, validated, and structured
    d. Requirements are verified and validated, and consensus is obtained from all stakeholders

6. The primary goal of functional decomposition is to—

    a. Realize the size and significance of business requirements at each phase of a solution development life cycle in a bottom-up approach

    b. Ensure that the problem or opportunity is broken down into subfunctions, processes, and activities that interact independently for a properly detailed analysis of all requirements

    c. Represent the activities of an organization in the form of a tree diagram

    d. Describe all business problems and their related processes in a logical breakdown, using a hierarchical diagram

7. The creation of a visual model representing sequential steps toward a business goal often complements functional decomposition. This is known as which type of structured analysis technique?

    a. Process modeling

    b. Logical data flow modeling

    c. Structured modeling

    d. Object-oriented modeling

8. Which of the following choices is NOT a recommendation for writing better requirements?

    a. Write in the passive voice to clearly describe the target of the action and not the doer of the action.

    b. Give every requirement a unique number.

    c. Express requirements as a verb or verb phrase to foster an active voice approach.

    d. Never assume that the reader is knowledgeable about the topic at hand.

9. Regardless of technique, which of the following choices should be avoided when creating diagrams or models?

    a. Crossing lines

    b. Labeling all diagrams and models with a title or reference point

    c. Creating elements of consistent size and shapes and colors

    d. Reading progression from top to bottom and left to right, with consideration of cultural environment

10. Which would be considered an appropriate modeling technique to capture high-level user requirements?

    a. State model

    b. Business rules

    c. Context diagram

    d. Flowchart

11. "As a result of cutbacks, the project manager is also acting in the capacity of a business analyst." This statement represents—

    a. An assumption

    b. A constraint

    c. Both

    d. None of the above

12. "Five business analysts are expected to be available as resources to participate in the requirements development and management of this project." This statement represents—

    a. An assumption
    b. A constraint
    c. Both
    d. None of the above

13. Verifying requirements can be best defined as—

    a. Identifying things that are believed to be true but cannot actually be verified
    b. Eliminating limitations or restrictions that prevent or limit the full capacity of a solution
    c. Linking high-level needs of the stakeholders to requirements
    d. Ensuring that requirements are clearly defined so that a solution can be designed and implemented

14. Which of the following requirements is most likely to be called into question for its ambiguity?

    a. The ATM machine will allow end users to withdraw or deposit money.
    b. The system will include workflow to verify that the end user has entered the correct personal identification number to access the account.
    c. The system shall provide a daily log of all client transactions. It should also be able to provide an end user with the option to check account balances for administrative purposes. The system will allow any bank employee to override any security features.
    d. The user interface must be designed for use on a 12-inch color screen.

15. Which statement most accurately describes the purpose of validating requirements?

    a. Validation ensures that prototypes and documentation are accepted by the project manager.
    b. Validation is done to ensure that the acceptance testing meets the customer's needs by achieving major milestones.
    c. Validation requires output from prototypes and documentation.
    d. Validation ensures that the overall business needs are met, that they are in alignment with the overall customer requirements, and that both business needs and customer requirements are traceable back to the originally proposed solution.

16. Activity diagrams, data flow diagram, and flowcharts are classified as which type of modeling technique?

    a. Data and behavior models
    b. Usage models
    c. Process/flow models
    d. Object-oriented models

17. Which of the following modeling techniques would help a business analyst to gain insight into a concept that considered a logical collection of information described by means of attributes and operations?

    a. Business rules
    b. Class diagram
    c. Flowchart
    d. Data flow diagram

18. What is wrong with the following data flow diagram (DFD)?

DFD – Online Order System

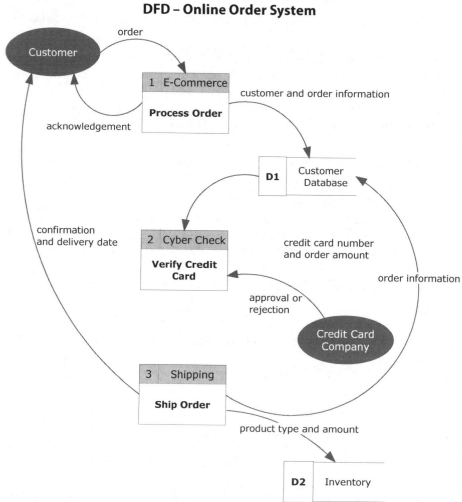

    a. Not all data flows are attached to a process.
    b. Not all incoming data are processed to produce an output.
    c. Not all data stores are involved with a data flow.
    d. Not all processes and data stores have one data flow in and one data flow out.

19. What is wrong with this flowchart?

Procedural Flowchart: Expense Reports

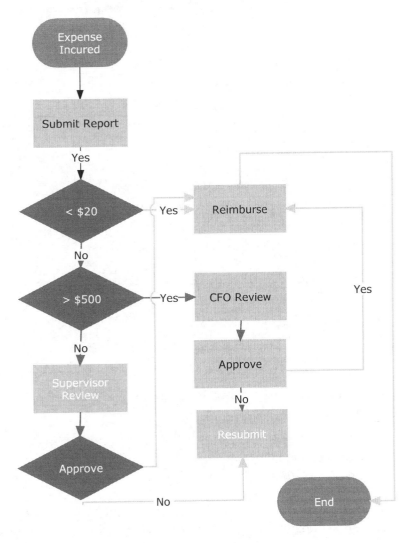

a. This is a state machine diagram.
b. The "Approve" notation should be a diamond.
c. Dollar values are unclear.
d. "Resubmit" is not connected to the entry point.

20. In this entity relationship diagram (ERD), what is the relationship and cardinality of "claim" to "policy"?

Entity Relationship Diagram:
Insurance Claim System

a. Claim is made against exactly one policy.
b. Claim is made against up to two policies.
c. Claim supports a minimum of zero policies.
d. Claim supports zero to many policies.

21. An alternative to metadata modeling would be—
a. Activity diagram
b. Data flow diagram
c. Flowchart
d. Class diagram

22. The first level of a data flow diagram is referred to as the—
a. Entity relationship diagram
b. Data flow diagram
c. State machine diagram
d. Context diagram

23. Which notation would Carrie consider using in an activity diagram to demonstrate the execution of parallel activities after a decision was made to execute them?
a. Merge
b. Fork
c. Branch
d. Joins

24. Ethan was asked to create an activity diagram for the new and improved login feature for the Bank of Millions. The new functionality will allow existing and new clients to pay their bills online. Upon reviewing his diagram, you find an error in the notation. What is the error?

UML Activity Diagram: Automated Banking

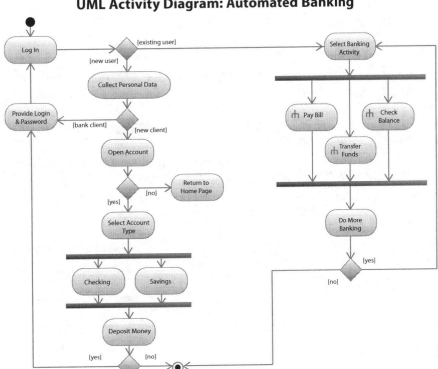

a. Improper use of end notation
b. Improper use of join notation
c. Improper use of decision notation
d. Improper use of fork notation

25. Which of the following choices is NOT a key feature of the state machine diagram?
a. Decisions are depicted with one filled-in arrowhead.
b. Events are labeled on transition lines.
c. Transition lines show how objects interact with other objects, considering the states.
d. States are depicted as boxes with rounded edges.

26. Ethan was assigned to a project where his client was extremely risk-averse to the development of their solution. He was regularly asked both to demonstrate his progress and to explore any user interface and system developments. As long as the feedback was positive, he would continue to develop the system from this foundation. This example illustrates which type of modeling technique?
a. Storyboarding
b. Prototyping
c. Workflow modeling
d. Use case descriptions

27. Which of the following choices is considered a type of collaborative prototyping without software code?

   a. Rapid prototyping
   b. Use case description
   c. Storyboards
   d. Use case diagram

28. Which of the following statements best describes a scenario?

   a. A text-based requirements-gathering technique describes a system from a stakeholder's point of view. The technique uses a series of written steps to be performed by a person, system, or event external to the system.
   b. A graphical representation of actors and their boundaries describes relationships of stakeholders with a system.
   c. A text-based requirements-gathering technique describes UML 2.0 standards for developing and refining data migration techniques.
   d. A graphical representation of a user interface aids software developers in understanding how stakeholders need to use a system.

29. According to unified modeling language standards, when creating a use case diagram, the primary actor should always be located where on the diagram?

   a. Bottom right
   b. Top right
   c. Top left
   d. Bottom left

30. _____ may be replaced by prototyping or may be complementary to storyboarding.

   a. State machine diagram
   b. Interface analysis
   c. Use case diagrams
   d. Workflow models

31. Ron was asked to evaluate his peers' use case diagram as part of the new coaching and mentoring program at XYZ Inc. He found a minor error in the diagram. What was it?

Use Case Diagram: Credit Card Processing

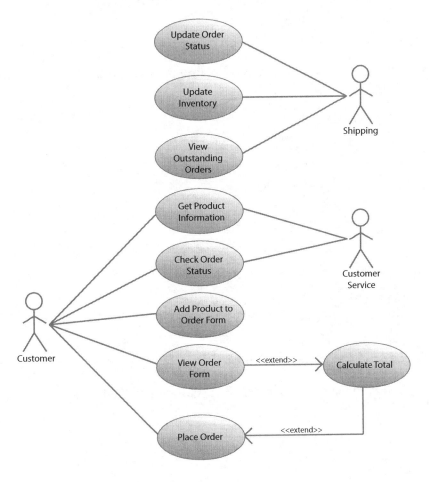

    a. Improper verb usage in use case
    b. Improper use of <<extend>> notation for View Order Form
    c. No boundary
    d. Improper use of <<extend>>notation for Place Order

32. When engaged in Requirements Analysis activities, a business analyst's primary goal is to—

    a. Analyze stated requirements
    b. Elicit requirements
    c. Manage business analysis performance
    d. Prioritize requirements

33. Development of a domain model is particularly useful for—

    a. Creating use case models
    b. Developing a business case
    c. Validating solution scope
    d. Verifying project scope

34. Which of the following choices is NOT considered a necessary task to complete Requirements Analysis activities?

    a. Structure requirements
    b. Model requirements
    c. Estimate requirements effort
    d. Verify requirements

35. Identify the missing task in the following Requirements Analysis task diagram.

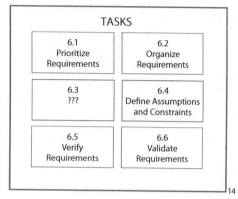

    a. Define Requirements
    b. Develop Business Case
    c. Prepare Solution Scope
    d. Specify and Model Requirements

36. This output is considered a deliverable resulting from requirements analysis activities:

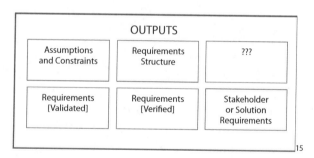

    a. BA process assets
    b. Required capabilities
    c. Requirements [Prioritized]
    d. Solution scope

---

14   Adapted from Figure 6-1, *BABOK® Guide* V2.0, 99.

15   Adapted from Figure 6-1, *BABOK® Guide* V2.0, 99.

37. After all the ideas have been generated in a brainstorming session, what is a recommended way for the group to evaluate the ideas?

 a. Force field analysis
 b. Questionnaire
 c. Decision analysis
 d. Gap analysis

38. According to the *BABOK® Guide* there are three types of diagrams to consider when modeling scope: a business process model, a use case model and a—

 a. Context diagram
 b. Non-functional requirements
 c. Sequence diagram
 d. State diagram

39. This technique textually describes what a solution must do to satisfy the people who will ultimately interact with it and is generally described in a high level of detail describing business value.

 a. Functional decomposition
 b. Scope modeling
 c. Use case diagrams
 d. User stories

40. Which of the following is NOT an element required to specify and model requirements?

 a. Descriptive text
 b. Matrix documentation
 c. Requirements attributes
 d. Risk analysis

ANSWER SHEET

1.	a	b	c	d	21.	a	b	c	d
2.	a	b	c	d	22.	a	b	c	d
3.	a	b	c	d	23.	a	b	c	d
4.	a	b	c	d	24.	a	b	c	d
5.	a	b	c	d	25.	a	b	c	d
6.	a	b	c	d	26.	a	b	c	d
7.	a	b	c	d	27.	a	b	c	d
8.	a	b	c	d	28.	a	b	c	d
9.	a	b	c	d	29.	a	b	c	d
10.	a	b	c	d	30.	a	b	c	d
11.	a	b	c	d	31.	a	b	c	d
12.	a	b	c	d	32.	a	b	c	d
13.	a	b	c	d	33.	a	b	c	d
14.	a	b	c	d	34.	a	b	c	d
15.	a	b	c	d	35.	a	b	c	d
16.	a	b	c	d	36.	a	b	c	d
17.	a	b	c	d	37.	a	b	c	d
18.	a	b	c	d	38.	a	b	c	d
19.	a	b	c	d	39.	a	b	c	d
20.	a	b	c	d	40.	a	b	c	d

ANSWER KEY

1. **d.** **Business objectives**

   Business needs often describe high-level goals or objectives of an organization or the output that a solution is expected to accomplish. It is also a required input for Requirements Analysis activities if a business case is not available as input.

   IIBA®, *BABOK® Guide* V2.0, 2009, 100, 224

2. **a.** **Elicitation activities**

   Through facilitated sessions or the input of documented organizational goals and objects, stated requirements are both defined and refined through Elicitation activities.

   IIBA®, *BABOK® Guide* V2.0, 2009, 61

3. **b.** **Upon completing the Enterprise Analysis phase, where the stakeholders' needs have been identified and a potential solution and its capabilities need to be defined**

   According to the *BABOK® Guide* V2.0, Requirements Analysis should occur upon completing the Enterprise Analysis activities, when the stakeholders' needs have been identified and a potential solution and its capabilities need to be defined.

   IIBA®, *BABOK® Guide* V2.0, 2009, 99

4. **d.** **Stakeholder list, roles, and responsibilities**

   Stakeholder list, roles, and responsibilities will provide a business analyst with guidance on who to involve in facilitated sessions where Requirements Analysis activities are performed.

   IIBA®, *BABOK® Guide* V2.0, 2009, 99

5. **d.** **Requirements are verified and validated, and consensus is obtained from all stakeholders**

   Verification ensures that the requirements have been clearly defined so that design implementation can begin. Validation makes certain that the clearly defined requirements meet the overall business need.

   IIBA®, *BABOK® Guide* V2.0, 2009, 114, 117

6. **b.** **Ensure that the problem or opportunity is broken down into subfunctions, processes, and activities that interact independently for a properly detailed analysis of all requirements**

   This is a top-down structured approach that can be done to understand systems development—a concept of operations where scope is clearly understood.

   IIBA®, *BABOK® Guide* V2.0, 2009, 106, 111, 126, 174

7.   a.   **Process modeling**

Process modeling involves creation of a visual model representing sequential steps to accomplish a business goal and often complements decomposition. The steps may represent the AS-IS state or the TO-BE state and can be demonstrated using a variety of graphical notations including UML.

Brûlé, Glenn, *Business Analysis Terms: A Working Glossary*, 2009, 136

IIBA®, *BABOK® Guide* V2.0, 106–107, 111, 126, 192–193

8.   a.   **Write in the passive voice to clearly describe the target of the action and not the doer of the action.**

You should always write your requirements in the active voice, where the subject of the verb performs the action. For example:

Glenn wrote the requirements. [active voice]

The requirements were written by Glenn. [passive voice]

IIBA®, *BABOK® Guide* V2.0, 2009, 108

9.   a.   **Crossing lines**

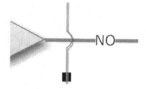

Crossing lines in diagrams and models can often be confusing and may mislead the reader of the requirements to misinterpret a connection or lack of connection. A little curve or "hop" over the line in question is recommended if the crossing of lines is unavoidable. This would demonstrate knowledge of proper notation to be used for the development of models.

Ambler, Scott W., *The Elements of UML™ 2.0 Style*, 2005, 5

IIBA®, *BABOK® Guide* V2.0, 2009, 110

10.   c.   **Context diagram**

A context diagram depicts a high-level interaction of the flow of information between internal and external entities. Context diagrams are used early in a project to get agreement on the scope under investigation. Context diagrams are typically included in a requirements document. These diagrams must be read by all project stakeholders and thus should be written in plain language so that the stakeholders can understand items within the document. Thorough decomposition should produce a level zero data flow diagram.

IIBA®, *BABOK® Guide* V2.0, 2009, 207

11. **b.** **A constraint**

Because the business analyst is a clearly defined profession, if a project manager were to take on a BA's responsibilities, this development could be considered to constrain the delivery of unambiguous requirements.

IIBA®, *BABOK® Guide* V2.0, 2009, 111–112

12. **a.** **An assumption**

This statement is believed to be true but cannot be verified. As such, it should be viewed as false and considered to be a risk with a potential to harm the project.

IIBA®, *BABOK® Guide* V2.0, 2009, 112

13. **d.** **Ensuring that requirements are clearly defined so that a solution can be designed and implemented**

Verifying requirements is necessary to ensure both their clarity and compliance to defined quality standards are met so that a solution can be implemented. Verification of requirements represents the business analyst's final check, which will be reviewed by the stakeholders.

IIBA®, *BABOK® Guide* V2.0, 2009, 114

14. **c.** **The system shall provide a daily log of all client transactions. It should also be able to provide an end user with the option to check account balances for administrative purposes. The system will allow any bank employee to override any security features.**

Because this requirement is ambiguous in its entirety, it should be broken out into its respective smaller requirements. This statement specifies more than one thing, without adequately explaining any of them, which violates the quality of cohesion.

IIBA®, *BABOK® Guide* V2.0, 2009, 115

15. **d.** **Validation ensures that the overall business needs are met, that they are in alignment with the overall customer requirements, and that both business needs and customer requirements are traceable back to the originally proposed solution.**

Validation allows defects to be identified before they cause problems and allows an opportunity to correct requirements by refining or rewriting them.

IIBA®, *BABOK® Guide* V2.0, 2009, 117

16. **c.** **Process/flow models**

Process flow models depict how a system behaves over a period of time with no human interaction. They are commonly referred to as dynamic models.

IIBA®, *BABOK® Guide* V2.0, 2009, 106–107, 192–193

17.   **b.**   **Class diagram**

Class diagrams demonstrate which entities are relevant to a solution, as well as show their structures and their relationships with other entities. They are one of two widely used data modeling techniques; the other is an entity relationship diagram.

IIBA®, *BABOK® Guide* V2.0, 2009, 163

18.   **d.**   **Not all processes and data stores have one data flow in and one data flow out.**

Notice that the arrow from the 2 process, "Cyber Check, Verify Credit Card" pointing toward the "Credit Card Company" is missing. The omission seems to indicate that there is no process to submit information to the credit card company for approval, and yet there is a process to reject or accept the credit card (indicated by the arrow pointing in the opposite direction). The D2 "Inventory" only has data populating it but nothing comes out of it or is used.

IIBA®, *BABOK® Guide* V2.0, 2009, 163

19.   **b.**   **The "Approve" notation should be a diamond.**

In flowchart notation, the diamond represents a decision-making point.

IIBA®, *BABOK® Guide* V2.0, 2009, 110, 193, 195

20.   **a.**   **Claim is made against exactly one policy.**
A claim can only be made against a minimum of one policy and a maximum of one policy (not many policies). This is represented by the 1 and only 1 symbol:

IIBA®, *BABOK® Guide* V2.0, 2009, 164

21.   **d.**   **Class diagram**

Class diagrams demonstrate the relationship between classes, their attributes and operations as they relate to an entity or entities, and their relevance to a solution. Class represents a logical collection of information or a distinct concept.

IIBA®, *BABOK® Guide* V2.0, 2009, 163–165

23.   **d.**   **Context diagram**

Data flow diagrams are evolved by decomposing a context diagram, which represents high-level interactions of a system or business area. These are decomposed into a single process to produce a DFD.

IIBA®, *BABOK® Guide* V2.0, 2009, 162

23. **b. Fork**

   A fork demonstrates the execution of parallel activities and is represented by parallel bars from a single flow into two or more parallel flows.

   IIBA®, *BABOK® Guide* V2.0, 2009, 194

24. **a. Improper use of end notation**

   If a user decides against opening a bank account, he or she is returned to the home page. This activity should be followed by a termination point otherwise known as "end notation":

   IIBA®, *BABOK® Guide* V2.0, 2009, 194

25. **a. Decisions are depicted with one filled-in arrowhead.**

   This would be the notation commonly referred to as a fork, used in a flowchart.

   IIBA®, *BABOK® Guide* V2.0, 2009, 210

26. **b. Prototyping**

   Prototyping is an iterative technique wherein the user interface development and progress are iteratively assessed. It may be decided that the prototype should be thrown away or that the development can be continued based on the existing foundation.

   IIBA®, *BABOK® Guide* V2.0, 2009, 111, 196

27. **c. Storyboards**

   Storyboards provide an early mock-up of an interface or a use case and are generally done as a collaborative effort. With no formal approach, a storyboard is often created using Post-it® notes, whiteboards, paper, and pens, pencils, or markers. Storyboards don't eliminate the formal functional requirements-gathering process, but rather they enhance the process. Generally a storyboard's targeted audience is the project stakeholders.

   IIBA®, *BABOK® Guide* V2.0, 2009, 197

28. **a. A text-based requirements-gathering technique describes a system from a stakeholder's point of view. The technique uses a series of written steps to be performed by a person, system, or event external to the system.**

   The usage scenario describes a potential business situation that may be faced by the stakeholders of a system. The focus is on behavioral requirements and not on technical design issues.

   IIBA®, *BABOK® Guide* V2.0, 2009, 111, 204

29. **c.** **Top left**

The most critical actors and functions should be placed at the top left of use case scenarios. In Western culture, this is the natural flow for reading.

Ambler, *The Elements of UML™ 2.0 Style*, 2005, 36

IIBA®, *BABOK® Guide* V2.0, 2009, 111, 206

30. **b.** **Interface analysis**

User interface design captures high-level ideas to generate requirements for user interactions with specific system elements.

IIBA®, *BABOK® Guide* V2.0, 2009, 111, 176

31. **b.** **Improper use <<extend>> notation for View Order Form**

Extend notation is used to depict the extension of behavior from another use case. In this case, View Order Form is also using the "Calculate Total" use case an "extension" to the parent use case. To make this diagram accurate the extend notation should be pointing towards the "View Order" Use Case and NOT away from it.

IIBA®, *BABOK® Guide* V2.0, 2009, 206

32. **a.** **Analyze stated requirements**

A business analyst will analyze stated requirements for both the current and future state so that stakeholder requirements and solution requirements may be crafted.

IIBA®, *BABOK® Guide* V2.0, 2009, 99

33. **c.** **Validating solution scope**

During Enterprise Analysis activities, it is likely that a business analyst will develop current state domain models for the purposes of validating solution scope, identification of potential areas of improvement for the business, and providing an overview of the current state of a business to stakeholders.

IIBA®, *BABOK® Guide* V2.0, 2009, 99

34. **c.** **Estimate requirements effort**

Because this is not a task of the Requirements Analysis phase, it should be done during the planning and management of requirements in collaboration with a project manager.

IIBA®, *BABOK® Guide* V2.0, 2009, 99

35. **d. Specify and model requirements**

Using a variety of techniques, including tables, matrices, diagrams and models, a business analyst will perform this task as part of the overall Requirements Analysis activities.

IIBA®, *BABOK® Guide* V2.0, 2009, 99

36. **c. Requirements [Prioritized]**

Producing documentation that would provide insight into requirements attributes and their criticality for implementation is part of the outputs produced during Requirements Analysis.

IIBA®, *BABOK® Guide* V2.0, 2009, 99

37. **c. Decision analysis**

Decision analysis allows a group of stakeholders to evaluate and come to an agreement where complex matters or uncertain situations need to be addressed.

IIBA®, *BABOK® Guide* V2.0, 2009, 166

38. **a. Context diagram**

According to the *BABOK®*, when modeling scope there are three diagrams that could be consider for use: a context diagram — Gane-Sarson Notation or Yourdon Notation — a use case model, and a business process model, which may also be considered as part of the scope modeling technique.

IIBA®, *BABOK® Guide* V2.0, 2009, 206–207

39. **d. User stories**

A high level of detail as described from a users point of view depicting how he or she will be satisfied by the proposed system and the business value it offers is a technique referred to by the *BABOK®* as a user story.

IIBA®, *BABOK® Guide* V2.0, 2009, 219

40. **d. Risk analysis**

Models, descriptive text, matrix documentation, requirements attributes and opportunities for improvement are all considered elements required to specify and model requirements. Risk analysis is likely to occur as a result of specifying and modeling requirements.

IIBA®, *BABOK® Guide* V2.0, 2009, 108–110

SOLUTION ASSESSMENT AND VALIDATION

STUDY HINTS

The essence of the Solution Assessment and Validation knowledge area lies with an understanding of how solution options satisfy the overall business need. Multiple solution options will have to be evaluated to ensure the best option is selected. Once the appropriate option is selected understanding how requirements will be delivered or allocated to ensure optimal efficiency in their delivery, as well as an organization's willingness or capability to take on the new solution, will require an in-depth understanding of techniques, including acceptance and evaluation criteria, decision analysis, and vendor assessment to name a few.

You can expect approximately 24 questions on Solution Assessment and Validation activities (that is, 16 percent of the exam). Figure 8 shows the inputs, tasks and deliverables for Solution Assessment and Validation. Each high-level task has an associated *BABOK® Guide* V2.0 section number and comprises many subtasks. The model provides a visual context; actual execution of some tasks may be parallel and iterative. Deliverables are also shown for further insight.

❖ ***Start your learning process by reviewing the overall task flow and deliverables of this knowledge area.***

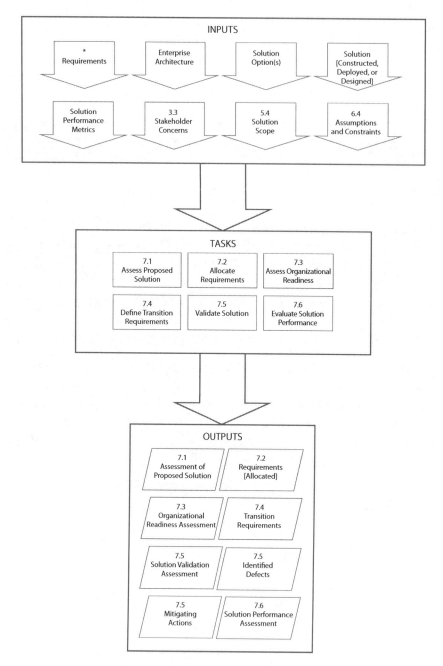

FIGURE 8. INPUTS, TASKS, AND OUTPUTS FOR SOLUTION ASSESSMENT AND VALIDATION[16]

NOTES: 1. AN * INSIDE AN ICON IN THE ABOVE DIAGRAM INDICATES THAT THE ITEM IN QUESTION WAS LIKELY PRODUCED AS A RESULT OF MULTIPLE TASKS, 2. A NUMBER X.Y CITED IN AN ICON IN THE ABOVE DIAGRAM INDICATES THE KNOWLEDGE AREA AND TASKS THAT EITHER PRODUCED THE ARTIFACT OR WILL USE THE ARTIFACT AS AN INPUT. 3. AN ICON WITH NO * OR NUMBER WAS PRODUCED EXTERNALLY.

---

16   Adapted from Figure 7-1, *BABOK® Guide* V2.0, 121.

FOCUS TOPICS FOR STUDY

❖ *Be able to contrast the business analyst negotiator and facilitator roles.*[17]

❖ *Define the business analyst role in Solution Assessment and Validation.*

❖ *Understand tools and techniques used to assess and validate solutions.*

❖ *Understand the importance of evaluating organizational readiness and the business analyst's role in it.*

❖ *Understand the importance of transition requirements and how they differ from other requirement types, and that transition requirements are temporary.*

❖ *Remember that Solution Assessment and Validation can be completed for one solution or for the purposes of comparing and evaluating multiple solution options against each other to articulate the solution that brings the greatest benefit to the sponsoring organization as prescribed by the goals and objectives.*

❖ *Understand that, although solution options are not implicitly cited as outputs for the assessment of the proposed solution, it is possible to uncover additional solution options that may not have been considered previously.*

❖ *Understand that the allocation of requirements relies heavily on such elements as resource availability, constraints, dependencies of solution components, business policies, business rules, release planning, and the various interdependencies of solution components that may be external to the solution being developed.*

❖ *Understand that, essentially, assessing organizational readiness is about understanding, defining, and preparing for how the solution will affect the overall business.* Consider how prepared the business and its resources are for handling the change in question.

❖ *Validation of solution considers the clarity and accuracy with which the solution and its corresponding requirements have been defined in order to meet the business need.* Should this expectation not be met, a plan to address defects is considered during this knowledge area's activities.

❖ *Understand that solution performance assessment is equivalent to post-implementation assessment.* These activities answer the question, "Is the solution performing according to expectations, have stakeholders been able to adapt to the solution and if so, to what degree have they changed any of their original needs that are not otherwise being utilized or are being circumvented in the actual solution?"

---

[17]   IIBA®, *BABOK® Guide* V2.0, 2009, 150.

INDEX OF SELECTIVE TERMS AND PHRASES

Be able to explain these terms and phrases listed in Table 6. One caveat: The *BABOK® Guide* V2.0 page(s) shown provides a definition, a description, or a use of the term or phrase. The term or phrase may also appear on other pages.

TABLE 6. SELECTIVE TERMS AND PHRASES FOR SOLUTION ASSESSMENT AND VALIDATION

Term or Phrase	BABOK® Guide V2.0 Page(s)
Acceptance and evaluation criteria	155–156
Assess defects an issues	135–136
Assess organizational readiness	127–131
Assess proposed solution	121–124
Allocate requirements	124–127
Cultural assessment	129
Define transition requirements	131–134
Enterprise architecture	128, 226
Evaluate solution performance	137–140
Force field analysis	130, 227
Investigate defective solution outputs	135
Opportunity cost	139
Organizational change	133
Organizational modeling	188–190
Organizational readiness assessment	131
Quality assurance	230
Release planning	126
Requirements [allocated]	124–127
Requirements [prioritized]	125, 134
Requirements [validated]	134–135
Requirements allocation	124
Solution [constructed]	134
Solution [deployed]	132
Solution [designed]	125, 132
Solution assessment and validation	121

Term or Phrase	BABOK® Guide V2.0 Page(s)
Solution components	125–126
Solution performance metrics	137
Stakeholder impact analysis	129
Sunk costs	139
Test plan	134, 136
Validate solution	134–137, 234
Vendor assessment	220–221

PRACTICE QUESTIONS

INSTRUCTIONS: Note the most suitable answer for each multiple-choice question in the appropriate space on the answer sheet.

1. A business analyst is primarily responsible for—
   a. Documenting all requirements
   b. Ensuring that the solution meets the business need
   c. Being a liaison between IT and the business
   d. Translating business needs into comprehensive models

2. Solution validation—
   a. Ensures that requirements have been captured according to organizational standards and or regulatory and compliance standards
   b. Is the process by which a solution is evaluated to ensure that all business needs are satisfied and that all defects are addressed accordingly
   c. Is a type of peer review
   d. Ensures that software code has been written according to software language syntax

3. Which of the following choices is NOT considered a task for Solution Assessment and Validation?
   a. Allocating requirements
   b. Assessing organizational readiness
   c. Defining transition requirements
   d. Developing a solution that meets the business needs

4. At which point during the project or phase should a business analyst consider planning for such issues as rollout strategies, defect reporting, and next-phase issues?
   a. During project planning
   b. Near the end of the project or phase completion
   c. During the quality assurance process
   d. At post-implementation

5. Kurt was assigned as the lead business analyst for a proposed new student registration system. As part of his planning for Solution Assessment and Validation, he considered using some documentation from his previous activities to do a cost-benefit analysis. From which phase of activities did Kurt draw upon for this documentation?
   a. Requirements Management and Communication
   b. Elicitation
   c. Enterprise Analysis
   d. Requirements Analysis

6. Who is responsible for customizing or developing the proposed solution?
    a. Project manager
    b. Business analyst
    c. Stakeholder
    d. Supplier

7. Which key audience must business analysts and implementers consider during the implementation of a solution and any resulting change management requests?
    a. Project managers
    b. Quality assurance testers
    c. End users
    d. Test manager

8. Dave knew that a key element required of his Solution Assessment and Validation activities would be critical to the product's success. What is that key element?
    a. Consensus and agreement on the solution from the implementers
    b. Approval from the end users to develop a product
    c. Prioritized and approved business requirements
    d. A clear and detailed understanding of all technical requirements

9. Which of the following choices is NOT part of Solution Assessment and Validation?
    a. Evaluation of RFP responses
    b. Development of RFP evaluation criteria
    c. Alignment of requirements to design
    d. Sign-off and approval by all stakeholders

10. The output of mapping requirements to design is—
    a. Requirements [allocated]
    b. Application architecture
    c. IT architecture
    d. Information architecture

11. _____ is a primary consideration when reviewing, selecting, and designing a solution as part of Solution Assessment and Validation knowledge area's activities.
    a. Adherence to UML 2.0 standards
    b. Clarity of written text
    c. Impact on the business environment
    d. Time to implement a solution

12. Usability can be best described as—
    a. The means by which an end user navigates through the proposed piece of software
    b. The ease with which a solution can be implemented into an existing infrastructure
    c. User acceptance
    d. Ease of use and the time it takes to become familiar with the proposed solution

13. Which sources of information did Carrie require to help her assess the usability of the proposed solution?

    a. Project charter
    b. Work breakdown structure
    c. Prioritized business requirements
    d. Description of overall business objectives

14. This documented information is required as an input for Solution Assessment and Validation tasks:

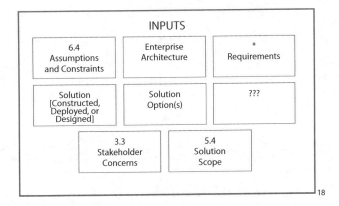

    a. Identified defects
    b. Requirements [allocated]
    c. Solution performance metrics
    d. Transition requirements

15. To properly assess the quality of a solution, a business analyst would require—

    a. Feedback from stakeholders
    b. A requirements communication plan
    c. Documentation regarding quality assurance standards and procedures
    d. The project manager's risk management plan

16. Part of the work required in supporting the changing requirements of a candidate solution is to—

    a. Write training manuals
    b. Perform impact analysis
    c. Perform gap analysis
    d. Perform integration testing

---

18   Adapted from Figure 7-1, *BABOK® Guide* V2.0, 121.

17. Laurie had completed the analysis and documentation of her requirements development phase for developing an intranet portal. Working with the solution development team and the stakeholders, Laurie quickly became aware of a disagreement between what the stakeholders and the solution team believed to be the best solution. Laurie could best manage this situation by—

    a. Allowing both groups enough time to realize what the right solution is
    b. Facilitating a force field analysis and, through multivoting, achieving consensus
    c. Revisiting all their supporting documentation and deciding for the team what the best solution is
    d. Conducting separate interviews to understand the constraints and proposing a change in scope to the project manager

18. What would be a key deliverable for supporting the implementation of a solution?

    a. Requirements [approved]
    b. Requirements [prioritized]
    c. Transition requirements
    d. Requirements [stated]

19. Articulating how the proposed solution will affect the business probably evolved from which set of business analyst activities?

    a. Assess the proposed solution
    b. Allocate requirements
    c. Assess organizational readiness
    d. Define transition requirements

20. True or false: A business analyst is responsible for deciding which solution is best for the stakeholders.

    a. True
    b. False

21. Solution assessment and validation is important to facilitate the—

    a. Accurate implementation of requirements
    b. Accurate implementation of specifications
    c. Development of user acceptance test plans
    d. Process of quality assurance

22. When considering having vendors provide alternative solutions via an RFP, a business analyst should think about—

    a. Having vendors demonstrate their products to stakeholders
    b. Understanding the evaluation criteria that will be used to assess the applicability of the proposed solution
    c. Hiring vendors that give credibility to the proposed solution
    d. Understanding how a vendor's solution will impact the existing infrastructure

23. What input is required for activities related to assessing organizational readiness?

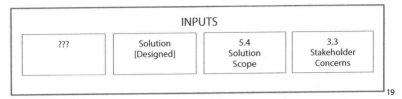

a. Assumptions and constraints
b. Enterprise architecture
c. Organizational process assets
d. Stakeholder list, roles and responsibilities

24. As a business analyst, you have options for ensuring that the usability of a proposed solution is sound. Which of the following techniques is NOT something that you would likely use to ensure usability?

a. Decision analysis
b. Focus groups
c. Observation
d. Data flow diagrams

25. The *BABOK® Guide* V2. 0 refers to demonstration of merit for the greatest business value in implementing a solution as which task?

a. Allocate requirements
b. Assess proposed solution
c. Evaluate solution performance
d. Validate solution

---

26.   What is the output produced by assessing a proposed solution used for?

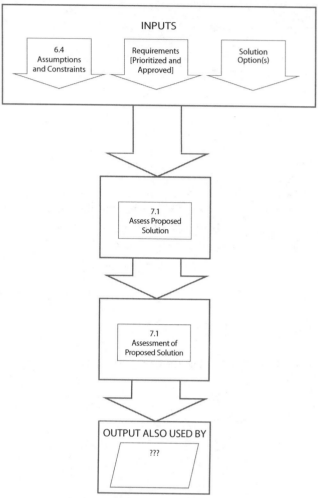

[20]

    a.   Developing implementation requirements
    b.   Developing user requirements
    c.   Solution selection or design
    d.   Validating solution performance

27.   When assessing a solution or solution options, a business analyst must also consider _____ to ensure that the most significant requirements are acknowledged and implemented.

    a.   Concise requirements
    b.   Prioritized requirements
    c.   Stakeholder requirements
    d.   Validated requirements

[20]   Adapted from Figure 7-2, *BABOK® Guide* V2.0, 122.

28. There are two essential elements to solution assessment: rating/ranking and identification of _____.
    a. Alternative solutions
    b. Capabilities not originally considered
    c. Implementation constraints
    d. Stakeholder risks

29. After all requirements had been defined for the customer relationship management application, the stakeholders of the EGB Company decided to implement a specific off-the-shelf product. In assessing the proposed solution, the business analyst would use which technique to ensure that the solution was worth implementing?
    a. Acceptance criteria
    b. Evaluation criteria
    c. Qualitative data from focus groups
    d. Quantification of implementation specifications

30. What type of business rule will allow a stakeholder to demonstrate noncompliance while that rule is attempting to be enforced?
    a. Operative
    b. Strategic
    c. Structural
    d. Tactical

31. Organizational assessment allows for the proper assessment of what?
    a. Benchmarking of how an organization is functioning prior to the implementation of the solution
    b. Effort required to deliver the solution
    c. Requirements necessary for training of the solution to be delivered
    d. Resources required to deliver the solution

32. What dictates how solution assessment and validation activities are conducted?
    a. Business analysis plans
    b. Enterprise architecture documentation
    c. The business analyst
    d. The project manager

33. The median tenure for an employee at the EAB Company was 17 years. When the implementation of a new system that would capture customer profiles through a Web-based interface was announced, there was much resistance to its launch. Employees claimed that such a move would remove much-valued personal customer interaction. Despite the resistance the IT team went ahead with the launch of the new product only to find eight months later that only a quarter of targeted employees and customers were actually using the new tool. This risk might have been identified if the following element of assessing organizational readiness had been considered—

   a. Cultural assessment
   b. Operational assessment
   c. Stakeholder impact analysis
   d. Technical assessment

34. How a solution performs post implementation is evaluated based on what?

   a. Stakeholder requirements
   b. Functional requirements
   c. Nonfunctional requirements
   d. Business requirements

35. Which input is required for the proper evaluation of solution performance?

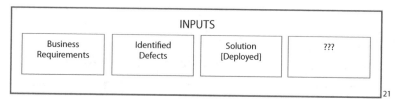

   a. Solution Design
   b. Solution Performance Metrics
   c. Solution Selection
   d. Stakeholder Concerns

36. When allocating requirements during solution assessment and validation activities, this technique will provide you with insight into how decisions are made; and constraints they may have on an organization—

   a. Acceptance and evaluation criteria
   b. Functional decomposition
   c. Business rules analysis
   d. Scenarios and use cases

---

[21]   Adapted from Figure 7-8, *BABOK® Guide* V2.0, 138.

37. At what point in a project life cycle does the allocation of requirements occur?

   a. After all requirements have been verified
   b. Before all requirements have been validated
   c. Early in the project life cycle and continuing until all valid requirements are allocated
   d. Prior to all requirements being verified and validated

38. When assessing organizational readiness Sean used which graphical diagram to depict to his stakeholders the potential positive and negative influences that may affect the implementation of a global wind farm monitoring software?

   a. Force field analysis
   b. Gap analysis
   c. Impact analysis
   d. SWOT analysis

39. Which of the following is not an activity considered during the assessment of organizational readiness?

   a. Performing cultural assessments
   b. Performing operational or technical assessment
   c. Performing budgetary reviews
   d. Performing stakeholder impact analysis

40. Which of the following are not required as a means to define transition requirements?

   a. Conduct a stakeholder impact analysis
   b. Evaluating data requirements
   c. Identifying ongoing work
   d. Managing organizational change

ANSWER SHEET

1.	a	b	c	d		21.	a	b	c	d
2.	a	b	c	d		22.	a	b	c	d
3.	a	b	c	d		23.	a	b	c	d
4.	a	b	c	d		24.	a	b	c	d
5.	a	b	c	d		25.	a	b	c	d
6.	a	b	c	d		26.	a	b	c	d
7.	a	b	c	d		27.	a	b	c	d
8.	a	b	c	d		28.	a	b	c	d
9.	a	b	c	d		29.	a	b	c	d
10.	a	b	c	d		30.	a	b	c	d
11.	a	b	c	d		31.	a	b	c	d
12.	a	b	c	d		32.	a	b	c	d
13.	a	b	c	d		33.	a	b	c	d
14.	a	b	c	d		34.	a	b	c	d
15.	a	b	c	d		35.	a	b	c	d
16.	a	b	c	d		36.	a	b	c	d
17.	a	b	c	d		37.	a	b	c	d
18.	a	b	c	d		38.	a	b	c	d
19.	a	b	c	d		39.	a	b	c	d
20.	a	b				40.	a	b	c	d

ANSWER KEY

1. **b.   Ensuring that the solution meets the business need**

    By bringing business needs together with solution providers, a business analyst is responsible for architecting and designing a solution to meet the business need.

    IIBA®, *BABOK® Guide* V2.0, 2009, 121

2. **b.   Is the process by which a solution is evaluated to ensure that all business needs are satisfied and that all defects are addressed accordingly**

    Validate solution is the final task identified by the *BABOK® Guide* V2.0 in the Solution Assessment and Validation knowledge area. Its objective it to ensure that the proposed solution satisfies the originally stated business need and where defects in the solution have been identified and an approach to address them is considered.

    IIBA®, *BABOK® Guide* V2.0, 2009, 134

3. **d.   Developing a solution that meets the business needs**

    Answer "d" is the only activity that is not part of Solution Assessment and Validation.

    IIBA®, *BABOK® Guide* V2.0, 2009, 121

4. **a.   During project planning**

    Planning for Solution Assessment and Validation activities should begin in the project planning phase. Early planning will ensure that time, effort, and resources are properly allocated to meet all business needs.

    IIBA®, *BABOK® Guide* V2.0, 2009, 121

5. **c.   Enterprise Analysis**

    The Enterprise Analysis phase is when Kurt would likely have created a high-level cost-benefit analysis while developing his business case.

    IIBA®, *BABOK® Guide* V2.0, 2009, 121

6. **d.   Supplier**

    Although it is the business analyst's responsibility to ensure that requirements satisfy the business needs of the stakeholders, the solution provider is likely to be the "construction" team. Although the project manager would probably be the project leader, the stakeholder would not necessarily have a role in customizing or developing the solution.

    IIBA®, *BABOK® Guide* V2.0, 2009, 123

7.   **c.   End users**

Business analysts should be sure to provide guidance to end users by participating in change management activities.

IIBA®, *BABOK® Guide* V2.0, 2009, 133

8.   **c.   Prioritized and approved business requirements**

Prioritized and approved business requirements, understanding of risks and constraints, and a high level of technical detail are some of the requirements for successfully executing Solution Assessment and Validation activities.

IIBA®, *BABOK® Guide* V2.0, 2009, 124

9.   **d.   Sign-off and approval by all stakeholders**

All elements except answer "d" are necessary to proceed with Solution Assessment and Validation activities. Signing off on requirements should happen before this group of activities because the requirements will dictate the type of solution required.

IIBA®, *BABOK® Guide* V2.0, 2009, 124

10.   **a.   Requirements [allocated]**

Requirements [allocated] ensures that the right requirements are implemented at the right time for the right reasons to the right business unit(s) to ensure that the maximum business benefit and financial implication are realized.

IIBA®, *BABOK® Guide* V2.0, 2009, 124

11.   **c.   Impact on the business environment**

A business analyst should have a detailed view of how the solution will impact the business environment when evaluating existing business processes, organizational structures, software applications and any other elements that may affect the solution.

IIBA®, *BABOK® Guide* V2.0, 2009, 121

12.   **d.   Ease of use and the time it takes to become familiar with the proposed solution**

Ease of use, frequency of use, adaptability, noncompliance, and error tolerance are all elements of usability. Usability is assessed and evaluated during assessment of organizational readiness and validation of the solution.

IIBA®, *BABOK® Guide* V2.0, 2009, 131

13. **c. Prioritized business requirements**

Prioritized and approved business requirements allow a business analyst to ascertain how well the solution might meet the usability categories that include ease of use, frequency of use, and so forth.

IIBA®, *BABOK® Guide* V2.0, 2009, 135

14. **c. Solution performance metrics**

This documentation represents the quantitative or qualitative data measurements necessary to ensure that the operation of the solution conforms to stakeholder expectations.

IIBA®, *BABOK® Guide* V2.0, 2009, 121

15. **c. Documentation regarding quality assurance standards and procedures**

Any standards, as defined by Six Sigma, the Capability Maturity Model® Integration (CMMI), the Sarbanes-Oxley Act of 2002 (SOX), and Institute of Electrical and Electronics Engineers, (IEEE), or any standards as defined by an organization, are a valuable if not critical predecessor to support the QA process.

IIBA®, *BABOK® Guide* V2.0, 2009, 134

16. **b. Perform impact analysis**

An impact analysis allows a business analyst to assess how particular changes will affect existing project plans and to articulate the impact to the stakeholders.

IIBA®, *BABOK® Guide* V2.0, 2009, 68–69, 135

17. **b. Facilitating a force field analysis and, through multivoting, achieving consensus**

Ultimately it is the business analyst's role to facilitate the group to a consensus. The techniques used should be appropriate to the audience and the issues at hand.

IIBA®, *BABOK® Guide* V2.0, 2009, 130

18. **c. Transition requirements**

Transition requirements are temporary requirements that are necessary to support the implementation of a solution, where the solution is replacing, updating, or adding components to an existing system. They generally consider the transition of data from an old system to a new system, downtime, transition time, training, and any other mechanisms that might ensure the successful implementation of the proposed solution.

IIBA®, *BABOK® Guide* V2.0, 2009, 131

19. **c.** **Assess organizational readiness**

    Assessing organizational readiness, a task identified with the Solution Assessment and Validation knowledge area, defines how an organization will respond, accept, and employ the newly proposed solution.

    IIBA®, *BABOK® Guide* V2.0, 2009, 127–128

20. **b.** **False**

    Although a business analyst is not responsible for decision making, he or she is, however, responsible for analyzing all solution options and objectively presenting them to the stakeholders to enable them to make the decision.

    IIBA®, *BABOK® Guide* V2.0, 2009, 121

21. **a.** **Accurate implementation of requirements**

    During these activities, it is a business analyst's primary role to employ techniques that would demonstrate how a proposed solution will meet stakeholders' needs and to ensure the integrity of solution components identified.

    IIBA®, *BABOK® Guide* V2.0, 2009, 121

22. **b.** **Understanding the evaluation criteria that will be used to assess the applicability of the proposed solution**

    The evaluation criteria that a business analyst uses to assess potential vendors and their solutions are most critical. All the other answers except "a" are likely to be a part of those criteria, as stakeholders may lose sight of the overall business need when presented with flashy solutions. The input required to evaluate the performance of a solution and how it meets the business expectations includes business requirements, identified defects, solution performance metrics, and solution [deployed].

    IIBA®, *BABOK® Guide* V2.0, 2009, 137

23. **b.** **Enterprise architecture**

    Documentation specific to the enterprise architecture should provide detail on the current state of the business including organizational structure, processes, customer value analysis, portfolio management considerations, system architecture, and so on. IIBA®, *BABOK® Guide* V2.0, 2009, 128

24. **d.** **Data flow diagrams**

    Data flow diagrams are a technique used to evaluate how information is delivered, processed, and stored by a system.

    IIBA®, *BABOK® Guide* V2.0, 2009, 129, 139, 161–162

25. **b.** **Assess proposed solution**

A business analyst may have the opportunity to evaluate either a single proposed solution or multiple solution options. The objective of this task is to ensure maximum business value for justifying implementation.

IIBA®, *BABOK® Guide* V2.0, 2009, 122

26. **c.** **Solution selection or design**

Solution selection, buy versus build, or the commencement of design and development of technical specifications are the outputs also used by activities conducted during the assessment of a proposed solution.

IIBA®, *BABOK® Guide* V2.0, 2009, 122

27. **b.** **Prioritized requirements**

Evaluating existing business processes, organizational structures, software applications, and any other elements may affect the solution. A business analyst should have a detailed view of how the solution will impact the business environment.

IIBA®, *BABOK® Guide* V2.0, 2009, 122

28. **b.** **Capabilities not originally considered**

Elements of solution assessment may include ranking of solution options and considering additional solution capabilities not originally identified by requirements but which may present themselves in solution options.

IIBA®, *BABOK® Guide* V2.0, 2009, 121

29. **a.** **Acceptance criteria**

Acceptance criteria is used to determine feasibility of a single solution and the minimal set of requirements required to implement it.

IIBA®, *BABOK® Guide* V2.0, 2009, 155

30. **a.** **Operative**

According to the IIBA®, operative rules must allow for the option of adherence or nonadherence by way of action or nonaction according to the prescribed instructions and or conditions presented to that individual.

IIBA®, *BABOK® Guide* V2.0, 2009, 159

31. **c.** **Requirements necessary for training of the solution to be delivered**

What training will be delivered, the impact of change, and how well an organization is able to cope with the magnitude of the change are all elements or assessing organizational readiness.

IIBA®, *BABOK® Guide* V2.0, 2009, 128

32. **a. Business analysis plans**

Business analysis plans chapter 2.3 and performance metrics 2.4 serve as an input into assessment and validation of proposed solution activities.

IIBA®, *BABOK® Guide* V2.0, 2009, 121

33. **a. Cultural assessment**

Whereas stakeholder analysis proposes to examine the impact of change that a solution might bring to a specific group, cultural assessment proposes to examine and evaluate the overall culture of an organization, as well as the general population's aversion to risk and their perception of the benefits that a solution might bring to them as individuals.

IIBA®, *BABOK® Guide* V2.0, 2009, 129

34. **d. Business requirements**

Business requirements are a necessary input to ensure that quantifiable business goals and objectives can be used as a benchmark to evaluate performance of a solution.

IIBA®, *BABOK® Guide* V2.0, 2009, 137

35. **b. Solution Performance Metrics**

Solution performance metrics, which are pre-determined prior to the solution being deployed, are expectations set by the stakeholders where quantitative and qualitative standards for performance are defined.

IIBA®, *BABOK® Guide* V2.0, 2009, 137

36. **c. Business rules analysis**

Business rules analysis will provide a business analyst with insight into the operative and structural rules that govern how an organization makes decisions. The allocation of requirements are likely dependant on a hierarchical structure or complexity of such rules and policies, thus dictating how they might be allocated to a given, project, phase or iteration of a project.

IIBA®, *BABOK® Guide* V2.0, 2009, 158-159

37. **b. Early in the project life cycle and continuing until all valid requirements are allocated**

Requirements should be validated as early as a solution approach has been determined. Allocation of requirements requires that trade-offs be made between requirements those requirements that bring the most value to the business and those that do not. Allocation of requirements will continue through the design and construction of a solution until all requirements are fully realized.

IIBA®, *BABOK® Guide* V2.0, 2009, 125

38. **a.**   **Force field analysis**

Force field analysis is a diagramming technique recommended by the BABOK to evaluate those forces for change and those forces opposing change. By using a quantification method, stakeholders can begin to quickly appreciate the effort required to increase the forces that are for change and lessen those that are opposing the change.

IIBA®, *BABOK® Guide* V2.0, 2009, 130

39. **c.**   **Performing budgetary reviews**

All activities identified in this question are considered during the assessment of organizational readiness – it's likely that performing budgetary reviews is something done by a project manager and stakeholders iteratively throughout the project life cycle.

IIBA®, *BABOK® Guide* V2.0, 2009, 129

40. **a.**   **Conduct a stakeholder impact analysis**

Conducting stakeholder analysis is an activity that is done during the requirements planning and monitoring activities.

IIBA®, *BABOK® Guide* V2.0, 2009, 24, 133

PRACTICE TEST 1

This practice test is designed to simulate IIBA's 150-question CBAP® certification exam. You have 3.5 hours to answer all questions.

INSTRUCTIONS: Note the most suitable answer for each multiple-choice question in the appropriate space on the answer sheet.

1. As a business analyst working on the design and development for an upgrade to the insurance quotation system, Melanie wanted to ensure that her requirements were signed off for the following reason:
   a. So that she could hold stakeholders accountable for their actions
   b. To ensure that no changes would be allowed to prevent scope creep
   c. So a baseline could be established for the tracking of future changes
   d. So that the requirements management plan could be defined

2. Gwen's organization determined that the most appropriate solution for the point of sale (POS) software would need to come from an external vendor. A business analyst's role in this situation is to—
   a. Have vendors demonstrate the capability of their product to the stakeholders
   b. Participate in the validation of the vendor's software code to demonstrate its performance in the desired specifications
   c. Evaluate the vendor's and their products' maturity in the marketplace
   d. Work with the stakeholders to identify evaluation criteria for determining the best solution to meet the business need

3. Deana was assigned to act as a lead business analyst for an internal project that was intended to develop a custom solution that would enable the call center to track the amount of time spent on the phone with prospective customers. During which set of business analysis activities does the *BABOK®* address how Deana should ascertain the most viable means to determine how to deliver the solution capabilities and provide input into the business case?
   a. Define the business need
   b. Determine solution approach
   c. Define business architecture
   d. Allocate requirements

4. Frances was asked to create a diagram based on the class diagram she had just completed. The class diagram identified an expense report and all of its characteristics and attributes. Frances knew that expense reports could be open, waiting for approval, waiting for explanation, under review, or be closed. The diagram Frances would use is a(n)—

   a. Use case diagram
   b. Sequence diagram
   c. Activity diagram
   d. State machine diagram

5. The development of a RACI matrix is done during which activities of Enterprise Analysis?

   a. Business architecture
   b. Scope development
   c. Decision package preparation
   d. None of the above

6. The major focus for Larry when working with a project manager to define the amount of effort needed for requirements activities should be—

   a. Types of elicitation and modeling activities to be used
   b. Identification of stakeholders and their respective roles
   c. Development of effort for the project
   d. Notification of all parties involved about their accountabilities

7. After working on an entity relationship diagram implementation for the last 10 months, the Chief Information Officer has asked that you prepare a presentation to the 30 stakeholders involved. With two days to prepare, your first task is to—

   a. Identify the audience and create or review their profiles
   b. Plan a presentation strategy
   c. Determine the objectives
   d. Determine the format for delivery

8. "The system must be developed on a .NET platform." This statement is considered a constraint. Which type of requirement is it?

   a. Business requirement
   b. User requirement
   c. Functional requirement
   d. Quality of service requirement

9. When creating a class diagram, there are three compartments that can be used to capture information about that class. They are—

   a. Class number, attribute, and operations
   b. Class number, attribute, and cardinality
   c. Class name, scaffolding code, and cardinality
   d. Class name, attribute, and operations

10. Management of requirements not only ensures that goals and objectives of the organization are mapped to the solution but also includes—

    a. Ensuring that all stakeholders participate in Elicitation and Requirements Analysis activities

    b. Ensuring that knowledge transfer of BA activities is shared for future performance improvement of the delivery of solutions

    c. The documentation of requirements after Elicitation activities are completed

    d. The planning and development of a requirements work plan

11. Demonstration of relationships between requirements is an activity that can best be described as which of the following choices?

    a. Organizing requirements

    b. Prioritizing requirements

    c. Specifying requirements

    d. Verifying requirements

12. For an international project, a business analyst must recognize circumstances where geographical and cultural differences are concerned. When creating a communication plan, emphasis should be placed on—

    a. Translation services for formal communication protocols

    b. Development of an approach to manage communications

    c. Development of a risk plan for sending out communications regarding performance issues

    d. Integration of communication activities into the work breakdown structure so that milestones and communication of them are not missed

13. Joan was developing her requirements package for the next release of the customer relationship management tool that her company developed two years ago. At a minimum, Joan needs to include—

    a. Business requirements

    b. Stakeholder requirements

    c. Data requirements

    d. Solution requirements

14. The number of business areas affected by a solution influences approach selection when considering what?

    a. Planning process

    b. Project complexity

    c. Requirements analysis tools

    d. Requirements prioritization

15. The stakeholders have asked that you present to them all the business rules that you have identified, those that you propose to be changed, and a look at the TO-BE state. The best way to present this information to them would be using—
    a. Activity diagrams
    b. Use case diagrams
    c. A combination of both text and diagrams
    d. Storyboards

16. Suzanne was determined to accurately collect unambiguous requirements for her clients. Her primary input to get started in this endeavor was—
    a. The business analysis approach artifacts
    b. Enterprise architecture
    c. Document analysis
    d. Stakeholder list, roles and responsibilities

17. Requirements envisioning is often conducted in what type of business analysis approach?
    a. Big design upfront
    b. Change-driven
    c. Lean
    d. Plan driven

18. Alison assembled a small group of stakeholders to evaluate the quality of the requirements that she had defined. This technique is known as—
    a. User acceptance testing
    b. Prototyping
    c. Usability testing
    d. Structured walkthrough

19. "If a supervisor does not approve or reject an expense report within 48 hours, the report will be routed via e-mail to the next approver." This statement describes a—
    a. User requirement
    b. Nonfunctional requirement
    c. Business rule
    d. System requirement

20. The primary reason that a business analyst would consider developing an activity diagram would be to—
    a. Depict data classified by classes and attributes
    b. Demonstrate a business process or rule and the detail behind a use case model
    c. Describe data attributes and structures and their flow through a system
    d. Demonstrate how a system might allow a user to interact with it and the tasks that it must perform

21. A business analyst should include a working _____ that identifies key business terms that have been mutually agreed upon by all stakeholders.

    a. Index
    b. Table of contents
    c. Library
    d. Glossary

22. This diagramming technique is used to help develop a high-level scope for a project and typically will precede the development of actors, data models, and use cases.

    a. Use case diagrams
    b. Context diagrams
    c. Entity relationship diagrams
    d. State diagrams

23. Dataflow diagrams, functional decomposition diagrams, and entity relationship diagrams are diagramming techniques typically employed using—

    a. Object-oriented analysis
    b. Business process analysis
    c. Structured analysis
    d. Impact analysis

24. According to the *BABOK® Guide* V2.0 standards, which of the following choices is the process for ensuring the correctness of how requirements have been articulated and predefined standards of quality?

    a. Requirements validation
    b. Requirements verification
    c. Requirements usability
    d. Requirements functionality

25. A key challenge that a business analyst will face when creating a business domain model is—

    a. Convincing project managers that you are responsible for the development of the scope statement
    b. Ensuring that you select the right elicitation techniques and the right stakeholders to acquire enough quantifiable information
    c. Having an accurate glossary of terms
    d. Obtaining consensus from stakeholders on the common tasks and activities they may perform in their business units and the interactions they may have across multiple business units along with any variances

26. Prior to allocating requirements, Carrie collected data related to costs for implementing each component of the solution. The data and input collected to support the allocation of requirements are referred to as what?

   a. Requirements categorized
   b. Requirements prioritized
   c. Solution [Designed]
   d. Solution Scope

27. What technique should Erin use to evaluate which approach would be most suitable for the project on which she was about to embark?

   a. Crawford slip
   b. Decision analysis
   c. Gap analysis
   d. Structured walkthrough

28. Which high-level diagramming technique can be used to depict a system's environment and any interactions with external entities, including people and systems?

   a. Swimlane diagram
   b. State diagram
   c. Class model
   d. Context diagram

29. A key challenge to consider when planning to interview stakeholders in an effort to profile them is that—

   a. The effort to complete the task is typically longer than applying an elicitation technique in a group-based setting
   b. Political agendas often will not allow for a detailed conversation to discover objective requirements
   c. Clearly articulated questions are always crafted in a closed-ended format that does not allow for creative responses
   d. Collecting data from questionnaires is easier than collecting data from interviews

30. In which of the following circumstances should a business analyst be more thorough and rigorous in eliciting requirements?

   a. In an outsourced environment
   b. Where the product or solution has been purchased from a vendor
   c. When customers are heavily involved in eliciting requirements
   d. Where the software development team has extensive experience and access to information that defines existing product information

31. The project manager with whom Aileen was working on the channel management customer portal was relieved to see the results of Aileen's interface analysis report because then he could—

    a. Include activities related to the analysis and documentation of effort in the WBS

    b. Coordinate efforts to develop this system with other projects that relied on dependencies from the output of this project

    c. Easily assess the complexity of this project compared with past projects

    d. Manage stakeholders' expectations about the quality of deliverables

32. Which Requirements Management and Communication task supporting the management of requirements and their relationship with all artifacts is missing in the graphic below?

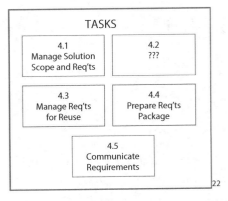

a. Assess capability gaps

b. Define solution scope

c. Determine solution approach

d. Manage requirements traceability

33. Which actionable directive supports a business policy?

    a. Business architecture

    b. Business method

    c. Business procedure

    d. Business rule

34. The overall objective of requirements allocation is—

    a. Appointing tasks and activities to the right resources

    b. Defining the critical path for project management activities

    c. Maximizing the cost-benefit ratio

    d. Ensuring that a proper balance of effort and resources is managed by the project manager

---

[22] Adapted from Figure 4-1, *BABOK® Guide* V2.0, 63.

35. Class models are typically employed in an object-oriented environment. In a non-object-oriented environment, an alternative to the class model would be a(n)—
    a. Activity diagram
    b. Data model
    c. CRUD matrix
    d. Use case diagram

36. A technique for defining the scope of a desired solution is—
    a. Focus group
    b. Work breakdown structure
    c. User task analysis
    d. Observation

37. When planning for a brainstorming session, you should ensure that your primary intended audience—
    a. Includes all stakeholders
    b. Is heterogeneous in nature
    c. Is homogenous in nature
    d. Is as objectively critical of the results as possible

38. This element is often considered a solution constraint during the allocation of requirements and may lead to a higher prioritization over elements.
    a. Business policies
    b. Business processes
    c. Business rules
    d. Regulatory requirements

39. Halfway through the requirements development phase of a project that proposed to introduce a new line of hockey equipment to the Canadian marketplace, Fred received an email announcing that, because the company had acquired a competitor, organizational changes required a freeze on all budgets and new hires for the next 18 months. Fred immediately documented this situation in collaboration with the project manager as—
    a. Nonfunctional requirements
    b. Functional requirements
    c. Assumptions
    d. Constraints

40. To complete the deliverable of the business architecture, Bill facilitated a session that identified the current state of the business and compared it to the company's desired goals. This best action describes which facilitation technique?
    a. Force field analysis
    b. Brainstorming
    c. Multivoting
    d. Gap analysis

41. When does a business analyst begin to plan such activities as Elicitation, Requirements Analysis, and Solution Assessment and Validation?
    a. After the project has been approved and a project manager has been assigned
    b. After a vendor has been selected and all stakeholders have signed off on the business requirements
    c. After a business analyst has validated all of his or her findings with the stakeholders
    d. After the decision package has been approved by the solution provider

42. To develop software requirements, a business analyst would require which of the following as a minimum input?
    a. Functional and nonfunctional requirements
    b. Business goals and system constraints
    c. Stakeholder and solution requirements
    d. Behavior models and structural models

43. "A Website that remembers my user preferences and provides ease of navigation would certainly encourage me to sign up for monthly music downloads. Being able to customize the look and feel of this site is also something that is very attractive to me." Lisa included this statement in her documented findings after having—
    a. Conducted a focus group
    b. Conducted a feasibility study
    c. Invited a vendor to demonstrate its product functionality
    d. Conducted a structured walk-through and user acceptance testing

44. Which one of the five outputs produced as a result of activities performed for the management and communication of requirements is missing in the graphic below?

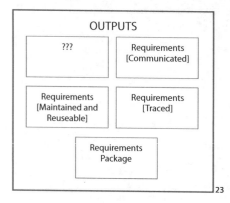

```
OUTPUTS

???                    Requirements
                       [Communicated]


Requirements           Requirements
[Maintained and        [Traced]
Reuseable]

        Requirements
        Package
```
23

   a. Requirements [Modeled]
   b. Requirements [Prioritized]
   c. Requirements [Approved]
   d. Requirements [Validated]

45. Which solution component is considered during the allocation of requirements?
   a. Business rules
   b. Constraints
   c. Dependencies
   d. Implementers

46. "The system shall produce batch reports between 2:00 a.m. and 5:00 a.m. every Thursday." This statement is an example of—
   a. Functional requirement
   b. Business requirement
   c. Process requirement
   d. Nonfunctional requirement

47. In a change-driven business analysis approach, communication with stakeholders is normally delivered—
   a. Formally
   b. Iteratively
   c. With the executive sponsor present
   d. To a governance committee before any decisions are made

---

23   Adapted from Figure 4-1, *BABOK® Guide* V2.0, 63.

48. Which input is required for understanding how a business analyst would prioritize requirements?

    a. Business case
    b. Business need
    c. Requirements
    d. Requirements management plan

49. To accurately prepare a business case, it is recommended that supporting documents from the _____ be required as input.

    a. Risk management plan
    b. Executive summary from the decision package
    c. Completed work breakdown structure
    d. Assess capability gaps output

50. Which one of the following choices is not a synonym for prototyping?

    a. Interface analysis
    b. Navigation flow
    c. Screen flow
    d. Storyboarding

51. To actively engage stakeholders in defining requirements for the purposes of solving a business need is known as—

    a. Requirements gathering
    b. Requirements elicitation
    c. Enterprise Analysis
    d. Requirements Analysis

52. Andy was assigned to develop requirements for customizing a commercial off-the-shelf-based solution. The existing service level agreement required that any changes to the existing software be approved by the vendor. To mitigate the risk of violating any legal agreements, Andy should—

    a. Review the risk management plan with the project manager and stakeholders
    b. Ensure that all team members are aware of the circumstances by outlining these nonfunctional requirements and the legal implications
    c. Have a legal team review the documentation so that they may explain the terms to the executive sponsor
    d. Transfer this responsibility to the project manager

53. The output of this business analysis activity describes the financial justification for moving forward with a proposed solution.

    a. Define business case
    b. Develop return on investment
    c. Determine solution approach
    d. Define solution scope

54. In which state should requirements be in order for them to be approved by stakeholders?

    a. [Modeled]
    b. [Specified]
    c. [Stated]
    d. [Verified]

55. You are working to develop requirements for a remote heart monitoring system. Because this is a plan-driven project, you want to identify a comprehensive list of risks. The best possible technique that you could consider using is—

    a. Document reviews
    b. Peer reviews
    c. Brainstorming
    d. Impact analysis

56. _____ is a means by which high-level scope can be determined in the scoping phases of the Enterprise Analysis activities.

    a. Pareto diagram
    b. Cause-and-effect diagram
    c. Root cause analysis
    d. Work breakdown structure

57. A test case can be best described as—

    a. The mapping of a solution and how it interacts with other systems
    b. The evaluation of a test scenario using predefined input and expected output
    c. Documentation that describes the criteria for which a solution has been selected
    d. Quality assurance documentation that adheres to imposed regulations set by an organization

58. Which elicitation technique did Rusty use to determine that the amount of physical space required to install the metal stamping machine would be a constraint in its implementation?

    a. Interview
    b. Questionnaire
    c. Joint application design session
    d. Observation

59. You've been asked to participate in a project to overhaul the software that provides communication to and from satellites monitoring weather patterns. You decide to use the solution scope to help you to identify risks because it—

    a. Defines the scope of work to be done to deliver the solution
    b. Identifies the project assumptions and constraints
    c. Was signed off on by all stakeholders and therefore must have all the risks identified
    d. References the product scope and the business requirements necessary to support the solution

60. During the development of the new satellite for broadcasting live weather reports, Hugh was careful to document both the government regulations and restrictions as nonfunctional requirements. With the growing popularity of satellite radio, however, he was also careful to document the possibility of changing regulations. This process is known as—
    a. Assumptions
    b. Constraints
    c. Nonfunctional requirements
    d. Functional requirements

61. Robert created a matrix to identify all the stakeholders from whom he would require participation in order to develop his requirements. He wanted to capture information about who would perform certain tasks, who would make decisions on the project, the liaison(s) who would provide input before the execution of activities, and who should be included in communications after the work was performed. Which tool did Robert use to capture this information?
    a. RACI matrix
    b. Work breakdown structure
    c. Organizational chart
    d. Context diagram

62. As Jamie prepared his risk management plan, he wanted to be sure to include all potential implementation risks that this opportunity might bring to the organization. Because of its global impact, Jamie should include—
    a. Organizational readiness
    b. Feasibility study
    c. Buy-versus-build approach
    d. Context diagram

63. When it comes to requirements development, the most common form of conflict is—
    a. Hidden political agendas
    b. Stakeholders insistent that their business units are more important than the others
    c. Poorly facilitated requirements workshops
    d. Misinterpretation of stated facts or requirements

64. Which of the following choices would you NOT likely find in a requirements document?
    a. Assumptions
    b. Effort required to deliver a system
    c. Organization chart
    d. Traceability matrix

65. Jed wanted to gain insight into the key elements and preliminary scope of a system idea that was brainstormed in previous facilitated sessions regarding the new business venture. The modeling technique that is recommended to examine these issues is—

    a. Organization charts
    b. Data flow diagram
    c. Root cause analysis
    d. Entity relationship diagrams

66. Three inputs are required for the allocation of requirements activities: _____ , Solution [Designed], and Solution Scope.

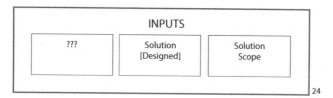

²⁴

    a. Business Analysis Approach
    b. Requirements [Prioritized and Approved]
    c. Requirements Management and Communication
    d. Solution Selection or Design

67. The approval of all requirements—

    a. Happens after every requirement is documented
    b. Is dependent on a group of stakeholders
    c. Is limited to those individuals with signatory authority
    d. Only happens at the end of the requirements activities

68. Which technique ensures a consistent understanding of requirements among the analysis team?

    a. Gap analysis
    b. Decomposition
    c. Interviews
    d. Structured walkthroughs

69. "The system will display the number of mileage points a user has accumulated after login credentials have been verified." This statement is an example of—

    a. Nonfunctional requirement
    b. Functional requirement
    c. Process requirement
    d. Business requirement

---

²⁴ Adapted from Figure 7-3, *BABOK® Guide* V2.0, 124.

70. The *BABOK®* describes a task that determines the point in time when requirements, their related solution components, releases, phases or iterations are delivered. This task is referred to as—

    a. Assess organizational readiness
    b. Define transition requirements
    c. Validate solution
    d. Allocate requirements

71. The type of tool set(s) that a business analyst selects for requirements management and development may influence the—

    a. Number of business areas affected
    b. Number of technical resources required
    c. Types of techniques employed
    d. Uniqueness of requirements captured

72. During a requirements workshop, Mark realized that he could not gain consensus from the group on whether to implement all 10 features at once or to select only the top five features. To achieve consensus, Mark—

    a. Dismissed the group, documented the results, and came to his own conclusions
    b. Decided that it would be best to hold one-on-one interviews instead
    c. Asked the group to participate in a multivoting exercise
    d. Asked the group to address each item in the list according to success criteria, impact, and effort

73. Which of the following choices is NOT something likely to be found in a business case?

    a. Identification of potential solutions and solution providers
    b. Risks, assumptions, and constraints
    c. Impact assessment report
    d. Financial metrics

74. Document analysis is limited to—

    a. The AS-IS state
    b. The TO-BE state
    c. All documentation on hand
    d. The previous phase or point release of the proposed solution

75. What does the acronym COTS stand for?

    a. Complete on time solution
    b. Commercial off-the-shelf
    c. Commercial on-the-shelf
    d. Clearly on target

76. At the beginning of an interview it is important that a business analyst—
    a. States the purpose of the interview
    b. Practices active listening
    c. Summarizes the questions
    d. Conducts a stakeholder analysis of the individual participating in the interview

77. The person in the organization who has overall responsibility for the financial and resource support of a project is often referred to as the—
    a. Executive sponsor
    b. Project manager
    c. Stakeholder
    d. Business analyst

78. Mary is working on a new call center implementation for cell phone subscribers. John is working on upgrading a new online application form for cell phone subscriptions. Both business analysts work at the same global telecommunications company. Considering that their projects are likely to share certain requirements and interdependencies, Mary's project could be categorized as a(n)—
    a. Agile project
    b. Change-driven project
    c. Plan-driven project
    d. RUP project

79. The most critical factor in facilitating a brainstorming session is—
    a. Prioritizing ideas as they are captured
    b. Allocating ideas as they are captured
    c. Not evaluating ideas during the session
    d. Encouraging group think

80. In a plan-driven business analysis approach, communication with stakeholders is normally delivered—
    a. Formally
    b. Iteratively
    c. Informally
    d. Only if there are decisions to be made required

81. A business analyst focuses his or her efforts on what type of requirements during requirements allocation activities?
    a. Business requirements
    b. Solution requirements
    c. System requirements
    d. Transition requirements

82. A software requirements specification document describes—

    a. How the software will be built to support the overall business needs
    b. Contractual requirements for prospective vendors to formally deliver a solution
    c. How the proposed solution must behave in order to satisfy business needs
    d. The overall scope of the solution created as an output of the Enterprise Analysis activities

83. Sally developed a context diagram for the proposed development of an online course registration system. To further define the scope of the solution and to consider its deployment and management, she created an inventory of subfunctions. This activity is referred to as—

    a. Goal decomposition
    b. Functional decomposition
    c. Feature list decomposition
    d. Dynamic decomposition

84. The stakeholders involved in the development of a new supply chain management system were very concerned about financial calculations that would reveal the amount of gain earned within a year and their organizations' total capital. This calculation is known as—

    a. Discounted cash flow
    b. Return on investment
    c. Average rate of return
    d. Net present value

85. Ted was adamant that charge card downloads should be the primary focus of implementing the travel and expense management solution, whereas John insisted that business rules and policies be redesigned to accommodate travel policies. As the business analyst on this project, you endeavor to resolve the conflict by—

    a. Allowing the stakeholders to resolve their differences through their own actions
    b. Asking the executive sponsor to sign off on the requirement that best suits his or her needs
    c. Facilitating communication using the appropriate technique to resolve the conflict
    d. Hosting a lottery to determine which requirement will be satisfied first

86. Functional requirements must be traceable back to the—

    a. Low-level requirements
    b. Design function
    c. Business requirements
    d. Nonfunctional requirements

87. A business analyst may conduct an informal presentation to—

    a. Ensure that the solution has been properly deployed
    b. Communicate requirements to another project team affected by an integrated project approach
    c. Have the quality assurance group sign off on functional specifications
    d. Complete prioritization of requirements so that an in-depth analysis of the TO-BE state may begin

88. Company ABC decided the following: "We will increase order processing time by 15 percent in the next 12 months." By definition, this statement is a—

    a. Requirement
    b. System requirement
    c. Business architecture
    d. Nonfunctional requirement

89. The development of a CRUD matrix depends on a(n)—

    a. Entity relationship diagram
    b. Use case diagram
    c. State diagram
    d. Well-defined glossary

90. In preparation for developing the business need, Michael is considering approaching the executive team in hopes of understanding the organization's current direction based on environmental and market trends. The documentation that Michael needs is referred to as—

    a. Existing business architecture
    b. Project scope
    c. Strategic plans
    d. Business case

91. Barry was involved in a project that would radically change the way music downloads could be purchased from the company Web site. After reviewing all existing documentation and facilitating a brainstorming session, Barry wanted to validate and continue to explore his findings using a qualitative method known as—

    a. Force field analysis
    b. Focus group
    c. Gap analysis
    d. Crawford slip

92. Jack assembled the team of stakeholders for the first meeting to kick off his Enterprise Analysis activities. His first order of business was to have the group come to a consensus by defining a common understanding of what the final solution would do for the organization. He wanted to be clear that the consensus should be aligned with the organization's goals and objectives. What was Jack determined to create?

    a. Project charter
    b. RACI chart
    c. Vision statement
    d. Binding contractual agreement

93. There are six inputs required for the management and communication of business analysis activities. Which activity is missing from the diagram below?

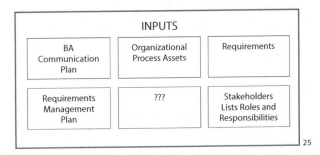

25

    a. Assumptions and constraints
    b. Solution performance assessment
    c. Solution scope
    d. Stakeholder concerns

---

25   Adapted from Figure 4-1, *BABOK® Guide* V2.0, 63.

94.   Which task is used as result of requirements prioritization?

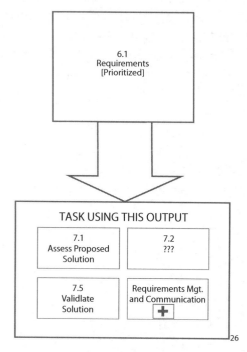

a.   Allocate Requirements
b.   Create Requirements Attributes
c.   Decompose requirements
d.   Prioritize Requirements

95.   "Uptime is 99-percent reliable." "The system takes up to 10 minutes to approve credit applications." "A decrease in time to approve credit applications would increase market share by 10 percent." "Competitors are currently processing all credit approvals in less than 2 minutes." All these statements are outputs of which type of analysis?

a.   Force field analysis
b.   Strengths, weaknesses, opportunities, and threats (SWOT) analysis
c.   Gap analysis
d.   Stakeholder analysis

96.   To ensure that his requirements were unambiguous, traceable, and consistent, Brad _____ his requirements.

a.   Rewrote
b.   Verified
c.   Prioritized
d.   Tested

---

26   Adapted from Figure 6-2, *BABOK® Guide* V2.0, 100.

97. When seeking to obtain sign-off from stakeholders, a business analyst should conduct a(n)—
    a. Survey
    b. Informal presentation
    c. Formal presentation
    d. Multivoting decision session

98. A change in this is most likely to have an impact on the change in solution scope?
    a. Business needs
    b. End users
    c. Stakeholders
    d. Technology

99. Business policies support _____.
    a. Business goal
    b. Business methods
    c. Business procedures
    d. Business rules

100. A business analysis approach _____ a project plan.
    a. Must be integrated into
    b. Has nothing to do with
    c. Must not consider
    d. Must remain independent of

101. True or false: Stakeholder requirements are critical in developing all proposed solutions and thus are mandatory information for a business requirements document.
    a. True
    b. False

102. When considering her upcoming assignment, Maria was told that all decisions, change requests, and approval of artifacts must be reviewed and approved by the product portfolio group. Given the scrutiny that her project was under, Maria decided that a _____ approach for her requirements management activities would prove to be the most appropriate.
    a. Plan-driven
    b. Change-driven
    c. Government imposed regulations
    d. Executive sponsorship approval

103. Requirements [Approved] is an output produced as a result of managing solution scope and requirements activities. This output is a required as an input in order to complete the missing activity below:

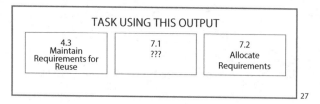

TASK USING THIS OUTPUT		
4.3 Maintain Requirements for Reuse	7.1 ???	7.2 Allocate Requirements

27

   a. Assess Proposed Solution
   b. Communicate Requirements
   c. Enterprise Architecture
   d. Manage Solution Scope and Requirements

104. When selecting which tools are most appropriate for a business analysis approach, a business analyst must consider—
   a. Vendor selection criteria
   b. Notation to be used
   c. Scope of the solution
   d. Training to be implemented

105. The ABC Company hired a consultant to provide subject matter expertise for the development of a Web-based travel and expense management solution to be deployed to all its offices worldwide. A plan-driven approached was used—
   a. To ensure frequent communication across geographical diversities
   b. To focus on the development of the solution and not the documentation
   c. To capture formal documentation
   d. To prioritize requirements as they evolve through the development of the solution

106. _____ is a technique for exploring a full range of potential solutions during a feasibility study.
   a. Gap analysis
   b. Brainstorming
   c. Force field analysis
   d. Root cause analysis

---

27   Adapted from Figure 4-2, *BABOK® Guide* V2.0, 65.

107. Allan's mandate was to increase market share through the acquisition of its competitors. In defining his business case, he wanted to be sure not only to include the cost of increasing market share and the quantified results but also to demonstrate how he arrived at the results and which options he considered. The necessary documentation and activities are referred to as—
    a. Feasibility study
    b. Scope decomposition
    c. Business architecture
    d. Scheduling and cost control

108. This technique is used to prioritize requirements and relies on the allocation of a fixed resource based on what a project team is capable of delivering for a specified duration during the development of a solution.
    a. Timeboxing/budgeting
    b. Metrics and key performance indicators
    c. Resource allocation
    d. Stakeholder analysis

109. The ultimate goal in creating a requirements package is to—
    a. Verify requirements
    b. Negotiate requirements
    c. Complement the overall project communication plan
    d. Gain consensus and approval from stakeholders

110. When it comes to requirements, who is ultimately responsible for achieving requirements as a solution?
    a. Business analyst
    b. Executive sponsor
    c. Project manager
    d. Quality assurance analyst

111. Rudy decided to sort out all contributing factors to the potential problems and risks in developing the online subscription newsletter request form. It is likely that he used which type of diagramming technique?
    a. Ishikawa diagram
    b. Pareto diagram
    c. Dataflow diagram
    d. POLDAT model

112. A requirements review is conducted—
    a. When all requirements are complete
    b. At the end of the Requirements Analysis activities
    c. Just before delivering the requirements to the implementation team
    d. At any time during the project

113. Although I may not be a direct user of the system, I would be most concerned about how the product might attract new customers to improve market share. I would also be concerned about regulatory compliance. I would not be concerned about the look and feel of reports produced as a feature of the new product. This stakeholder profile best describes a(n)—

    a. Business analyst
    b. Project manager
    c. End user
    d. Executive sponsor

114. The primary purpose of conducting a peer review is to—

    a. Reduce risk that results from ambiguous requirements manifesting themselves into defects
    b. Educate stakeholders on possible areas for improvement
    c. Identify inconsistencies and ensure that stakeholders' needs are being met
    d. Ensure that quality assurance policies and practices are adhered to

115. When working with a design team to formalize a plan for developing a solution, a business analyst must consider—

    a. The clarity of the requirements and how they have been written
    b. A review of functional and nonfunctional requirements
    c. Stakeholder profiles
    d. Costs of effort to produce the solution

116. _____ is a technique for identifying the uncertainty of proposed solutions.

    a. Environmental impact
    b. Cost-benefit analysis
    c. Risk analysis
    d. Benchmarking

117. Michelle was asked to act as the lead business analyst on a project that proposed to completely redesign their global supply change management system. What technique should Michelle use in selecting the most appropriate approach to address the requirements for this project?

    a. Decision analysis
    b. Document analysis
    c. Interface analysis
    d. Requirements analysis

118. When creating an entity relationship diagram, relationships are annotated to show—
    a. Cardinality
    b. Entities
    c. Attributes
    d. Unique identifiers

119. To identify an individual's characteristics and role in a project is a technique commonly referred to as—
    a. Gap analysis
    b. Stakeholder analysis
    c. Force field analysis
    d. Impact analysis

120. Newly passed government legislation mandates that all pharmaceutical companies must be in compliance with the means by which they document the development of trial narcotics. As a result, all processes and procedures for the project on which Carrie is working will be audited on a regular basis by federally appointed auditors. Carrie's choice in approach for business analysis activities is most likely to be—
    a. Big design up-front approach
    b. Change-driven approach
    c. Plan-driven approach
    d. Lean approach

121. Models may be an output of what Requirements Management and Communication activity?
    a. Define assumptions and constraints
    b. Prepare the requirements package
    c. Prioritize requirements
    d. Validate requirements

122. _____ rules are intended to ensure that compliance is met specifically regarding knowledge of the organization rather than the behavior of individuals.
    a. Operative
    b. Strategic
    c. Structural
    d. Tactical

123. Government agencies frequently elicit requirements from vendors in the form of a Request for Proposals (RFP). When the vendors have been short-listed, the sponsoring government entity often invites vendors to demonstrate their ability in meeting the defined objectives of the RFP. This requirements assessment approach is—
    a. Acceptance testing
    b. Benchmarking
    c. Evaluation criteria
    d. User testing

124. Risk mitigation can be best described as—

    a. The minimization of a threat by eliminating its probable cause
    b. The transference of all or part of the risks to a third party by means of insurance
    c. The development of a contingency plan, assuming there is no way to avoid or deflect the risk
    d. The decrease of a risk by lowering the probability or impact of the risk event

125. As part of corporate standards Steve was required to treat each change request as though it were a project unto itself to ensure that the change request did not have any significant impact on the project scope. The formality of this process is an indication that this requirements approach is a—

    a. Big design up-front approach
    b. Change-driven approach
    c. Plan-driven approach
    d. Lean approach

126. Eric knew that the group of stakeholders that he invited to his facilitated workshop had demonstrated animosity among themselves in previous projects. To facilitate generating creative ideas, Eric—

    a. Used an icebreaker to reduce animosity
    b. Had participants fill in a questionnaire before the workshop
    c. Conducted a force field analysis with the group
    d. Employed the Crawford slip brainstorming technique

127. The management of requirements is dependent on the output from which activity?

    a. Requirements Management Plan
    b. Elicitation activities
    c. Preparation of the decision package
    d. Requirements traceability

128. When evaluating solution performance stakeholders may be reluctant to eliminate an already existing solution based on expenses already incurred to keep the solution, this element is referred to as—

    a. Consumer price index
    b. Inflation
    c. Opportunity cost
    d. Sunk costs

129. One purpose of the communication plan is to provide information about the—

    a. The experience and skill level of all team members
    b. All facilitation and modeling techniques that will be employed during the solution development life cycle
    c. Methods that will be used to convey information
    d. Methods used to dismiss resources that are no longer needed

130. The difference between a focus group session and a requirements workshop is the—
    a. Number of participants
    b. Point at which the techniques are used in the solution development life cycle
    c. Types of requirements each produces
    d. Types of information produced as a result of the session

131. Anna knew that adding the credit card download module to the existing travel and expense management system would be a cultural challenge for end users, who would be the largest audience affected by the implementation. What would be an effective means for Anna to elicit feedback about the module's functionality?
    a. Horizontal prototype
    b. Throwaway prototype
    c. Iterative prototype
    d. Vertical prototype

132. When Mary conducted her initial interview with Jason from the sales department, she asked, "What are some reasons that you and your colleagues would use this customer relationship management tool?" It was Mary's intention to discover—
    a. User profiles
    b. Business requirements
    c. Stakeholder requirements
    d. System requirements

133. The goal of verifying functional design is to—
    a. Ensure traceability back to user requirements
    b. Calculate costs related to developing a solution
    c. Determine a buy-versus-build strategy
    d. Ensure that risk is mitigated by ensuring that all business rules are implemented

134. Angela prepared to quantify high-level business requirements. She considered the time value of income and expenditures at a given interest rate using the following formula: $NPV = \sum_{t=0}^{n} \frac{C_t}{(1+r)^t}$. Angela used this technique to prepare—
    a. Schedules and cost control
    b. Risks
    c. Business case
    d. Project scope

135. Which of the following choices represents a context diagram?
    a. Level 0 data flow diagram
    b. State diagram
    c. Process map
    d. Dialogue map

136. Stakeholders often set budget and time constraints for the delivery of a solution. Which technique is the most appropriate to use and provide input into the prioritization of requirements?

    a. MoSCoW Method
    b. Risk Analysis
    c. Timeboxing
    d. Voting

137. Jim wanted to get a sense from his stakeholders of their interface and graphical user interface requirements for an application that would integrate their resource allocation management system, including their project management dashboard and their library of policies, procedures, and life cycle management tools. Although he was able to demonstrate the look and feel of the product, the business logic had yet to be developed. What was Jim doing to further elicit requirements for this solution?

    a. Demonstrating a horizontal prototype
    b. Demonstrating a vertical prototype
    c. Demonstrating a throwaway prototype
    d. Demonstrating an evolutionary prototype

138. According to the *BABOK® Guide* V2.0, how many activities are there to complete Enterprise Analysis?

    a. Four
    b. Five
    c. Six
    d. Seven

139. A business analyst is trying to understand answers given during an interview. To clearly understand the process that a user describes, a BA might—

    a. Send an agenda before a meeting
    b. Observe the user performing his or her tasks while conducting an interview
    c. Send a questionnaire before a meeting
    d. Ensure that the end user has the proper skill level to perform the task

140. A means by which a business analyst can bring a group of stakeholders to a consensus on requirements priorities is—

    a. Through voting
    b. Through a third-party arbitrator
    c. By enlisting the support of the project manager, as this is his or her responsibility
    d. By using a method called "draw n' point"

141. There is often a great deal of emphasis placed on the _____ of requirements in a change-driven approach.
    a. Approval
    b. Change management process
    c. Documentation
    d. Prioritization

142. Multivoting is a technique best used during which phase of Enterprise Analysis?
    a. Maintaining or developing the business architecture
    b. Determining solution approach
    c. Defining the project scope
    d. Assessing the initial risk

143. To capture functional requirements, UML 2.0 describes 13 types of diagrams, broken into three categories. If you were to create a use case or class diagram, into which category would these types of diagrams fall?
    a. Interaction diagram
    b. Structure diagram
    c. Method diagram
    d. Behavior diagram

144. Through Elicitation activities, Erin determined that the proposed solution, a fingerprint security system, would be critical in maintaining security and access to personal information about the bank's existing clients. This component would be the top priority in the stakeholders' minds for the desired solution. Considering the complexity of this type of solution, Erin should document this as a(n)—
    a. Assumption
    b. Requirement attribute
    c. Constraint
    d. Nonfunctional requirement

145. Which of the following choices is NOT considered a requirements activity within the IIBA's *BABOK® Guide* V2.0?
    a. Requirements analysis
    b. Project communication
    c. Solution assessment
    d. Solution validation

146. In July Audrey was assigned as a business analyst to evaluate and allocate requirements for the launch of her company's new mobile phone application, just in time for Christmas. Among other elements that she must consider, what particular element would certainly influence how and when components of the solution would be developed?

    a. Business rules
    b. Project management plan
    c. Release planning
    d. Stakeholder availability for implementation

147. The UML version of a process flow diagram is a—

    a. Class diagram
    b. Flowchart
    c. Object diagram
    d. Activity diagram

148. When does the allocation of requirements typically begin?

    a. After all requirements have been documented
    b. After all functional business units have been identified through stakeholder analysis
    c. After all resources have been committed to a project
    d. Upon completion of the development of solution scope

149. Because decision analysis is a recognized technique for the assessment of a proposed solution, business analysts must consider both advantages and disadvantages of using this technique given their stakeholders. One such disadvantage may be—

    a. That it's often difficult to get buy-in from all stakeholders
    b. That multivoting is a better technique to gain consensus from all stakeholders
    c. That after a decision is made, it is then considered irreversible
    d. The overall impact of effort on the project

150. One way to prioritize and categorize requirements is to use—

    a. Use case diagrams
    b. Their behavior
    c. MoSCoW technique
    d. Unspecified nouns

ANSWER SHEET FOR PRACTICE TEST 1

1.	a	b	c	d
2.	a	b	c	d
3.	a	b	c	d
4.	a	b	c	d
5.	a	b	c	d
6.	a	b	c	d
7.	a	b	c	d
8.	a	b	c	d
9.	a	b	c	d
10.	a	b	c	d
11.	a	b	c	d
12.	a	b	c	d
13.	a	b	c	d
14.	a	b	c	d
15.	a	b	c	d
16.	a	b	c	d
17.	a	b	c	d
18.	a	b	c	d
19.	a	b	c	d
20.	a	b	c	d

21.	a	b	c	d
22.	a	b	c	d
23.	a	b	c	d
24.	a	b	c	d
25.	a	b	c	d
26.	a	b	c	d
27.	a	b	c	d
28.	a	b	c	d
29.	a	b	c	d
30.	a	b	c	d
31.	a	b	c	d
32.	a	b	c	d
33.	a	b	c	d
34.	a	b	c	d
35.	a	b	c	d
36.	a	b	c	d
37.	a	b	c	d
38.	a	b	c	d
39.	a	b	c	d
40.	a	b	c	d

41.	a	b	c	d
42.	a	b	c	d
43.	a	b	c	d
44.	a	b	c	d
45.	a	b	c	d
46.	a	b	c	d
47.	a	b	c	d
48.	a	b	c	d
49.	a	b	c	d
50.	a	b	c	d
51.	a	b	c	d
52.	a	b	c	d
53.	a	b	c	d
54.	a	b	c	d
55.	a	b	c	d
56.	a	b	c	d
57.	a	b	c	d
58.	a	b	c	d
59.	a	b	c	d
60.	a	b	c	d

61.	a	b	c	d
62.	a	b	c	d
63.	a	b	c	d
64.	a	b	c	d
65.	a	b	c	d
66.	a	b	c	d
67.	a	b	c	d
68.	a	b	c	d
69.	a	b	c	d
70.	a	b	c	d
71.	a	b	c	d
72.	a	b	c	d
73.	a	b	c	d
74.	a	b	c	d
75.	a	b	c	d
76.	a	b	c	d
77.	a	b	c	d
78.	a	b	c	d
79.	a	b	c	d
80.	a	b	c	d

81.	a	b	c	d
82.	a	b	c	d
83.	a	b	c	d
84.	a	b	c	d
85.	a	b	c	d
86.	a	b	c	d
87.	a	b	c	d
88.	a	b	c	d
89.	a	b	c	d
90.	a	b	c	d
91.	a	b	c	d
92.	a	b	c	d
93.	a	b	c	d
94.	a	b	c	d
95.	a	b	c	d
96.	a	b	c	d
97.	a	b	c	d
98.	a	b	c	d
99.	a	b	c	d
100.	a	b	c	d

101.	a	b		
102.	a	b	c	d
103.	a	b	c	d
104.	a	b	c	d
105.	a	b	c	d
106.	a	b	c	d
107.	a	b	c	d
108.	a	b	c	d
109.	a	b	c	d
110.	a	b	c	d
111.	a	b	c	d
112.	a	b	c	d
113.	a	b	c	d
114.	a	b	c	d
115.	a	b	c	d
116.	a	b	c	d
117.	a	b	c	d
118.	a	b	c	d
119.	a	b	c	d
120.	a	b	c	d

121.	a	b	c	d
122.	a	b	c	d
123.	a	b	c	d
124.	a	b	c	d
125.	a	b	c	d
126.	a	b	c	d
127.	a	b	c	d
128.	a	b	c	d
129.	a	b	c	d
130.	a	b	c	d
131.	a	b	c	d
132.	a	b	c	d
133.	a	b	c	d
134.	a	b	c	d
135.	a	b	c	d
136.	a	b	c	d
137.	a	b	c	d
138.	a	b	c	d
139.	a	b	c	d
140.	a	b	c	d

141.	a	b	c	d
142.	a	b	c	d
143.	a	b	c	d
144.	a	b	c	d
145.	a	b	c	d
146.	a	b	c	d
147.	a	b	c	d
148.	a	b	c	d
149.	a	b	c	d
150.	a	b	c	d

ANSWER KEY FOR PRACTICE TEST 1

1. **c.** **A baseline could be established for the tracking of future changes**

   Often, with the approval of requirements, a baseline is established (or in some cases re-established) to ensure that any changes made to the requirements are managed appropriately, monitored, and tracked with scrutiny.

   IIBA®, *BABOK® Guide* V2.0, 2009, 66

2. **d.** **Work with the stakeholders to identify evaluation criteria for determining the best solution to meet the business need**

   The business analyst's primary role in a situation where the solution is being provided by a third-party vendor is to ensure that the product meets all the requirements that support the business need. He or she should work with the stakeholders to determine the criteria to be used for making a decision.

   IIBA®, *BABOK® Guide* V2.0, 2009, 121

3. **b.** **Determine solution approach**

   Determining solution approach is necessary to understand the solution will be realized and the most effective and efficient means by which this will be accomplished. This activity is one of 5 cited in the Enterprise Analysis knowledge area

   IIBA®, *BABOK® Guide* V2.0, 2009, 88

4. **d.** **State machine diagram**

   State machine diagrams demonstrate various states of an object (in this question, an expense report) and any transitions that may occur between states.

   IIBA®, *BABOK® Guide* V2.0, 2009, 209

5. **d.** **None of the above**

   Development of a RACI matrix is usually done during Business Analysis Planning and Monitoring activities.

   IIBA®, *BABOK® Guide* V2.0, 2009, 29

6. **b.** **Identification of stakeholders and their respective roles**

   Identifying stakeholders and their respective roles will allow Larry to prepare and manage effort, responsibilities, and accountabilities and to prepare the types of requirements activities appropriate for the respective target audience. This will serve as the platform for all future planning and management activities.

   IIBA®, *BABOK® Guide* V2.0, 2009, 24–25

7.   c.   **Determine the objectives**

Understanding the objectives for the meeting will allow you to easily plan a strategy, a format, and a means by which you can address all issues that stakeholders may have.

IIBA®, *BABOK® Guide* V2.0, 2009, 37-38

8.   d.   **Quality of service requirement**

Quality of service is also referred to as a nonfunctional requirement describing quality that is not visible to the user, constraints and limitations in how the solution is to be designed, and any interactions that a solution may have with external systems.

IIBA®, *BABOK® Guide* V2.0, 2009, 6

9.   d.   **Class name, attribute, and operations**

When creating a class diagram, the topmost compartment should indicate the name of the class. The second compartment, which is optional, should list the attributes of the class, such as the descriptions of the possible states, data, or functionality required to support the class. Operations, the third compartment, describes what the class can do—that is, its functionality—for example, save, print, or report.

IIBA®, *BABOK® Guide* V2.0, 2009, 165

10. b.   **Ensuring that knowledge transfer of BA activities is shared for the future performance improvement of the delivery of solutions**

Documenting and capturing both the current and future states of the proposed solution can provide a business analyst and respective project teams with reusable requirements for future solution initiatives and can potentially reduce the time it takes to produce or deliver any subsequent solutions.

IIBA®, *BABOK® Guide* V2.0, 2009, 63

11. a.   **Organizing requirements**

There are two primary objectives on which a business analyst should focus when organizing requirements: demonstration of relationships and interdependencies between requirements; and identification of models that are best satisfy the need of the solution for an organization.

IIBA®, *BABOK® Guide* V2.0, 2009, 103

12. **b.** **Development of an approach to manage communications**

Having a consistent means to communicate, especially on a global scale, is sure to mitigate any risks across both cultural and global geographies.

IIBA®, *BABOK® Guide* V2.0, 2009, 38, 39–40

13. **d.** **Solution requirements**

When upgrading an existing system, any technical requirements should be included in her decision package. All other documented requirements should be readily available if requested.

IIBA®, *BABOK® Guide* V2.0, 2009, 6

14. **b.** **Project complexity**

When selecting an approach that will best serve the delivery of requirements analysis and management practices, the number of business units may increase project complexity when considering risk, number of resources required, number of systems affected, and the uniqueness of requirements.

IIBA®, *BABOK® Guide* V2.0, 2009, 22–23

15. **c.** **A combination of both text and diagrams**

The best approach here is to use a combination of text and diagrams. Activity diagrams and use case scenarios would be ideal to compare the issues in this situation to ensure consistency of requirements.

IIBA®, *BABOK® Guide* V2.0, 2009, 66, 72

16. **d.** **Stakeholder list, roles and responsibilities**

Stakeholder list, roles and responsibilities would provide a business analyst with guidance in understanding who, should be involved, the frequency and best means to engage a stakeholder or group of stakeholders, geographical considerations, cultural considerations, etc. All information from the stakeholder list, roles and responsibilities should serve as a primary source to get started in the requirements elicitation process.

IIBA®, *BABOK® Guide* V2.0, 2009, 54

17. **b.** **Change-driven**

Requirements envisioning is a technique used in an iterative or change-driven approach for the development of solutions. Its intention is to develop an initial list of requirements that over the duration of the project will continuously be developed and refined.

IIBA®, *BABOK® Guide* V2.0, 2009, 20

18. **d.** **Structured walkthrough**

Business analysts use peer reviews to validate requirements. Structured walkthroughs can be done at any time during the requirements development phase.

IIBA®, *BABOK® Guide* V2.0, 2009, 212

19. **c.** **Business rule**

A business rule addresses business policies to describe how a proposed solution should comply with definitions, constraints, or actions required.

IIBA®, *BABOK® Guide* V2.0, 2009, 106, 158–159

20. **b.** **Demonstrate a business process or rule and the detail behind a use case model**

An activity diagram portrays the flow or sequence of activities for high-level business processes. It is categorized as a behavior model by UML 2.0 standards.

IIBA®, *BABOK® Guide* V2.0, 2009, 195–196

21. **d.** **Glossary**

A glossary of terms is a best practice that a business analyst should use to ensure that all in the project can agree upon and understand a common set of business terms by. The glossary may also lend more clarity concerning the problem or opportunity.

IIBA®, *BABOK® Guide* V2.0, 2009, 58, 160

22. **b.** **Context diagrams**

A context diagram depicts a proposed system and any interaction that it may have with other systems or actors. It provides context to stakeholders and the business analyst about project scope.

IIBA®, *BABOK® Guide* V2.0, 2009, 28, 206–207

23. **c.** **Structured analysis**

Using structured analysis, business analysts focus on eliciting requirements based on a collection of processes and the data that support them. DFDs, ERDs, and functional decomposition are all techniques of structured analysis.

IIBA®, *BABOK® Guide* V2.0, 2009, 106, 162

24. **b.** **Requirements verification**

Verification is the process by which requirements are checked to ensure that they meet organizational or regulatory standards of quality and, as such, have been deemed to have been defined correctly. Verification can be achieved in a number of ways including inspections and walk-throughs.

IIBA®, *BABOK® Guide* V2.0, 2009, 114, 231

25. **d.** **Obtaining consensus from stakeholders on the common tasks and activities they may perform in their business units and the interactions they may have across multiple business units along with any variances**

The business domain model should be part of a business analyst's initial effort to begin diagramming the AS-IS state of the business to identify high-level or organizational structure and the processes and data needed to begin developing the TO-BE state. Main business entities and their relationships, described with nouns and noun phrases, should be used in coordination with terms documented in the already developed glossary.

IIBA®, *BABOK® Guide* V2.0, 2009, 224

26. **c.** **Solution [Designed]**

In order for requirements to be allocated considering the maximum business value, a solution and its elements must be clearly mapped out. Solution [designed], by *BABOK® Guide* definition, is a detailed description of a solution, its components, and associated costs and efforts related to deploying the solution in question.

IIBA®, *BABOK® Guide* V2.0, 2009, 125

27. **b.** **Decision analysis**

Decision analysis is a technique that can be applied to evaluate multiple methodologies or approaches that would be most suitable given the environmental circumstances that surround the development of a solution

IIBA®, *BABOK® Guide* V2.0, 2009, 23, 166

28. **d.** **Context diagram**

An effective diagramming technique to depict requirements uncovered from Business Analysis Planning and Monitoring Activities is the context diagram, a diagram that is identified as a Scope Modeling Technique. By developing a context diagram, a business analyst may begin to develop use cases and data models.

IIBA®, *BABOK® Guide* V2.0, 2009, 28, 206–207

29. **a.** **The effort to complete the task is typically longer than applying an elicitation technique in a group-based setting**

    Because interviews are conducted one-on-one, business analysts can conduct only one at a time. Therefore much more effort is required to elicit objective responses and to clarify conflicting messages.

    IIBA®, *BABOK® Guide* V2.0, 2009, 58, 177

30. **a.** **In an outsourced environment**

    In a situation where an organization has outsourced its software development, physical and geographical locations and the lack of day-to-day interactions should dictate more detailed requirements in cases where verification of requirements might be conducted intermittently.

    IIBA®, *BABOK® Guide* V2.0, 2009, 55

31. **b.** **Coordinate efforts to develop this system with other projects that relied on dependencies from the output of this project**

    Because the outputs of interface analysis are expected to identify any other system to be built or affected by the solution, a project manager would be happy to collaborate with other projects to consider impact on delivery date, risks, constraints, and dependencies.

    IIBA®, *BABOK® Guide* V2.0, 2009, 53, 56–57, 176

32. **d.** **Manage requirements traceability**

    Activities conducted during the management of requirements for traceability ensure that the relationships between all artifacts developed during business analysis activities support the overall solution definition. All other items listed in the answer are tasks for Enterprise Analysis activities.

    IIBA®, *BABOK® Guide* V2.0, 2009, 63, 67–68

33. **d.** **Business rule**

    A business rule supports a business policy and is specific to an actionable item. It can be tested, can be simple or complex in nature, and may be independent or interdependent on other business rules. Business rules analysis is a technique that may provide guidance and insight into the allocation of requirements.

    IIBA®, *BABOK® Guide* V2.0, 2009, 159

34. **c.** **Maximizing the cost-benefit ratio**

    The ultimate goal and objective for the allocation of requirements is to ensure that costs are minimized, impact is increased, and the overall solution is developed for adherence.

    IIBA®, *BABOK® Guide* V2.0, 2009, 125

35. **b.** **Data model**

Like a class model, a data model depicts the entities and attributes of objects, but it does not include behavior and relationships between entities. The notation that depicts these relationships is different for the two models. Unlike a class model, a data model does not describe design specifications of object-oriented software.

IIBA®, *BABOK® Guide* V2.0, 2009, 106, 163

36. **b.** **Work breakdown structure**

A WBS provides a hierarchical approach and understanding of what is required to achieve the business objectives. At this point, the level of detail is likely to be limited to two to three levels.

IIBA®, *BABOK® Guide* V2.0, 2009, 35

37. **b.** **Is heterogeneous in nature**

A heterogeneous audience would encourage a broader depth of creative ideas given the broad range of backgrounds and experience.

IIBA®, *BABOK® Guide* V2.0, 2009, 157

38. **d.** **Regulatory requirements**

All items listed in this answer are in fact elements of allocation of requirements activities. Regulatory requirements, however, is the only choice not considered a solution component. As such, they address potentially imposed constraints on the desired solution.

IIBA®, *BABOK® Guide* V2.0, 2009, 126

39. **d.** **Constraints**

Any limitations imposed on a project that may restrict the outcome of a solution must be documented as constraints.

IIBA®, *BABOK® Guide* V2.0, 2009, 112

40. **d.** **Gap analysis**

Gap analysis results in a desired output or deliverable upon the completion of the business architecture. Its objective is to get a clear understanding of current state versus future state and of what needs to be accomplished to get to the future state.

IIBA®, *BABOK® Guide* V2.0, 2009, 85–86, 227

41. **a.** **After the project has been approved and a project manager has been assigned**

A project must be approved directly either by the stakeholders or the portfolio management team before planning activities can begin. After the PM has been assigned, he or she should begin working with a business analyst to begin planning the development and management of requirements.

IIBA®, *BABOK® Guide* V2.0, 2009, 17

42. **c.** **Stakeholder and business requirements**

To develop software requirements, a business analyst must have clearly defined and understood both the solution and stakeholder requirements.

IIBA®, *BABOK® Guide* V2.0, 2009, 5

43. **a.** **Conducted a focus group**

Focus groups are intended to produce qualitative results; the output is likely to include quotations from participants to support major themes or issues.

IIBA®, *BABOK® Guide* V2.0, 2009, 58, 172

44. **c.** **Requirements [Approved]**

Approved requirements by stakeholders may provide input to supporting tasks and activities

IIBA®, *BABOK® Guide* V2.0, 2009, 63, 66

45. **a.** **Business rules**

Business rules, policies, processes, applications, organizational structure, and those individuals responsible for maintaining and operating a solution are considered elements of solution components during the allocation of requirements.

IIBA®, *BABOK® Guide* V2.0, 2009, 125

46. **d.** **Nonfunctional requirement**

A nonfunctional requirement provides a description of a product's features that may not be evident to the end user and generally demonstrates characteristics including quality attributes, design or implementation constraints, and any external interactions with users, systems, or hardware.

IIBA®, *BABOK® Guide* V2.0, 2009, 6, 184

47. **b.**   **Iteratively**

Frequency of communication versus formality of communication are characteristic of a change-driven business analysis approach.

IIBA®, *BABOK® Guide* V2.0, 2009, 22

48. **d.**   **Requirements management plan**

The requirements management plan is an artifact produced for the purpose of defining which processes are to be followed according to a set of tasks and activities.

IIBA®, *BABOK® Guide* V2.0, 2009, 99

49. **d.**   **Assess capability gaps output**

The feasibility study provides a basis from which benefits and costs of the solution can be quantified.

IIBA®, *BABOK® Guide* V2.0, 2009, 85–86

50. **a.**   **Interface analysis**

Interface analysis is an elicitation technique that is intended to describe how two systems will interact with each other. Navigation flow, screen flow and story boarding are considered types of prototyping techniques that can be used as a throw away or evolutionary process when developing requirements.

IIBA®, *BABOK® Guide* V2.0, 2009, 53, 176

51. **b.**   **Requirements elicitation**

Elicitation is the term used to define requirements; it means to draw forth or bring out.

IIBA®, *BABOK® Guide* V2.0, 2009, 53

52. **b.**   **Ensure that all team members are aware of the circumstances by outlining these nonfunctional requirements and the legal implications**

Collaboration and coordination of information with all team members will ensure that proper courses of action are planned for developing and managing requirements, particularly around the types of requirements. This best practice is cited in the *BABOK® Guide* in the Requirements Management & Communication knowledge area.

IIBA®, *BABOK® Guide* V2.0, 2009, 63

53. **a.** **Define business case**

Defining the business case demonstrates financial justification for the development or procurement of a desired solution. This activity is the final activity cited in the Enterprise Analysis knowledge area.

IIBA®, *BABOK® Guide* V2.0, 2009, 94–95

54. **d.** **[Verified]**

At any point during requirements activities, requirements are managed for the sake of ensuring that solution scope is maintained. Signing off on requirements by stakeholders is generally an activity that is done after the requirements have been verified and validated.

IIBA®, *BABOK® Guide* V2.0, 2009, 64

55. **c.** **Brainstorming**

Brainstorming allows stakeholders to quickly identify a large number of risks in a short period of time. These risks can then be categorized, evaluated, and prioritized based on probability and impact.

IIBA®, *BABOK® Guide* V2.0, 2009, 28

56. **d.** **Work breakdown structure**

A WBS is a hierarchical, structured grouping of project elements. At this level of planning, it is likely that only two to three elements are required to help determine project scope and initial cost estimates.

IIBA®, *BABOK® Guide* V2.0, 2009, 35

Ward, J. LeRoy. *Dictionary of Project Management Terms*, 3rd ed., 2008, 470

57. **b.** **The evaluation of a test scenario using predefined input and expected output**

A test scenario is meant to provide verification of each requirement and what it is intended to do. A test case provides the data for the requirement to act or react to certain conditions and parameters. One test scenario will often have multiple test cases to ensure that all possibilities for success and failure are realized.

IIBA®, *BABOK® Guide* V2.0, 2009, 155–156, 234

58. **d.** **Observation**

Rusty likely realized that more space would be needed to install the solution during observation of the floor production staff.

IIBA®, *BABOK® Guide* V2.0, 2009, 58, 186

59. **b.** **Identifies project assumptions and constraints**

As part of developing project scope, a business analyst identifies assumptions and constraints as part of the initial risk identification of the overall project.

IIBA®, *BABOK® Guide* V2.0, 2009, 92

60. **a.** **Assumptions**

Anything that is believed to be true but unverifiable and which may have a negative impact on the project should be documented as an assumption and consequently be evaluated as a risk.

IIBA®, *BABOK® Guide* V2.0, 2009, 112

61. **a.** **RACI matrix**

A RACI matrix identifies who is responsible, who is accountable, who must be consulted, and who should be informed with reference to the project, including developing and managing requirements.

IIBA®, *BABOK® Guide* V2.0, 2009, 29

62. **a.** **Organizational readiness**

As part of his risk plan, Jamie needs to identify organizational readiness in terms of resource capability and the overall enterprise architecture, either already in place or required for developing the desired solution.

IIBA®, *BABOK® Guide* V2.0, 2009, 127–128

63. **d.** **Misinterpretation of stated facts or requirements**

Clearly defined requirements, consensus on all terms stated and defined in a glossary of terms, a highly skilled facilitator, and stakeholder involvement are all ways to avoid misinterpreting stated facts and requirements.

IIBA®, *BABOK® Guide* V2.0, 2009, 61

64. **b.** **Effort required to deliver a system**

Any project deliverable information, including scheduling and cost control, need not be included in the requirements document.

IIBA®, *BABOK® Guide* V2.0, 2009, 17, 72–74

65. **d.** **Entity relationship diagrams**

Domain modeling provides iterative input into the development of entity relationship diagramming, and can be used to visualize business areas and the potential scope of an initiative.

IIBA®, *BABOK® Guide* V2.0, 2009, 163

66. **b.** **Requirements [Prioritized and Approved]**

The *BABOK® Guide* V2.0 implicitly states that allocation of requirements may occur at any stage of requirements management and development activities. Requirements must be prioritized and approved prior to their being allocated.

IIBA®, *BABOK® Guide* V2.0, 2009, 125

67. **c.** **Is limited to those individuals with signatory authority**

Only those stakeholders who have signing authority for the approval of requirements should be involved in signing off on requirements or managing business analysis activities. The challenges that they may face include changes to solution scope.

IIBA®, *BABOK® Guide* V2.0, 2009, 64

68. **d.** **Structured walkthroughs**

Structured walkthroughs are an interactive process that can occur at any stage of the solution development life cycle. During the planning stages, peer reviews may be used as a means by which a business analyst can transfer knowledge to the rest of his or her team members. At the same time, he or she may also have the team verify the clarity of already defined business requirements.

IIBA®, *BABOK® Guide* V2.0, 2009, 212

69. **b.** **Functional requirement**

A functional requirement describes how a system will perform, the behavior that the solution must manage, or the response of the system.

IIBA®, *BABOK® Guide* V2.0, 2009, 6

70. **d.** **Allocate Requirements**

The allocation of requirements is important to business analysis activities as it ensures the timeliness and efficiency of the delivery of requirements, to ensure the maximum business value is given throughout the development of the proposed solution.

IIBA®, *BABOK® Guide* V2.0, 2009, 124

71. **c.** **Types of techniques employed**

   Consider the example of brainstorming: There are a great number of tools that can be used to facilitate brainstorming activities, some of which can be used in a virtual environment while others are meant to be used where participants are colocated. Some tools may not be able to accommodate some brainstorming techniques, such as the Crawford slip technique or the nominal group technique.

   IIBA®, *BABOK® Guide* V2.0, 2009, 22

72. **c.** **Asked the group to participate in a multivoting exercise**

   Mark probably worked with the stakeholders to create a decision grid for objectively evaluating each item on the list based on success criteria, effort to implement, or impact on the organization. Multivoting is used to prioritize requirements.

   IIBA®, *BABOK® Guide* V2.0, 2009, 102

73. **a.** **Identification of potential solutions and solution providers**

   Identification of potential solutions or solution providers is an activity that evolves from Solution Assessment and Validation activities.

   IIBA®, *BABOK® Guide* V2.0, 2009, 96–97, 121

74. **a.** **The AS-IS state**

   Document analysis can provide an understanding only of the AS-IS state and the current documentation.

   IIBA®, *BABOK® Guide* V2.0, 2009, 170

75. **b.** **Commercial off-the-shelf**

   In some cases, near the end of the solution development life cycle phase, requirements are prepared in the form of a request for proposals (RFP) or a request for information (RFI) to solicit responses from vendors who might be able to resolve the requirements by a packaged solution, referred to as a commercial off-the-shelf- or COTS-based solution.

   IIBA®, *BABOK® Guide* V2.0, 2009, 41, 225

76. **a.** **States the purpose of the interview**

   Stating the purpose of the interview, addressing any initial concerns of the interviewee and explaining the process to be taken during the interview are all activities that a business analyst considers as they begin this activity.

   IIBA®, *BABOK® Guide* V2.0, 2009, 179

77. **a. Executive sponsor**

The executive sponsor or "project champion" is the individual in the organization whose responsibility for funding and resources directs the starting or stopping of a project(s).

IIBA®, *BABOK® Guide* V2.0, 2009, 13

78. **c. Plan-driven project**

Mary's project would be considered a plan-driven project, because of the criticality of maintaining a certain quality of support, the potential critical impact on the business in the event of a failure to manage all complex requirements across a potentially large geographical area, and the potential number of team members involved.

IIBA®, *BABOK® Guide* V2.0, 2009, 19–22

79. **c. Not evaluating ideas during the session**

Evaluating ideas during a brainstorming session can be counterproductive because it may prevent individuals from participating, discourage creativity by focusing on solution output instead of possible resolutions, and prevent real ideas from surfacing or evolving.

IIBA®, *BABOK® Guide* V2.0, 2009, 157–158

80. **a. Formally**

Formal documentation is often retained for plan-driven projects and most often requires approval and sign-off. Formal documentation is normally recorded as a means of tracking project history.

IIBA®, *BABOK® Guide* V2.0, 2009, 22

81. **b. Solution requirements**

Solution and stakeholder requirements are evaluated and assessed for their contribution to business value and the order in which they will be implemented against alternatives to maximize on cost benefits.

IIBA®, *BABOK® Guide* V2.0, 2009, 124

82. **a. A description of how the software will be built to support the overall business needs**

A software requirements specification document demonstrates both the behavior and the implementation of a software application. Its targeted audience is the technology or implementation team responsible for delivering the solution.

IIBA®, *BABOK® Guide* V2.0, 2009, 73–75

83. **b.** **Functional decomposition**

Functional decomposition is an activity that examines high-level functions of an organization, starting at the business unit level, and refines them into subfunctions or activities. This process could be referred to as understanding the lowest common denominator required to complete a process or series of processes. These processes can be depicted in a functional decomposition diagram, which resembles an organization chart in terms of hierarchy.

IIBA®, *BABOK® Guide* V2.0, 2009, 85, 174–175

84. **b.** **Return on investment**

ROI is calculated by dividing total capital into earnings before interest, taxes, and dividends.

IIBA®, *BABOK® Guide* V2.0, 2009, 96, 232

Ward, *Dictionary of Project Management Terms*, 2008, 382

85. **c.** **Facilitating communication using the appropriate technique to resolve the conflict**

Any number of facilitated communication techniques can be used to resolve the conflict between the stakeholders including decision analysis.

IIBA®, *BABOK® Guide* V2.0, 2009, 65

86. **c.** **Business requirements**

Functional requirements must be traced back to business requirements or features to prevent a misunderstanding of a customer's needs.

IIBA®, *BABOK® Guide* V2.0, 2009, 5-6

87. **b.** **Communicate requirements to another project team affected by an integrated project approach**

Although the criticality of communicating requirements to a dependent project team is important, an informal presentation may be sufficient if sign-off from all stakeholders has been approved.

IIBA®, *BABOK® Guide* V2.0, 2009, 80

88. **a.** **Requirement**

A requirement is a condition or capability needed by a stakeholder to solve a business problem or achieve an objective.

IIBA®, *BABOK® Guide* V2.0, 2009, 4–6

89. **a.** **Entity relationship diagram**

A CRUD matrix defines different levels of data manipulation on entities within a system and how the data may be created, read, updated, or deleted. Any diagram that includes information about data and its attributes, including ERDs and class diagrams or a data dictionary, may serve as the input for developing a CRUD matrix.

IIBA®, *BABOK® Guide* V2.0, 2009, 164

90. **c.** **Strategic plans**

Strategic plans are required as a source of input to the development of the business architecture. The strategic plans may also include any ongoing business problems, competitive disadvantages, and desired profitability and efficiencies or lack thereof.

IIBA®, *BABOK® Guide* V2.0, 2009, 83

91. **b.** **Focus group**

A focus group is a form of qualitative elicitation used to understand ideas and attitudes towards a specific product or service.

IIBA®, *BABOK® Guide* V2.0, 2009, 58, 172

92. **c.** **Vision statement**

A vision statement sets the stage for good product and project definition and is considered a best practice. It provides the context for the purpose of the project and should include, but not be limited to, organizational goal alignment, key stakeholders, and a quick snapshot of the purpose of the project.

IIBA®, *BABOK® Guide* V2.0, 2009, 94

93. **c.** **Solution scope**

Solution scope is a critical input to the management and communication of requirements activities. Solution scope and the supporting documentation provide insight on what requirements can be approved in order to support meeting the objectives of solution scope.

IIBA®, *BABOK® Guide* V2.0, 2009, 63–64

94. **a.** **Allocate Requirements**

Prioritized requirements allow for the distribution of requirements across iterations or releases of the solution or solution components.

IIBA®, *BABOK® Guide* V2.0, 2009, 99

95. **b.** **Strengths, weaknesses, opportunities, and threats (SWOT) analysis**

The statements listed in this question depict outputs of SWOT (strengths, weaknesses, opportunities, and threats) analysis.

IIBA®, *BABOK® Guide* V2.0, 2009, 88, 217

96. **b.** **Verified**

Verification of requirements ensures that requirements have been clearly defined and understood so that an implementation team can begin to develop a solution. Verifying requirements considers traceability, consistency, correctness, ambiguities, prioritization, and other characteristics.

IIBA®, *BABOK® Guide* V2.0, 2009, 114, 234

97. **c.** **Formal presentation**

A formal presentation to review all critical documentation, including an executive summary of the business needs and the alignment with goals and objectives before developing the solution, is best for obtaining sign-off.

IIBA®, *BABOK® Guide* V2.0, 2009, 80

98. **a.** **Business needs**

If the business needs change during the development of a solution, so then must solution scope. Requirements must be evaluated, approved, and signed off to support the revised scope.

IIBA®, *BABOK® Guide* V2.0, 2009, 64

99. **a.** **Business goal**

A business policy is a stated or implied means by which a business conducts day-to-day operations. Policies are non-actionable directives that support business goals and enforced by business rules.

IIBA®, *BABOK® Guide* V2.0, 2009, 159

Brûlé, *Business Analysis Terms: A Working Glossary*, 2009, 27

100. **a.** **Must be integrated into**

Business analysis represents only a portion of the overall development of a solution and is in many cases only a phase in the evolution of a solution and the project plan necessary to realize the development of the proposed solution.

IIBA®, *BABOK® Guide* V2.0, 2009, 22

101. **b.** **False**

Some organizations do not call for stakeholder requirements as a separate deliverable. However, it should be noted that stakeholder requirements define software requirements from a stakeholder's perspective and serve as an important link between business and solution requirements.

IIBA®, *BABOK® Guide* V2.0, 2009, 5

102. **a.** **Plan-driven**

A change-driven approach often requires documentation with much less formality than a plan-driven approach. Often, documented requirements are captured in a list format and are sequenced according to stakeholder priorities or as a form of acceptance criteria; and formal documentation of the solution is captured post-implementation to facilitate the transfer of knowledge to the solutions stakeholders.

IIBA®, *BABOK® Guide* V2.0, 2009, 21–22

103. **a.** **Assess Proposed Solution**

Requirements [Approved] are an input necessary for the execution of assessing a proposed solution in business analysis.

IIBA®, *BABOK® Guide* V2.0, 2009, 65, 121–122

104. **b.** **Notation to be used**

Different tools use different modeling notation and syntax to capture their requirements. In addition, different tools are intended to capture requirements for different levels of formality and using a variety of different approaches.

IIBA®, *BABOK® Guide* V2.0, 2009, 22

105. **c.** **To capture formal documentation**

Given the complexity of the project and the engagement with a contracted individual, the ABC Company selected a plan-driven approach to ensure the formal documentation of all requirements and project activities so that information about the solution may be readily available after the contractor has completed his or her work.

IIBA®, *BABOK® Guide* V2.0, 2009, 22

106. **b.** **Brainstorming**

Brainstorming is recommended for exploring all the potential solution options for meeting requirements by allowin g stakeholders the means to express ideas freely. This technique is not meant to solve problems or opportunities or to evaluate the ideas; ideas should not be evaluated during the brainstorming session.

IIBA®, *BABOK® Guide* V2.0, 2009, 58, 157

107. **a.** **Feasibility study**

A feasibility study explores all possible options for satisfying a business opportunity. Activities include but are not limited to conducting current state assessment, identifying potential solutions and the feasibility of each solution, and determining the scope, effort, and techniques to conduct the research.

IIBA®, *BABOK® Guide* V2.0, 2009, 90–91

108. **a.** **Timeboxing/Budgeting**

Timeboxing and budgeting is a technique uniquely identified in the Requirements Analysis knowledge area specific to the prioritization of requirements. This technique is allows for a business analyst to assess the relative priority of a requirement(s) based on the amount of effort needed to implement a requirement and any potential fixed costs associated with the implementation of the requirement in question. Essentially two factors are considered while using this technique – time and cost.

IIBA®, *BABOK® Guide* V2.0, 2009, 102

109. **d.** **Gain consensus and approval from stakeholders**

To resolve a business problem or opportunity, a business analyst needs to consider a means to communicate with all stakeholders in such a way that they may reach a consensus and sign off on the requirements to produce the desired deliverables.

IIBA®, *BABOK® Guide* V2.0, 2009, 72

110. **c.**   **Project manager**

Although a business analyst's role includes developing and managing requirements, a project manager is ultimately responsible for managing the entire team, including the BA. The PM is responsible for delivering goods and services under the constraints of time, cost, quality, and scope.

IIBA®, *BABOK® Guide* V2.0, 2009, 12

111. **a.**   **Ishikawa diagram**

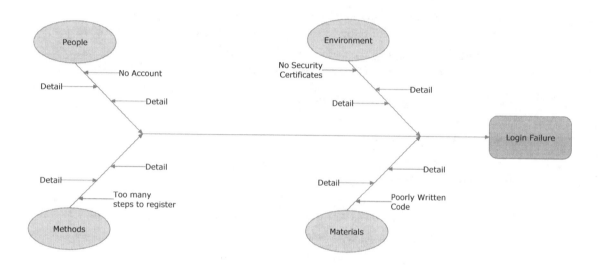

The Ishikawa diagram is also known as a fishbone diagram or a cause-and-effect diagram. The head of the fish identifies the risk and the "fishbones" represent potential causes and effects.

IIBA®, *BABOK® Guide* V2.0, 2009, 202–203

112. **d.**   **At any time during the project**

A requirements review is an iterative process, and therefore it may be held at any point during the requirements development and management activities.

IIBA®, *BABOK® Guide* V2.0, 2009, 116

113. **d.**   **Executive sponsor**

The executive sponsor has a stake in the solution that is typically tied to an organization's goals and vision. The executive sponsor is accountable for overall adherence to organizational performance according to regulatory affairs, and as a result, any government-imposed regulations are a concern. The look and feel of the product is something for which end users—rather than the executive sponsor—have a high regard.

IIBA®, *BABOK® Guide* V2.0, 2009, 13

114. **c.** **Identify inconsistencies and ensure that stakeholders' needs are being met**

Peer reviews help to prevent unnecessary cost overruns by identifying inconsistencies and unmet stakeholders' needs.

IIBA®, *BABOK® Guide* V2.0, 2009, 229

115. **b.** **A review of functional and nonfunctional requirements**

A review of both functional and nonfunctional requirements gives a business analyst insight into how they can be mapped to the design of the solution and which type of user class considerations need to be made.

IIBA®, *BABOK® Guide* V2.0, 2009, 114-117

116. **c.** **Risk analysis**

Risk management can be used as a feasibility technique to identify the probability and impact of risks, assumptions, and constraints associated with potential solutions.

IIBA®, *BABOK® Guide* V2.0, 2009, 200–201

117. **a.** **Decision analysis**

Decision analysis supports the making of decisions where complex conditions exists or may exist during the development of a solution.

IIBA®, *BABOK® Guide* V2.0, 2009, 23, 166

118. **a.** **Cardinality**

Cardinality depicts the minimum and maximum number of relationships that one entity may have on another entity. One example: A student may enroll in one or more courses, and a course may have more than one student. However, a course cannot have "no students," but may have only one course code.

IIBA®, *BABOK® Guide* V2.0, 2009, 111, 164–165

119. **b.** **Stakeholder analysis**

Stakeholder analysis allows a business analyst to identify such factors as interests, risks, and success criteria needed to discover and develop requirements.

IIBA®, *BABOK® Guide* V2.0, 2009, 24

120. **c.** **Plan-driven approach**

In this case where detailed documentation and the formality of how it is captured is required, a plan-driven approach with distinct "stop and start" phases is likely to be the most appropriate.

IIBA®, *BABOK® Guide* V2.0, 2009, 21–22

121. **b.** **Prepare the requirements package**

The *BABOK® Guide* V2.0 recommends that the preparation and delivery of the requirements package is likely to be presented in one of thee formats: formalize documentation, a presentation, or and models.

IIBA®, *BABOK® Guide* V2.0, 2009, 63, 73

122. **c.** **Structural**

Structural rules are those types of rules that may change over time, but which cannot not be violated. They are generally based on logical conditions, which in turn are based on data and knowledge supplied by the organization.

IIBA®, *BABOK® Guide* V2.0, 2009, 159–160

123. **c.** **Evaluation criteria**

Evaluation criteria are used when multiple solution options are considered for the selection of a solution that best meets the needs of the business.

IIBA®, *BABOK® Guide* V2.0, 2009, 155

124. **d.** **The decrease of a risk by lowering the probability or impact of the risk event**

Risk mitigation is defined as decreasing the probability of the risk event or the impact of its occurrence.

IIBA®, *BABOK® Guide* V2.0, 2009, 36, 201

Ward, *Dictionary of Project Management Terms*, 2008, 274

125. **c.** **Plan-driven approach**

The more formal an approach to the requirements activities is, then more likely it is that a conscientious decision was made to proceed with a plan driven approach.

IIBA®, *BABOK® Guide* V2.0, 2009, 21–22

126. **d.** **Employed the Crawford slip brainstorming technique**

Eric could use the Crawford slip technique of anonymous brainstorming to promote creative ideas by having his audience generate ideas anonymously on slips of paper. They can then build on each others' ideas by adding their own ideas to previously submitted thoughts. Crawford slip is a nonverbal exercise meant to minimize conflict.

IIBA®, *BABOK® Guide* V2.0, 2009, 157–158

Ward, *Dictionary of Project Management Terms*, 2008, 108

127. **a.** **Requirements Management Plan**

The output of business analysis performance metrics activities and business analysis plans are required input for the management and communication of all business analysis activities.

IIBA®, *BABOK® Guide* V2.0, 2009, 63

128. **d.** **Sunk cost**

Sunk costs are an element of consideration when validating an existing solution, and may influence decisions regarding the elimination and or replacement of a solution

IIBA®, *BABOK® Guide* V2.0, 2009, 139

129. **c.** **Methods that will be used to convey information**

Target audience, types of communication, frequency, how and where information will be stored, and the method for keeping all documentation up-to-date are all elements of the communication plan.

IIBA®, *BABOK® Guide* V2.0, 2009, 78

130. **d.** **Types of information produced as a result of the session**

A focus group produces reports with qualitative results, whereas requirements workshop allow a group of stakeholders to reach consensus using a variety of techniques that include logical data models, functional decomposition diagrams, and data flow diagrams, a more quantitative approach.

IIBA®, B*ABOK® Guide* V2.0, 2009, 172, 198

131. **d.** **Vertical prototype**

A vertical prototype is best used to elicit requirements to demonstrate compatibility with existing systems or lack thereof and is focused on one particular aspect of the entire application.

IIBA®, *BABOK® Guide* V2.0, 2009, 56, 196

132. **c.** **Stakeholder requirements**

Stakeholder requirements are intended to capture the needs of a specific stakeholder or a group/category of stakeholders and how they might interact with a proposed solution.

IIBA®, *BABOK® Guide* V2.0, 2009, 5

133. **a.** **Ensure traceability back to user requirements**

Traceability truly begins when functional design is assessed and evaluated against user requirements. User requirements must be fully incorporated into the functional design. If they are not, then they need either to be removed or re-evaluated, or the functional design specifications need to be rewritten.

IIBA®, *BABOK® Guide* V2.0, 2009, 68

134. **c.** **Business case**

A business case can help to identify the net present value of the proposed business needs. Typically used for capital budgeting, a business case could be used in this situation to help assess how much value the solution might bring to the organization.

IIBA®, *BABOK® Guide* V2.0, 2009, 95–96, 167

135. **a.** **Level 0 data flow diagram**

The context diagram is also known as a level 0 DFD depicting interactions of a system with other entities and is typically used to help define project scope.

IIBA®, *BABOK® Guide* V2.0, 2009, 161–162

136. **c.** **Timeboxing**

Timeboxing is a particularly useful technique for prioritizing requirements where a fixed resource has been allocated to a predetermined approach for delivery of a solution. There are three different timebox approaches that may be applied: All In, All Out, and Selective.

IIBA®, *BABOK® Guide* V2.0, 2009, 102

137. **a.** **Demonstrating a horizontal prototype**

A horizontal prototype elicits requirements using a mock-up of the system with a wide view of the functionality but with little or no business logic behind it.

IIBA®, *BABOK® Guide* V2.0, 2009, 56, 196–197

138. **b.** **Five**

There are five activities prescribed in the *BABOK® Guide* to complete in the Enterprise Analysis Knowledge Area.: Define the business need, assess capability gaps, determine solution approach, define solution scope and define the business case..

IIBA®, *BABOK® Guide* V2.0, 2009, 81

139. **b.** **Observe the user performing his or her tasks while conducting an interview**

As part of an interview, a business analyst may ask to observe an end user while he or she participates in activities that might help to discover requirements about an existing business process. By combining both elicitation techniques, a BA can quickly resolve any descriptive ambiguities that might become apparent only in an interview with the end user.

IIBA®, *BABOK® Guide* V2.0, 2009, 58, 186

140. **a.** **Through voting**

Voting is a democratic decision-making process in which stakeholders choose or rank by priority their desired requirements.

IIBA®, *BABOK® Guide* V2.0, 2009, 102–103

141. **d.** **Prioritization**

The prioritization of requirements is often a driver of solution development as each iteration is completed. This demonstrates how stakeholders are directly involved with the evolution of the solution and often a means by which the traditional change requests are facilitated.

IIBA®, *BABOK® Guide* V2.0, 2009, 21

142. **b.** **Determining solution approach**

Multivoting is likely to be used after all possible solutions have been brainstormed in order to either prioritize or select those solutions identified and to help bring a group of stakeholders to consensus.

IIBA®, *BABOK® Guide* V2.0, 2009, 90–91

143. **d.** **Behavior diagram**

Use case or class diagrams depict the behavioral features of a business process or a system including its relationships with users or systems.

IIBA®, *BABOK® Guide* V2.0, 2009, 105–106

144. **b.** **Requirement attribute**

Requirements complexity, acceptance criteria, urgency, or priority must be documented as an attribute of the requirement.

IIBA®, *BABOK® Guide* V2.0, 2009, 58

145. **b.**   **Project communication**

Overall project communication is the responsibility of the project manager. Requirements communication, however, is a subset of requirements activities and is the responsibility of the business analyst.

IIBA®, *BABOK® Guide* V2.0, 2009, 37

146. **c.**   **Release planning**

Release planning takes into consideration many different elements that include schedules, project budgets, launch dates, periods of time were business is halted for implementation purposes or business cycles, including launching new products for Christmas sales.

IIBA®, *BABOK® Guide* V2.0, 2009, 126

147. **d.**   **Activity diagram**

In an object-oriented environment, an activity diagram shows how data move through a system as input or output and are stored or processed. Activity diagrams are used in much the same way as data flow diagrams are used in a non–object-oriented environment.

IIBA®, *BABOK® Guide* V2.0, 2009, 194

148. **d.**   **Upon completion of the development of solution scope**

Allocation of requirements is an iterative activity that may occur throughout the identification, development, and management of requirements and physical development of the solution. It can begin as early as the completion of the solution scope development.

IIBA®, *BABOK® Guide* V2.0, 2009, 125

149. **c.**   **That after a decision is made, it is then considered irreversible**

If stakeholders are not made aware of all limitations, risks assumptions, and constraints, it is likely that not only will they be reluctant to reassess or evaluate decisions, but they may make decisions with a false degree of certainty.

IIBA®, *BABOK® Guide* V2.0, 2009, 168–169

150. **c.** **MoSCoW technique**

At a high level, a business analyst may begin prioritizing requirements and their attributes to evaluate them by examining the imperatives used to describe them. Imperatives may include such words as "Must—requirement must be included and satisfied; Should—represents a requirement of high priority, but may be resolved using a different approach or by other means; Could—desired but not necessary; and Won't—a requirement that will not be implemented as stated by stakeholders." A business analyst may later use a more structured approach to prioritize the requirements.

IIBA®, *BABOK® Guide* V2.0, 2009, 102

Practice Test 2

This practice test is designed to simulate IIBA's 150-question CBAP® certification exam. You have 3.5 hours to answer all questions.

INSTRUCTIONS: Note the most suitable answer for each multiple-choice question in the appropriate space on the answer sheet.

1. Business analysts often describe requirements as the "what" of a solution versus the "how" of a solution, with "how" most often being determined by the technical team. In the case of a discrepancy of these levels of abstraction, a business analyst would be most concerned with—

    a. The amount of effort required to implement a requirement
    b. How the requirements have been prioritized
    c. The business stakeholder's perspective
    d. Ensuring that requirements related to implementation of the solution are accurate

2. During the decomposition of scope, Gerry quickly realized that the proposed solution would need to pass information to an external system and receive information from another. A further understanding of these efforts and the detailed requirements to achieve them is known as—

    a. Interface analysis
    b. SWOT analysis
    c. Requirements analysis
    d. Specification analysis

3. A requirements workshop ideally should be facilitated by a—

    a. Executive sponsor
    b. Project manager
    c. Business analyst
    d. Neutral facilitator

4. Which particular technique is useful during the assessment of organizational readiness to understand issues that may prevent the solution from being accepted into the organization and those issues that may promote the solution in being adapted into the organization?

   a. Force field analysis
   b. Gap analysis
   c. Root cause analysis
   d. SWOT analysis

5. A business analyst is likely to consider using this element to schedule requirements activities.

   a. Project scope statement
   b. Activity list
   c. Requirements source list
   d. Stakeholder list

6. These are considered to be the perceived needs of stakeholders and must be further investigated to ensure alignment with goals and objectives of the organization as they evolve into business requirements.

   a. Requirements [prioritized]
   b. Requirements [stated]
   c. Requirements [validated]
   d. Requirements [verified]

7. This evolutionary technique is often used to elicit requirements, define assumptions and constraints, and validate requirements. In some cases the results are discarded, and in other cases the results are cumulative and evolutionary. Storyboards and dialogue maps are considered a type of this technique.

   a. Decision tree
   b. Prototype
   c. Peer reviews
   d. Use case models

8. During an interview, it is considered a best practice to ask questions in a particular order. Which of the following choices demonstrates the best order?

   a. How many hours do you spend on expense reports? Who in your organization submits expense reports? Are expenses reimbursed using direct deposit or by check?
   b. Who in your organization submits expense reports? What is the maximum amount allowed for a per diem? Does your organization use corporate cards?
   c. Who codes the expense reports with general ledger codes? Are the reports created in a spreadsheet or a word processing program? Who reconciles the receipts?
   d. Tell me about the expense reporting process. Who in your organization submits expense reports? Who is responsible for approving those reports? After the expense reports are approved, who reconciles the receipts against expenses submitted?

9. A business analyst's primary role regarding alternate solution selection is to—

    a. Facilitate vendor selection by identifying criteria that will meet the business need
    b. Direct the technical team on the appropriate technology to use based on the business need
    c. Ensure that the technical specifications found in the business requirements document are implemented properly
    d. Ensure that quality standards comply with imposed regulations

10. A project manager may be considered a key stakeholder in Requirements Management and Communication activities for what reason?

    a. To help provide clarity around which elicitation techniques may be most appropriate for the delivery of key requirements artifacts
    b. To develop a risk response plan to any proposed changes made to requirements
    c. To ensure that funding is readily available for any changes to the solution scope
    d. To provide signatures and sign off on solution scope changes

11. Cohesive, complete, and consistent are characteristics that are _____ while ensuring syntactical correctness during this Requirements Analysis activity.

    a. Verified
    b. Validated
    c. Categorized
    d. Prioritized

12. When interviewing stakeholders, it is your goal to understand—

    a. Whether your solution will be bought from a vendor or developed in house
    b. Organizational alignment
    c. Stakeholder involvement in the project
    d. Who is financially responsible for the project

13. Determining which elicitation technique to use and to whom to apply it is identified in which knowledge area?

    a. Solution Assessment and Validation
    b. Elicitation
    c. Enterprise Analysis
    d. Business Analysis Planning and Monitoring

14. The identification of requirements issues and the documentation supporting how they are managed is a technique commonly referred to as what?

    a. Decision record
    b. Ishikawa diagram
    c. Pareto analysis
    d. Problem tracking

15. A stakeholder could be a(n)—

    a. Government entity
    b. Internal system
    c. External system
    d. Service level agreement

16. The requirements management plan is an output produced during Business Analysis Planning and Monitoring activities. Why might this serve as an input for elicitation activities?

    a. A business analyst will want to ensure that all requirements, requests, and results elicited from stakeholders are delivered appropriately.
    b. A project manager will want to be clear on the effort required to do so for cost-control purposes.
    c. The stakeholders can then schedule enough time to commit to the project.
    d. Miscommunication of requirements will cause the scope of the project to creep.

17. What is a key output resulting from activities of defining the business analysis approach?

    a. Performance analysis
    b. Stakeholder analysis
    c. Stakeholder elicitation plan
    d. Team roles

18. Through Requirements Management and Communication activities, a business analyst may need to—

    a. Sign off on the requirements package
    b. Liaise with a project manager to take on this responsibility
    c. Make amendments to the original scope document
    d. Adjust any changes made to the project schedule as a result of poor communication

19. The primary objective of conducting Elicitation activities is to—

    a. Develop relationships with stakeholders to ensure that all business needs are met
    b. Understand the TO-BE state for the desired solution
    c. Understand the AS-IS state for the desired solution
    d. Provide data and information for developing requirements

20. Which of the following are considered requirements attributes?

    a. Ambiguous, concise, and traceable
    b. Unambiguous, concise, and source
    c. Source, stability, and priority
    d. Cost, ambiguity, and priority

21. Describing what a system will do to satisfy stakeholder needs is the characteristic of—
    a. Quality of service requirements
    b. Business requirements
    c. System requirements
    d. Functional requirements

22. Which of the following choices should NOT be considered potential reference material when trying to identify project stakeholders?
    a. Service level agreement
    b. Company directory
    c. Project charter
    d. Organization chart

23. Documentation necessary as input into the Solution Assessment and Validation activities includes but is not limited to—
    a. A conversion plan
    b. Enterprise architecture
    c. An RFP/RFQ
    d. A test plan

24. When describing a focus group, what is one of the characteristics that you would include?
    a. It is a form of qualitative research.
    b. It is a form of quantitative research.
    c. It employs a disciplined decision-making process to prioritize requirements.
    d. It requires a group of stakeholders to reach consensus over whatever period of time is necessary to do so.

25. This input is required in order for the validation of a solution to be successful.
    a. Organizational process assets
    b. Requirements [stated]
    c. Requirements [prioritized and validated]
    d. Requirements [stated, confirmed]

26. Under what conditions would analysis of transition requirements NOT be necessary?
    a. Stakeholders have come to consensus on organizational change management issues.
    b. The initiative has been imposed by government regulations and must be implemented regardless of the impact it might have.
    c. The requirements have been validated as being accurate.
    d. Solution is adding a capability to the organization where that capability did not exist.

27. A formal sign-off on requirements may be an indication that—
    a. Regulatory compliance is governing the actions of this project
    b. Stakeholders are risk-averse to the proposed solution
    c. This is a change-driven project
    d. This project is using an agile approach to deliver its solution

28. When considering interface analysis, a business analyst should not expect to achieve results that would reveal or give insight to—
    a. Business processes
    b. Inputs
    c. Outputs
    d. Key data

29. Although interviews may be very effective in establishing rapport with stakeholders, they also have their limitations. Which of the following choices describes one of those limitations?
    a. Actions speak louder than words
    b. Interpretation of data collected during the interview
    c. Limited use of open-ended questions
    d. Too much information from interviewee when asked too many open-ended questions

30. Michael was assigned as a business analyst to a project that proposed to add functionality to an existing application. How might this issue affect planning considerations?
    a. Michael would need to consider developing a complete requirements package.
    b. Michael would need to consider a buy-versus-build approach.
    c. Michael would need to create the TO-BE state based on existing documentation (AS-IS state) and consider conducting a gap analysis to determine the best approach.
    d. Michael would need to consider using existing functional requirements and mapping them to a requirements trace matrix.

31. Which model would give stakeholders insight into how business analysis work is defined and about the type of work involved in a business analysis approach?
    a. Data models
    b. Object oriented models
    c. Organizational models
    d. Process models

32. The ability to depict the origins, assignment, and associations of requirements can be best described as—
    a. Traceability
    b. A data dictionary
    c. Evolution
    d. A glossary of terms

33. Evaluation of a solution to determine its alignment with a business need and consider reconciling any uncovered defects is referred to as what?
    a. Delineation
    b. Justification
    c. Verification
    d. Validation

34. One primary output from creating or selecting the requirements activities would include a—
    a. Project work breakdown structure
    b. List of logical dependencies
    c. Selection of activities from Enterprise Analysis to Solution Assessment and Validation
    d. Complete list of all project resources required to produce the solution

35. Dale was a business analyst on a project that was going to implement new security features to an existing mail system. During his interview with the Chief Technology Officer, he was told that, for the purposes of protecting intellectual property and misuse of email, a 5 MB restriction on all incoming and outgoing email was to be imposed. Dale was careful to capture this technical requirement as a(n)—
    a. Assumption
    b. Constraint
    c. Attribute
    d. User requirement

36. In creating categories for your stakeholders, you created a category for subject matter experts. Which type of stakeholders would you expect to list under this category?
    a. Project managers
    b. Executive sponsor
    c. Buyers
    d. Trainers

37. Which of the following choices would NOT likely be a metric used when evaluating the success of the requirements development and management life cycle?

    a. Schedule
    b. Number of defects
    c. Number of requirements
    d. Resources

38. This modeling technique is typically employed so that stakeholders may begin to understand the hierarchal breakdown of organizational processes.

    a. Class model
    b. Activity diagram
    c. Business policies
    d. Context diagram

39. When running a focus group, your discussion guide should include—

    a. A glossary of terms
    b. Stakeholder profiles
    c. Time allotted for conversations
    d. Goals and objectives of the session

40. During the identification of stakeholders, Harold discovered a group of individuals who, as a result of the proposed solution, would receive biannual reports of forecasted revenue. Beyond this activity, they would have no other interactions with the system. Harold categorized these users as—

    a. Advisors
    b. Product champions
    c. Indirect users
    d. Providers

41. An effective way to maintain and manage risks and requirements is to—

    a. Use a communication plan to send frequent risk evaluation to the stakeholders
    b. Conduct frequent structured walkthroughs to detect any inconsistencies that may arise while the requirements are being developed
    c. Ensure that the quality analysis team understands the business requirements and that they receive a link to the specifications
    d. Ensure that risk documentation is distributed to all stakeholders and project team members

42. When creating your stakeholder lists, you used the following categories to identify stakeholders: owner, producer, and reviewer. Under the column heading "develop user requirements," you are likely to categorize a software developer as a(n)—

    a. Owner
    b. Approver
    c. Producer
    d. Reviewer

43. Complex business rules are likely to be depicted using what type of model?

    a. Process map
    b. Actor map
    c. Decision tree
    d. State chart diagram

44. Forward traceability of a requirement is also known as what?

    a. Allocation
    b. Cardinality
    c. Derivation
    d. Evolution

45. Which input is required to help define transition requirements?

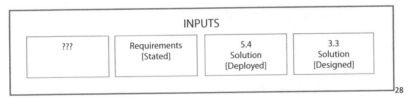

    a. Assumptions and Constraints
    b. Business Analysis Approach
    c. Organizational Readiness Assessment
    d. Stakeholder Concerns

46. Estimating reduced costs, accelerated processes, decreased defects, and activity costs could provide a business analyst with a(n)—

    a. SWOT analysis
    b. Gap analysis
    c. Activity based costing
    d. Return on investment

---

47. Approval or sign-off on requirements may come from a stakeholder or—

    a. A business analyst
    b. The director of IT
    c. Groups of stakeholders
    d. The project manager

48. Which one of the following statements is true for the specification and modeling of requirements?

    a. A business analyst should be fluent in UML 2.0 modeling language
    b. Inputs required include Requirements [Stated] and Requirements Structure
    c. A business analyst should engage a subject matter expert to define which level of abstraction is most appropriate
    d. Input required includes enterprise architecture documentation

49. Inez was assigned to a project that was expected to cost her organization $350,000 over a 24-month period. Inez did some research, including scope decomposition, to learn that if the solution was implemented according to the requirements specifications, her organization would benefit from an increase in revenues estimated to be $500,000 over a 36-month period. Inez came to this conclusion by—

    a. Conducting activity-based costing
    b. Scrutinizing the estimated effort of the project against the cost to develop the overall solution
    c. Interviewing stakeholders to understand their financial commitment to the project
    d. Comparing the cost of implementing the solution to the potential revenue realized by implementing the solution

50. A business analyst should be careful to understand stakeholder authority and signatories because of which reason stated below?

    a. Compliance with the business analysis approach
    b. To avoid forgeries
    c. To avoid having stakeholders sign off on subsets of requirements where they have no authority
    d. To ensure that all stakeholders are held accountable for their actions

51. Large groups of requirements requiring simultaneous implementation should be scrutinized for project risk because—

    a. The project may be complex and may require a team of expert resources to implement
    b. The project may be expensive to implement
    c. Requirements may be missed, and project failure is unavoidable
    d. Many change requests may lead to project scope creep

52. When describing steps involved in executing a system, such as logging into the system with a password, by using either text, models or matrixes, a business analyst is describing a—

    a. Business requirement
    b. Functional requirement
    c. Transition requirement
    d. Stakeholder requirement

53. When involved in Solution Assessment and Validation activities, a business analyst is expected to—

    a. Sign off on the requirements package and hand over his or her documents to the implementation team
    b. Deliver the training to end users who will use the system
    c. Negotiate service level agreements
    d. Provide guidance to the quality assurance team to ensure compliance with the business needs and any imposed regulations

54. Which modeling concept can be best described as an internal or external transaction that may be scheduled to manipulate or activate an existing business process?

    a. Abstraction
    b. Processes
    c. Rules
    d. Event

55. A technique that could be used during interface analysis to understand a user's interaction with the system is—

    a. White-box reverse engineering
    b. Glass-box reverse engineering
    c. Prototyping
    d. Interview

56. An organization decided that the most appropriate solution to meet its goals and objectives was to purchase a commercial off-the-shelf-based solution. A business analyst would use which documentation to help prepare a list of stakeholders that are likely candidates to contribute to the development of requirements for delivering the most appropriate solution?

    a. Enterprise architecture
    b. Feasibility study reports
    c. Project scope documentation
    d. Work breakdown structure

57. System performance is always a consideration that business analysts and design teams face. During the solution selection activities, system performance can be categorized as a—

    a. Functional requirement

    b. Feature

    c. Nonfunctional requirement

    d. User requirement

58. Which diagramming technique is often used to depict the visualization of use case diagrams and their extended steps?

    a. Data flow diagram

    b. Activity diagram

    c. Flowchart

    d. Entity relationship diagram

59. Requirements are said to have been _____ after all stakeholders agree that the proposed product can undergo development.

    a. Unambiguous

    b. Verified

    c. Prioritized according to risk

    d. Formalized

60. When identifying the means of eliciting requirements from stakeholders, a business analyst should pay attention to—

    a. Political alliances

    b. Ulterior motives

    c. Role versus job title

    d. Full-time employees versus contractors

61. Which of the following choices listed below is NOT a technique used for root cause analysis?

    a. Fishbone diagram

    b. Five whys technique

    c. Brainstorming

    d. Process modeling

62. If a requirement is not _____ and_____, it cannot be verified as being a valid requirement.

    a. Testable; traceable

    b. Ambiguous; measurable

    c. Necessary; traceable

    d. Concise; uses acronyms

63. When conducting interviews with stakeholders, you should avoid—

    a. Asking closed-ended questions
    b. Observing them while they conduct their work
    c. Asking for permission to follow up with clarification
    d. Asking leading questions

64. A diagram used to understand a top-level process and all of its subprocesses is referred to as a—

    a. Functional decomposition diagram
    b. State machine diagram
    c. Use case diagram
    d. Activity diagram

65. Kevin decided to do what, so that he could track any variances or alterations to the requirements deliverables for comparative purposes?

    a. Baseline the requirements
    b. Ensure that a scribe was present at all meetings
    c. Provide a central repository for all documentation on the corporate intranet
    d. Videotape all business analysis activities

66. The following modeling technique may be used to help identify elements for consideration when assessing organizational readiness of a solution to be implemented—

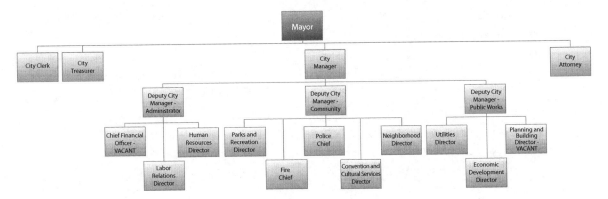

    a. Data flow diagram
    b. Object model
    c. Organizational model
    d. Process model

67. Levels of requirements abstraction can vary based on the—
    a. Business case
    b. Methodologies
    c. Number of requirements
    d. Operational assets

68. Which of the following choices would NOT be included in a requirements document?
    a. Quality attributes
    b. Impact analysis report
    c. Project charter
    d. Costs and efforts

69. You have been asked to present no less than four solution options as a result of your enterprise analysis efforts. So that the stakeholders are clear about factors such as risk, costs, and customer value, you present your findings using which type of modeling technique?
    a. Use case diagrams
    b. Requirements attributes
    c. Risk analysis
    d. Criteria matrix

70. The description of solution characteristics is also referred to as—
    a. Functional requirements
    b. Business requirements
    c. Transition requirements
    d. Nonfunctional requirements

71. What might be a tool that a business analyst considers so that she or he may understand the rationale for signing off on the allocation of requirements?
    a. Business requirements document
    b. Decision record
    c. RACI chart
    d. Solution Development Life Cycle

72. Elicitation is not limited only to stakeholders. Elicitation of requirements for existing solutions can also be done considering—
    a. Document analysis
    b. An independent study by a third party
    c. Informal conversations
    d. Analysis of the work breakdown structure

73. When preparing a questionnaire to identify stakeholders, you may be able to identify stakeholders who you have not yet considered. How might this be possible?

    a. By sending your questionnaire to a mass mailing list
    b. By sending your questionnaire to all the people in the company
    c. By soliciting advice from other business analysts and project managers
    d. By having questionnaire respondents identify potential stakeholders

74. "A service the system provides to fulfill one or more stakeholders' needs" is the definition of what?

    a. Function
    b. Feature
    c. Design
    d. Scope

75. As part of the Requirements Management and Communication activities, a business analyst might consider developing which type of model to demonstrate the relationships between business needs and goals and any of the final product components?

    a. Context diagram
    b. State machine diagram
    c. Sequence diagram
    d. Requirements coverage matrix

76. A business analyst can prevent scope creep by—

    a. Implementing a policy for requirement change requests after a baseline has been established
    b. Ensuring that there are enough resources to deliver a quality product
    c. Asking stakeholders for more funding to support the project
    d. Documenting all requirements using a variety of diagramming techniques

77. Every strategic goal should be reviewed and assessed by the business analyst so that it is—

    a. Depicted in a use case model
    b. Approved by all stakeholders
    c. Included in all requirements documentation
    d. Written to be measurable

78. Ultimately functional requirements must be traceable back to—

    a. Low-level requirements
    b. Design function
    c. Business requirements
    d. Nonfunctional requirements

79. When conducting a requirements workshop, consideration for which method should be given?

    a. Crawford slip

    b. Nominal group technique

    c. Brainstorming technique

    d. Any combination of these techniques may be suitable

80. Which task uses transition requirements as input for its activities?

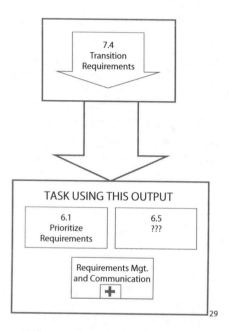

    a. Allocate Requirements

    b. Analyze Requirements

    c. Validate Requirements

    d. Verify Requirements

---

[29] Adapted from Figure 7-6 BABOK® Guide V2.0, 132.

81. The following modeling technique may be used to help identify elements for consideration when assessing organizational readiness of a solution to be implemented:

Online Order System

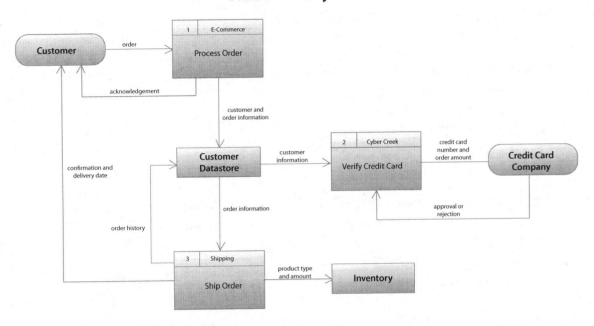

a. Data flow diagram
b. Entity relationship diagram
c. Object-oriented model
d. Use case model

82. Four items are critical when developing the initial solution scope: assumptions and constraints, business need, required capabilities, and—

a. An initial outline of business rules
b. A buy-versus-build decision
c. A solution approach
d. Feasibility study results

83. "Are you directly affected by the output of the project deliverables?" This is an example of a(n)—

a. Open-ended question
b. Closed-ended question
c. Implication question
d. Derogatory question

84. The application of tools and templates is determined during which *BABOK® Guide* V2.0 knowledge area?

    a. Requirements Analysis
    b. Enterprise Analysis
    c. Business Analysis Planning and Monitoring
    d. Elicitation

85. A hierarchical depiction of activities and interrelated events best describes which modeling technique?

    a. Process modeling
    b. Scope modeling
    c. Use cases
    d. User stories

86. Which diagram is used to enhance the view of a context diagram in conjunction with "verb-object structure" to demonstrate the conversion, combination, or re-ordering of information?

    a. Data flow diagram
    b. Entity relationship diagram
    c. DRD
    d. EFT

87. When working with the implementation team to deploy a solution, a business analyst should be careful to consider the—

    a. Skills of the resources implementing the solution
    b. Clarity of all models developed and how they are mapping to the solution
    c. Transition of data from one format to another
    d. Cost of the solution as it is outlined in the Enterprise Analysis activities

88. The rectangle that encompasses a use case diagram is intended to describe—

    a. The software to be developed
    b. The scope of the system being modeled
    c. The finite area in which a user completes a single task
    d. Nothing (as it is used for organizational and aesthetic purposes only)

89. An alternate means to the observation technique for understanding how a user functions in his or her work environment might be—

    a. Use case diagramming
    b. Storyboarding
    c. Active/visible observation
    d. Data modeling

90. The determination of how information will be provided to stakeholders is decided by a business analyst—
    a. When he or she is considering the Enterprise Analysis activities
    b. When the stakeholders complete a questionnaire and provide feedback
    c. After the project manager has determined the best delivery method to use
    d. When he or she is satisfied with how the communication plan is developed

91. Financial constraints realized during Enterprise Analysis may be an indicator of—
    a. The complexity of the project
    b. An unwillingness to allow scope to creep
    c. A lack of stakeholder commitment
    d. An unwillingness to take on any risk that the solution may pose

92. When interviewing your stakeholders, it is a best practice to—
    a. Ask closed-ended questions
    b. Use the stakeholders' own terminology
    c. Provide them with the results from previous stakeholder interviews
    d. Avoid confrontation by asking open-ended questions

93. The primary purpose of managing requirements for traceability is to—
    a. Ensure delivery in a hierarchical fashion
    b. Demonstrate historical activities
    c. Ensure that requirements have referable points to related solution artifacts and business requirements
    d. Provide a description of prioritized requirements

94. Catalogued, categorized, and scoped are characteristics that can be used to describe which output produced after requirements have been organized?
    a. [Stated] Requirements
    b. Information architecture
    c. Requirements structure
    d. Requirements specification

95. After Ben finished developing a RACI chart, his boss quickly pointed out an error. Which of the following choices is the error that was found?
    a. Application architects were to be consulted on Enterprise Analysis activities.
    b. The project manager and business analyst were assigned "A" for requirements management.
    c. The business architect was assigned to do the work.
    d. The end users were to be informed of activity progress.

96. Frequency of use, ease of navigation, and intuitiveness are typical types of—

    a. Functional requirements

    b. Nonfunctional requirements

    c. Stability requirements

    d. Design requirements

97. Why would a business analyst consider involving customers in the development of a business analysis approach?

    a. Availability

    b. To ensure that compliance is adhered to

    c. To facilitate user acceptance testing

    d. To provide insight to compatibility with other ongoing initiatives

98. What modes are particularly useful as input for the development of organizational models?

    a. Events

    b. Profiles

    c. Relationship

    d. Rules

99. Which input is required so that a solution or set of solutions may be validated?

    a. Identified defects

    b. Mitigation actions

    c. Solution [constructed]

    d. Solution validation assessment

100. There are six inputs required for Elicitation activities to be delivered. Which input is missing in the diagram below?

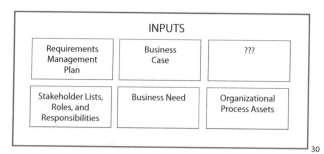

30

    a. Scheduled resources

    b. Solution scope

    c. Stakeholder concerns

    d. Supporting materials

---

30   Adapted from Figure 3-2, *BABOK® Guide* V2.0, 54.

101. Your target audience for a structured walkthrough of requirements will be the implementers of the solution. As you carefully construct the presentation, you tailor the communication style to be—

    a. Indirect
    b. Spirited
    c. Systematic
    d. Considerate

102. Templates, polices, procedures, and governance standards—some of the inputs required for stakeholder analysis—are commonly and collectively referred to as what?

    a. Business interaction assets
    b. Functional process assets
    c. Organizational process assets
    d. Project management assets

103. The deconstruction of an organizational unit into its collective group of interrelated activities is a requirements analysis technique commonly referred to as what?

    a. Data flow diagramming
    b. Data modeling
    c. Functional decomposition
    d. Organizational modeling

104. Beside signing off on requirements, a stakeholder may also be required to sign off on which requirements related activity?

    a. Conduct stakeholder analysis
    b. Glossary of terms
    c. Model requirements
    d. Problem resolution

105. A primary source of data for a business analyst when considering presentation delivery methods is the—

    a. Project charter
    b. Risk management plan
    c. Stakeholder profiles
    d. User task analysis

106. Demonstrating how a requirement evolves from concept to solution and back is known as a—

    a. Lateral verification
    b. Traceability
    c. Solution Assessment and Validation
    d. Risk analysis

107. A modeling technique that a business analyst might consider during goal decomposition is—
   a. Use case diagram
   b. Tree diagram
   c. Activity diagram
   d. State machine diagram

108. "To call forth or draw out" is the definition of—
   a. Gathering requirements
   b. Eliciting requirements
   c. Modeling requirements
   d. Testing requirements

109. The primary output of Enterprise Analysis is—
   a. A work breakdown structure
   b. Business requirements
   c. A context diagram
   d. A risk mitigation plan

110. Any presentation that you, as a business analyst, may be called upon to deliver, must be clearly defined by its—
   a. Objectives and audience
   b. Clarity and content
   c. Stakeholders' needs and compliance with corporate presentation standards
   d. Requirements types and use of diagrams

111. A stakeholder can be best described as an—
   a. Individual who provides funding for a project
   b. Individual who can influence the outcome of the project deliverables
   c. Individual who is affected by the project's outcome
   d. Individual on the portfolio management team, which decides on the approval or rejection of all projects

112. A business analyst would rely on what input as a source for developing assumptions and constraints?
   a. Organizational process assets
   b. Stakeholder concerns
   c. Solution scope
   d. Requirements structure

113. What is a popular user interface simulation technique that is absent of software code?
   a. Vertical prototyping
   b. Horizontal prototyping
   c. Glass box re-engineering
   d. Storyboarding

114. The agile methodology fosters which prototyping technique?

    a. Horizontal prototype
    b. Vertical prototype
    c. Throwaway prototype
    d. Evolutionary prototype

115. Business goals are _____, long term and ongoing statements, objectives are _____ and linked to quantitative measures of success.

    a. Qualitative, quantitative
    b. SMART, organizational
    c. Business unit focused, subjective
    d. Finite, qualitative

116. Costs that are based on a description of the proposed product and history of the same type of project are known as—

    a. Bottom-up costing
    b. Activity-based costing
    c. Top-down costing
    d. Wideband Delphi technique

117. True or False: Formal sign off on requirements must be done in person with a written signature.

    a. True
    b. False

118. When considering the delivery of a formal review of requirements you may consider which of the following choices as a source for determining your format for delivery?

    a. Business analysis plans
    b. Organizational process assets
    c. Project charter
    d. Software development team

119. While prioritizing requirements you decide that you will remove all requirements that prevent budgets and time constraints from being realized. This iterative technique is referred to as—

    a. All In
    b. All Out
    c. Selective
    d. Won't

120. The purpose of which activity is to identify what individuals in a project share common goals and outcomes?

    a. Development of an organizational chart
    b. Planning of the business analysis approach
    c. Requirements analysis
    d. Stakeholder analysis

121. "Defining requirements traceability derivation" can also be referred to as what?

    a. Backwards traceability
    b. Cardinality
    c. Exclusivity
    d. Forward traceability

122. Immediately after the deployment of a loan application, Erin realized that systems users weren't exactly following the procedures outline in the training delivered prior to them using the application. However, they were certainly effective in processing loans. Erin realized that this was a result of what?

    a. The evaluation of solution performance
    b. An increase in applications being approved
    c. The validation of transition requirements
    d. The verification of business requirements

123. Which elicitation technique may be considered during an organizational readiness assessment, particularly where cultural implications may be concerned?

    a. Acceptance and evaluation criteria
    b. Focus groups
    c. Process models
    d. Survey/questionnaire

124. If the proposed solution selected has been determined to be a commercial off-the-shelf-based solution, a business analyst should give particular consideration in his or her documentation to—

    a. Stakeholder requirements
    b. Amount of effort required by the implementers to install a solution
    c. Open source code
    d. Existing service level agreements

125. When are requirements that were overlooked or missed during Elicitation activities likely to be discovered?

    a. During Enterprise Analysis activities
    b. During Requirements Analysis
    c. During Solution Assessment and Validation
    d. During stakeholder sign-off

126. Uncovering or refining requirements using a simulated interface is referred to as—

    a. Observation
    b. Prototyping
    c. User task analysis
    d. Storyboarding

127. What is the expected output from activities described for the "management of solution scope and requirements" task?

    a. Requirements [approved]
    b. Requirements management plan
    c. Solution scope
    d. Stakeholder lists, roles and responsibilities

128. The following technique may be used to understand the source of defect(s) uncovered during the validation of a solution:

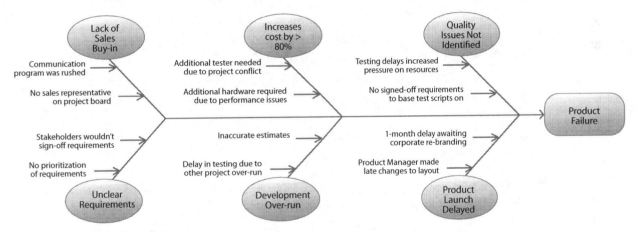

    a. Five whys diagram
    b. Pareto diagram
    c. Fishbone diagram
    d. Use-case diagram

129. When describing an individual or group of individuals who need to solve a problem that would allow them to interact more efficiently with a system, a business analyst might be describing a—

    a. Quality of service requirement
    b. Functional requirement
    c. Stakeholder requirement
    d. Business requirement

130. Hugh was involved in the global deployment of a company-wide intranet for which there were multi-language, date, and time considerations. When documenting these needs, Hugh categorized them as—

    a. Functional requirements
    b. Business requirements
    c. Quality of service requirements
    d. Stakeholder requirements

131. While developing the solution scope for an enterprise-wide project, you created a context diagram. What information were you trying to display using this diagramming technique?

    a. Interaction of business units with each other
    b. Conditions that might have a negative impact on the domain
    c. High-level description of the AS-IS and/or TO-BE models
    d. Functional requirements clarifying what a user needs to do to interact with a system

132. When creating your descriptions for stakeholders, you have clearly defined the difference between a customer and a user as—

    a. Customers pay for the product and users interact with it
    b. Users want business benefits, and customers provide insight into the product specifications
    c. Users interact with output as a result of customer input
    d. None of the above

133. If you are told that the information that you will deliver at your next focus group will be to a homogeneous audience, this means that—

    a. The type of information that you will present must appeal to a diverse audience
    b. All stakeholders involved are concerned only about meeting the business need
    c. Because all stakeholders reside in the "home office," the mode of delivery will be consistent using electronic media, including presentation packages
    d. The type of information that you will present must appeal to a very specific audience

134. When working on a project that considers a collaborative approach with other projects that are dependent on the outputs of your project, a business analyst should consider—

    a. Developing a requirements communication plan
    b. Including all stakeholders from all projects in his or her planning activities
    c. Ensuring that he or she has access to all requirements-capturing tools used across all projects
    d. Negotiating the effort required to develop models that will integrate all project activities

135. A business analyst would consider a _____ as a resource to begin developing data flow diagrams.

    a. Use case diagram
    b. Context diagram
    c. CRUD matrix
    d. Project charter

136. When preparing to conduct Elicitation activities, a business analyst should consider—

    a. His or her availability
    b. Any administrative charges, including long-distance telephone costs
    c. Buy-versus-build requirements
    d. Stakeholders' willingness to come to a consensus

137. Much effort must be put into facilitating a joint application design session. The most critical planning effort should be focused on—

    a. Who will be the participants in the session
    b. The session length
    c. Documentation method
    d. A means by which consensus will be reached

138. "The system must produce an insurance quotation in less than three minutes from the time a user submits his or her query." "The priority rating is 3." "Stakeholders require the implementation of this requirement by February 11." "This requirement is still under review by its owner, John Smith."

    The preceding statements are examples of—

    a. Requirement attributes
    b. Functional constraints
    c. Technical assumptions
    d. Nonfunctional requirements

139. IIBA's *BABOK® Guide* V2.0 refers to a collective library of requirement documents as—

    a. A requirements package
    b. A portfolio of requirements
    c. Packaged specifications
    d. A dossier of deliverables

140. Which of the following choices is NOT something that would likely be included in the solution scope statement?

    a. Business need
    b. Project costs
    c. Implementation approach
    d. Dependencies

141. The examination of user manuals, training manuals, service level agreements, or regulatory documentation is an elicitation technique known as what?

    a. Document analysis
    b. Interface analysis
    c. Observation
    d. Survey/questionnaire

142. When considering planning activities, the business analyst would take into account an organization's solution development life cycle to determine—

    a. Project costs
    b. Project duration
    c. The nature of the project complexity and therefore its risk
    d. What deliverables will be produced and when

143. To understand the current state of the business architecture, Paul documented which of the following choices as a deliverable?

    a. A work breakdown structure
    b. A feasibility study
    c. Decomposed business functions
    d. A risk analysis

144. So that the scope of a solution may be determined, a business analyst would require which documentation as input?

    a. Solution approach
    b. Assumptions and constraints
    c. A work breakdown structure
    d. Recommendations

145. What information is it critical to include in your questionnaire before sending it out for feedback?
    a. Purpose and deadline
    b. Purpose and consent to use the data
    c. Deadline and incentive to complete
    d. Deadline and instructions on how to complete the questionnaire

146. Stan realized that the implementation of the new online insurance quotation application automated much of the manual labor that currently collected insurance quotes. As a result, the number of insurance specialists would be reduced, and the number of technical support staff would need to be increased to support the application. This realization is considered to be what element of defining transition requirements?
    a. Data
    b. Functional decomposition
    c. Organizational change
    d. Ongoing work

147. A document used to describe how a system might be implemented and how it may produce deliverables based on stakeholder requirements is often referred to as a—
    a. Request for proposals (RFP)
    b. Business requirements document (BRD)
    c. Software requirements specification (SRS)
    d. Request for quotations (RFQ)

148. Transition requirements are unique in nature because they—
    a. Are developed for a unique target audience of implementers
    b. Can be re-used for subsequent software development initiatives
    c. Can only be developed after the solution has been defined
    d. Specifically address the training required to become familiar with the new solution

149. The following modeling technique may be used to help identify elements for consideration when assessing organizational readiness of a solution to be implemented:

Online Ticket Service

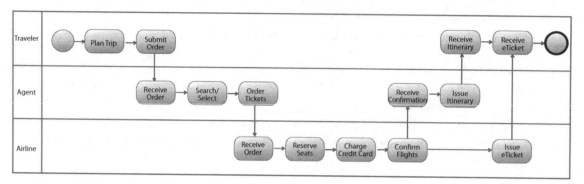

a. Data model

b. Process model

c. Prototype

d. Use case model

150. IIBA's *BABOK® Guide* V2.0 describes how many different types of requirements?

a. Four

b. Five

c. Six

d. Seven

ANSWER SHEET FOR PRACTICE TEST 2

1.	a	b	c	d
2.	a	b	c	d
3.	a	b	c	d
4.	a	b	c	d
5.	a	b	c	d
6.	a	b	c	d
7.	a	b	c	d
8.	a	b	c	d
9.	a	b	c	d
10.	a	b	c	d
11.	a	b	c	d
12.	a	b	c	d
13.	a	b	c	d
14.	a	b	c	d
15.	a	b	c	d
16.	a	b	c	d
17.	a	b	c	d
18.	a	b	c	d
19.	a	b	c	d
20.	a	b	c	d

21.	a	b	c	d
22.	a	b	c	d
23.	a	b	c	d
24.	a	b	c	d
25.	a	b	c	d
26.	a	b	c	d
27.	a	b	c	d
28.	a	b	c	d
29.	a	b	c	d
30.	a	b	c	d
31.	a	b	c	d
32.	a	b	c	d
33.	a	b	c	d
34.	a	b	c	d
35.	a	b	c	d
36.	a	b	c	d
37.	a	b	c	d
38.	a	b	c	d
39.	a	b	c	d
40.	a	b	c	d

41.	a	b	c	d
42.	a	b	c	d
43.	a	b	c	d
44.	a	b	c	d
45.	a	b	c	d
46.	a	b	c	d
47.	a	b	c	d
48.	a	b	c	d
49.	a	b	c	d
50.	a	b	c	d
51.	a	b	c	d
52.	a	b	c	d
53.	a	b	c	d
54.	a	b	c	d
55.	a	b	c	d
56.	a	b	c	d
57.	a	b	c	d
58.	a	b	c	d
59.	a	b	c	d
60.	a	b	c	d

61.	a	b	c	d
62.	a	b	c	d
63.	a	b	c	d
64.	a	b	c	d
65.	a	b	c	d
66.	a	b	c	d
67.	a	b	c	d
68.	a	b	c	d
69.	a	b	c	d
70.	a	b	c	d
71.	a	b	c	d
72.	a	b	c	d
73.	a	b	c	d
74.	a	b	c	d
75.	a	b	c	d
76.	a	b	c	d
77.	a	b	c	d
78.	a	b	c	d
79.	a	b	c	d
80.	a	b	c	d

81.	a	b	c	d
82.	a	b	c	d
83.	a	b	c	d
84.	a	b	c	d
85.	a	b	c	d
86.	a	b	c	d
87.	a	b	c	d
88.	a	b	c	d
89.	a	b	c	d
90.	a	b	c	d
91.	a	b	c	d
92.	a	b	c	d
93.	a	b	c	d
94.	a	b	c	d
95.	a	b	c	d
96.	a	b	c	d
97.	a	b	c	d
98.	a	b	c	d
99.	a	b	c	d
100.	a	b	c	d

101.	a	b	c	d
102.	a	b	c	d
103.	a	b	c	d
104.	a	b	c	d
105.	a	b	c	d
106.	a	b	c	d
107.	a	b	c	d
108.	a	b	c	d
109.	a	b	c	d
110.	a	b	c	d
111.	a	b	c	d
112.	a	b	c	d
113.	a	b	c	d
114.	a	b	c	d
115.	a	b	c	d
116.	a	b	c	d
117.	a	b	c	d
118.	a	b	c	d
119.	a	b	c	d
120.	a	b	c	d

121.	a	b	c	d
122.	a	b	c	d
123.	a	b	c	d
124.	a	b	c	d
125.	a	b	c	d
126.	a	b	c	d
127.	a	b	c	d
128.	a	b	c	d
129.	a	b	c	d
130.	a	b	c	d
131.	a	b	c	d
132.	a	b	c	d
133.	a	b	c	d
134.	a	b	c	d
135.	a	b	c	d
136.	a	b	c	d
137.	a	b	c	d
138.	a	b	c	d
139.	a	b	c	d
140.	a	b	c	d

141.	a	b	c	d
142.	a	b	c	d
143.	a	b	c	d
144.	a	b	c	d
145.	a	b	c	d
146.	a	b	c	d
147.	a	b	c	d
148.	a	b	c	d
149.	a	b	c	d
150.	a	b	c	d

ANSWER KEY FOR PRACTICE TEST 2

1. **c. The business stakeholder's perspective**

   In the case where this is a discrepancy of the level of abstraction for requirements and the uncertainty about the what versus the how, a business stakeholder's perspective should be clarified, because requirements must be aligned with their perspective to ensure these criteria meet their needs for solution development.

   IIBA®, *BABOK® Guide* V2.0, 2009, 105

2. **a. Interface analysis**

   Interface analysis is the study of two or more systems and their abilities to communicate with each other to help refine and define scope and the amount of effort required to create the solution.

   IIBA®, *BABOK® Guide* V2.0, 2009, 111, 176

3. **d. Neutral facilitator**

   A neutral facilitator will ensure objectivity of the participants and the objectives. A business analyst may attend the workshop as a participant.

   IIBA®, *BABOK® Guide* V2.0, 2009, 56, 198

4. **a. Force field analysis**

   Force field analysis during the assessment of organizational readiness is intended to graphically depict supportive and opposing influences that may promote or prevent the successful deployment of a solution. Each force should be evaluated and ranked to clearly understand where the greatest influence lies and what the potential output of that force may be.

   IIBA®, *BABOK® Guide* V2.0, 2009, 130

5. **b. Activity list**

   A WBS is the primary source to schedule activities and to define the activity list.

   IIBA®, *BABOK® Guide* V2.0, 2009, 35

6. **b. Requirements [stated]**

   Requirements [stated] are high-level descriptions of stakeholder needs and serve as an input to defining business needs during enterprise analysis activities.

   IIBA®, *BABOK® Guide* V2.0, 2009, 83

7   **b.   Prototype**

There are several kinds of prototypes: throw-away, evolutionary, horizontal and vertical. The kind you use will be based on the nature, complexity, and level of risk of your project. The kind of prototype used may also help address any technical constraints or risks.

IIBA®, BABOK® Guide V2.0, 2009, 196–197

8.   **d.   Tell me about the expense reporting process. Who in your organization submits expense reports? Who is responsible for approving those reports? After the expense reports are approved, who reconciles the receipts against expenses submitted?**

During an interview, a business analyst needs to consider the order in which he or she asks questions. Starting with general questions and moving the conversation to more detailed questions is the most effective way to elicit requirements necessary to gain a complete understanding of the business need. This sequence will prove helpful in identifying the flow of business processes and rules and the data needed to support them.

IIBA®, BABOK® Guide V2.0, 2009, 177–178

9.   **a.   Facilitate vendor selection by identifying criteria that will meet the business need**

A business analyst will want to ensure that the chosen vendor is able to meet all business, user, and system requirements and that the vendor can easily define the success criteria necessary to meet these needs.

IIBA®, BABOK® Guide V2.0, 2009, 123

10.   **b.   To develop a risk response plan to any proposed changes made to requirements**

Any changes to requirements, which may represent a change in solution scope that stakeholders accept or reject, must take into consideration the amount of risk associated with the overall project.

IIBA®, BABOK® Guide V2.0, 2009, 67

11.   **a.   Verified**

Verification of requirements is an activity meant to ensure that requirements adhere to quality standards imposed by an organization. The questions asked during verification of requirements should be: "Have these requirements been written correctly?" "Do they provide accurate information so that the solution can be further developed?" and "Are they ready for validation by stakeholders?"

IIBA®, BABOK® Guide V2.0, 2009, 114

12. **c.** **Stakeholder involvement in the project**

Understanding a stakeholder's involvement in a project may lead to an understanding of that stakeholder's authority and the impact the project may have on him or her.

IIBA®, BABOK® Guide V2.0, 2009, 28, 177–178

13. **d.** **Business Analysis Planning and Monitoring**

By identifying key stakeholders and their roles and responsibilities during the Business Analysis Planning and Monitoring phase, a business analyst can determine what techniques are most appropriate.

IIBA®, BABOK® Guide V2.0, 2009, 24

14. **d.** **Problem tracking**

Time, cost, corporate culture, geographical diversity, and complexity of solution are all elements that Barry would consider when selecting what elicitation techniques would be most appropriate for conducting Elicitation activities. This information provided to Barry was likely the outputs produced during the Business Analysis Planning and Monitoring activities. All other items listed in the answer are considered outputs of Elicitation activities.

IIBA®, BABOK® Guide V2.0, 2009, 66

15. **a.** **Government entity**

A government entity may impose regulations on the project that would require input or feedback for the development of requirements. Tax laws or insurance regulations are two such cases of government involvement.

IIBA®, BABOK® Guide V2.0, 2009, 11

16. **a.** **A business analyst will want to ensure that all requirements, requests, and results elicited from stakeholders are delivered appropriately.**

The requirements management plan can provide insight for business analysts to select elicitation techniques that are best suited to the stakeholders, which provides a business analyst with a level of confidence that the expectations will be met and that the stakeholders will be appropriately involved. Information in the plan that helps identify the most appropriate elicitation techniques includes how requirements will be stored, traceability considerations, expectations on level of formality with requirements attributes, prioritization process, formality, participation from stakeholders, etc.

IIBA®, BABOK® Guide V2.0, 2009, 43–48

17. **d.** **Team roles**

Team roles, frequency of interaction, and proposed techniques for the approach are often required output for the development of a business analysis approach.

IIBA®, *BABOK® Guide* V2.0, 2009, 23

18. **c.** **Make amendments to the original scope document**

Throughout the requirements development phase, a business analyst may uncover additional opportunities or may not be able to bring the group of stakeholders to consensus. If the group can't reach consensus, the BA may need to revisit the scope of the solution and make changes accordingly.

IIBA®, *BABOK® Guide* V2.0, 2009, 42, 64–65

19. **d.** **Provide data and information for developing requirements**

Elicitation is most often conducted in parallel with requirements analysis. It is the goal of carefully considered and planned elicitation techniques to produce models based on output from these activities so that he or she can produce TO-BE state models.

IIBA®, *BABOK® Guide* V2.0, 2009, 53

20. **c.** **Source, stability, priority**

Source, stability, and priority will help a business analyst to determine such things as risk involved, difficulty to implement, impact of changes, and the types of resources required for implementation.

IIBA®, *BABOK® Guide* V2.0, 2009, 45

21. **d.** **Functional requirements**

Functional requirements are often characterized by "shall" statements (or imperatives), such as "the system shall produce 100 invoices per hour," and describe how the user requirements will be met. They also serve as an input to the development of system requirements by describing a system behavior.

IIBA®, *BABOK® Guide* V2.0, 2009, 6

22. **b.** **Company directory**

The company directory may prove to be neither up to date nor exhaustive in terms of effort to review the material. It will probably not provide much more information than names and numbers. All other items listed in the answer are likely to be considered organizational process assets, which may provide further insight into identifying stakeholders.

IIBA®, *BABOK® Guide* V2.0, 2009, 24–25

23. **b.** **Enterprise architecture**

Enterprise architecture documentation is especially useful for determining the organizational readiness of an organization. This documentation can provide a business analyst with insight into the current state of an organization, including structure, systems, and processes.

IIBA®, *BABOK® Guide* V2.0, 2009, 121

24. **a.** **It is a form of qualitative research.**

A focus group is characterized as a form of qualitative research in which a carefully selected group of stakeholders is assembled to elicit requirements or to provide feedback on proposed goods and services. The feedback given is subjective.

IIBA®, *BABOK® Guide* V2.0, 2009, 58, 172

25. **c.** **Requirements [prioritized and validated]**

Requirements [prioritized and validated] are necessary to validate a solution. They provide insight into acceptance criteria and the scope for acceptability of output produced by the solution in question.

IIBA®, *BABOK® Guide* V2.0, 2009, 134

26. **d.** **Solution is adding a capability to the organization where that capability did not exist.**

The analysis of transition requirements is typically an activity reserved for solutions that are considered to be extending, updating, or improving existing operations or systems. Where a capability or solution does not exist, the analysis of transition requirements is not necessary.

IIBA®, *BABOK® Guide* V2.0, 2009, 132

27. **a.** **Regulatory compliance is governing the actions of this project**

Formal sign-off on projects may be required for conformity of organizational regulation or compliance of government-imposed regulations.

IIBA®, *BABOK® Guide* V2.0, 2009, 67

28. **a.** **Business processes**

Interface analysis is intended to reveal how a system interacts with a user or another system or hardware. Given these considerations, it is expected that only input or output of data and the confines within which those data operate are revealed. This concept is similar to black-box re-engineering.

IIBA®, *BABOK® Guide* V2.0, 2009, 111, 176

29. **b.** **Interpretation of data collected during the interview**

Depending on the expertise of the business analyst working within the business domain, he or she may not gather all information necessary to formulate unambiguous requirements by asking enough questions or the right questions. If the BA lacks the appropriate expertise, misinterpretations are imminent.

IIBA®, *BABOK® Guide* V2.0, 2009, 58, 180

30. **c.** **Michael would need to create the TO-BE state based on existing documentation (AS-IS state) and to consider conducting a gap analysis to determine the best approach.**

If Michael were to work on an enhancement-type project, the minimal development of the AS-IS state based on existing documentation should be considered, along with a gap analysis and the review of models, including business rules, diagrams, and data models.

IIBA®, *BABOK® Guide* V2.0, 2009, 85–87

31. **d.** **Process models**

Process models may be used as a technique to help define, develop, and document an approach to the requirements development and management approach.

IIBA®, *BABOK® Guide* V2.0, 2009, 23, 192–193

32. **a.** **Traceability**

Traceability, or more specifically requirements traceability, is the demonstration of a requirement's lineage, allocation, and relationship to other interdependent requirements.

IIBA®, *BABOK® Guide* V2.0, 2009, 67–68, 231

33. **d.** **Validation**

Validation, an activity cited in the Solution Assessment and Validation knowledge area, ensures that the solution prescribed meets the overall business need and where it does not, it ensures reconciliation where appropriate.

IIBA®, *BABOK® Guide* V2.0, 2009, 134

34. **b.** **List of logical dependencies**

Although the business analyst is responsible for creating a work breakdown structure for his or her activities, a WBS is not likely to be needed for all project activities—rather, only those activities from Elicitation to Solution Assessment and Validation. A list of resources would be limited to those people contributing to the development and management of requirements. The answer here would be a listing of logical dependencies, particularly where the evolution of requirements are concerned.

IIBA®, *BABOK® Guide* V2.0, 2009, 32–33

35. **b.** **Constraint**

Constraints are limitations imposed on the delivery of a solution. In this particular case, message size can be categorized as a technical constraint.

IIBA®, *BABOK® Guide* V2.0, 2009, 112–113

36. **d.** **Trainers**

A trainer may be sought to provide insight and advice on the AS-IS state of the system and any common defects, or on well-received features of the existing product. He or she may also provide advice on how users will accept or reject the system.

IIBA®, *BABOK® Guide* V2.0, 2009, 12, 31, 130   –131

37. **c.** **Number of requirements**

When considering assessments using metrics, a business analyst might consider time, cost, resources, features, and qualities. The number of requirements is likely to be taken into consideration when assessing the degree of risk a project may have.

IIBA®, *BABOK® Guide* 2009 V2.0, 2009, 123

38. **b.** **Activity diagram**

Behavior models are used to depict the how of a business or system in question. Activity diagrams are specifically used to elaborate on use case diagrams, particularly extending their views to all steps—in short, to define the details of the process.

IIBA®, *BABOK® Guide* V2.0, 2009, 106–107, 194, 223

39. **d.** **Goals and objectives of the session**

Your discussion guide serves as an agenda. Goals, objectives, and questions to be addressed should be identified in the discussion guide.

IIBA®, *BABOK® Guide* V2.0, 2009, 54

40. c. **Indirect users**

Indirect users are generally not involved frequently with a system and may be affected only sometimes by the output of its deliverables.

IIBA®, *BABOK® Guide* V2.0, 2009, 24–28

41. b. **Conduct frequent structured walkthroughs to detect any inconsistencies that may arise while the requirements are being developed**

Structured walkthroughs are meant to be conducted iteratively so that the project team has an opportunity to assess and evaluate any inconsistencies, errors, or risks.

IIBA®, *BABOK® Guide* V2.0, 2009, 117, 211

42. d. **Reviewer**

The business analyst really should be responsible for producing user requirements. A software developer can provide feedback when called upon to do so.

IIBA®, *BABOK® Guide* V2.0, 2009, 24–28

43. c. **Decision tree**

Business rules address the development of the why requirements, or behavior requirements, and can be visually represented using a decision table or tree.

IIBA®, *BABOK® Guide* V2.0, 2009, 85, 158–159, 168

44. a. **Allocation**

Allocation is also known as the forward traceability of a requirement.

IIBA®, *BABOK® Guide* V2.0, 2009, 68

45. c. **Organizational readiness assessment**

Organizational readiness assessment documentation provides insight into what changes will be made where in the organization, including any models that may have been developed.

IIBA®, *BABOK® Guide* V2.0, 2009, 132

46. d. **Return on investment**

Return on investment (ROI) is the ratio of money gained to money spent.

IIBA®, *BABOK® Guide* V2.0, 2009, 96, 170

47. **c.** **Groups of stakeholders**

    A single stakeholder or groups of stakeholders may have the authority to sign off on requirements.

    IIBA®, *BABOK® Guide* V2.0, 2009, 66–67

48. **b.** **Inputs required include requirements [stated] and requirements structure.**

    Requirements [stated] are a necessary input into specifying and modeling requirements so that stakeholder needs can be clearly captured and articulated. A requirements structure ensures requirements are documented appropriately and demonstrates all relationships between requirements models.

    IIBA®, *BABOK® Guide* V2.0, 2009, 108

49. **d.** **Comparing the cost of implementing the solution to the potential revenue realized by implementing the solution**

    Inez did a cost-benefit analysis by quantifying both the costs to implement and the benefits realized. Cost benefit analysis is typically conducted during Enterprise Analysis activities, specifically during the development of a business case. The technique described by the *BABOK®* that addresses cost benefit analysis is Decision Analysis (9.8).

    IIBA®, *BABOK® Guide* V2.0, 2009, 96, 166–168

50. **c.** **To avoid having stakeholders sign off on subsets of requirements where they have no authority**

    Although a stakeholder may be in agreement with subsets and complementary groupings of requirements, a business analyst needs to ensure that the stakeholder has signing authority for what they are signing off on.

    IIBA®, *BABOK® Guide* V2.0, 2009, 67

51. **a.** **The project may be complex and may require a team of expert resources to implement**

    The more complex a project is, then the more scrutiny there should be toward risk. A more formal approach to delivering requirements must be considered. Requirements Allocation is an activity cited in the *BABOK®* that takes into consideration how requirements are allocated for a particular iteration based on cost, complexity, risk, etc.

    IIBA®, *BABOK® Guide* V2.0, 2009, 124

52. b. Functional requirement

A functional requirement describes how a system behaves with users or other systems and the events that trigger these behaviors.

IIBA®, *BABOK® Guide* V2.0, 2009, 6

53. d. Provide guidance to the quality assurance team to ensure compliance with the business needs and any imposed regulations

Based on his or her in-depth knowledge of the proposed business solution, a business analyst would work collaboratively with the QA team to ensure that the solution both complies with regulations and meets the overall business need.

IIBA®, *BABOK® Guide* V2.0, 2009, 121

54. d. Event

Process models, state diagrams, and use case and scope models may all serve to represent events that may take place within an organization.

IIBA®, *BABOK® Guide* V2.0, 2009, 106

55. c. Prototyping

Prototyping, storyboarding, and sometimes observation are all techniques that can be applied to elicit requirements to understand the interaction of users with internal or external systems or with hardware devices.

IIBA®, *BABOK® Guide* V2.0, 2009, 196

56. a. Enterprise architecture

An input required for conducting stakeholder analysis is the enterprise architecture. This documentation can provide a business analyst with an understanding of both the structure of organizational business units and their respective actions, including actions and responsibilities involving stakeholders, customers, and suppliers.

IIBA®, *BABOK® Guide* V2.0, 2009, 24

57. c. Nonfunctional requirement

Quality of service requirements or nonfunctional requirements must be carefully considered when developing alternate solutions, particularly if the design team cites nonfunctional requirements as additional costs or as impacts on the scope of the project, or on other related projects.

IIBA®, *BABOK® Guide* V2.0, 2009, 6

58. **b.** **Activity diagram**

An activity diagram, a UML 2.0 standard, depicts a sequence of activities and their logic and extends the views of use case diagrams.

IIBA®, *BABOK® Guide* V2.0, 2009, 194

59. **b.** **Verified**

Verification ensures that requirements have been developed clearly enough to allow the development of the solution to begin.

IIBA®, *BABOK® Guide* V2.0, 2009, 114

60. **c.** **Role versus job title**

A business analyst should focus his or her efforts on such issues as how the user will interact with and be affected by the system and how the BA's ability and expertise can contribute to the overall requirements development.

IIBA®, *BABOK® Guide* V2.0, 2009, 24–28, 54

61. **c.** **Brainstorming**

Generally, brainstorming is a technique used to cultivate a large volume of ideas to solve a business problem or address a business opportunity.

IIBA®, *BABOK® Guide* V2.0, 2009, 157

62. **a.** **Testable; traceable**

A means to verify requirements is to ensure that they are both testable and traceable back to the original business needs.

IIBA®, *BABOK® Guide* V2.0, 2009, 115–116

63. **d.** **Asking leading questions**

Asking a stakeholder leading questions during an interview removes the objectivity from the resulting answers.

IIBA®, *BABOK® Guide* V2.0, 2009, 58, 177

64. **a.** **Functional decomposition diagram**

A functional decomposition diagram or tree diagram breaks down a high-level function into its smallest subfunctions or processes. The same purpose can be served by using a table and numbering the functions.

IIBA®, *BABOK® Guide* V2.0, 2009, 36, 174

65. **a.** **Baseline the requirements**

Baselining requirements is an activity that allows a business analyst to track all changes or additions to the requirements development and management activities to ensure that they can be compared to the baselined state, as well as to understand the nature of the changes and who was involved.

IIBA®, *BABOK® Guide* V2.0, 2009, 66

66. **c.** **Organizational model**

Groups of stakeholders, who may impacted by the impending solution and the order of magnitude of those changes or interdependencies between groups, can be identified for the purposes of assessing organizational readiness.

IIBA®, *BABOK® Guide* V2.0, 2009, 190

67. **b.** **Methodologies**

Change-driven or plan-driven methods and approaches to requirements management and development activities can determine the level of requirements abstraction required to produce deliverables.

IIBA®, *BABOK® Guide* V2.0, 2009, 105

68. **d.** **Costs and efforts**

Typical items included in a requirements document might include quality attributes, an impact analysis report, and a project charter, but not costs and efforts, which are likely to be included in the overall project plan.

IIBA®, *BABOK® Guide* V2.0, 2009, 75, 224

69. **d.** **Criteria matrix**

A requirements criteria matrix can be created using a variety of elicitation techniques. Requirements can be evaluated using the criteria matrix by means of symbols identifying the ranking type or calculations based on assigned values for cost and risk, or by simple "must have, would like to have, and not on your life" evaluations.

IIBA®, *BABOK® Guide* V2.0, 2009, 109

70. **d.** **Nonfunctional requirements**

Nonfunctional requirements or quality of service requirements describe system attributes and are considered constraints. More often than not, these conditions are not related in any way to a system's ability to perform desired tasks.

IIBA®, *BABOK® Guide* V2.0, 2009, 6

71. **b.** **Decision record**

    A decision record may be a tool that a business analyst uses to track all signatures, dates, rationales, and who was involved in the decision that was made.

    IIBA®, *BABOK® Guide* V2.0, 2009, 66–67

72. **a.** **Document analysis**

    Document analysis considers the elicitation from a variety of existing documentation, including but not limited to service level agreements, training manuals, competitive profiles, market studies, and so forth.

    IIBA®, *BABOK® Guide* V2.0, 2009, 58, 169

73. **d.** **By having questionnaire respondents identify potential stakeholders**

    It is likely that your carefully crafted stakeholder questionnaire will elicit responses from your stakeholders on who the other stakeholders are that you have not yet considered.

    IIBA®, *BABOK® Guide* V2.0, 2009, 214

74. **b.** **Feature**

    The question provides the definition of feature. Features are carefully consider during activities cited in the solution assessment and validation knowledge area of the *BABOK®*.

    IIBA®, *BABOK® Guide* V2.0, 2009, 119, 227

75. **d.** **Requirements coverage matrix**

    A requirements coverage matrix demonstrates the relationship of requirements to the final output and software deliverables. These diagrams demonstrate the bi-directional relationships from business goals to software design and back. Typically a requirements coverage matrix is used when the number of requirements is relatively low.

    IIBA®, *BABOK® Guide* V2.0, 2009, 70

76. **a.** **Implementing a policy for requirement change requests after a baseline has been established**

    A business analyst needs to scrutinize all requirements carefully. By baselining requirements, a BA and his or her team can be conscientious of the extent and magnitude of changes made or being made to the baseline.

    IIBA®, *BABOK® Guide* V2.0, 2009, 64

77. **d.**   **Written to be measurable**

All strategic goals should contain measurable qualities, including outcome, measurement and time frame. In short, strategic goals are generally decomposed into measurable objectives.

IIBA®, *BABOK® Guide* V2.0, 2009, 83-84

78. **c.**   **Business requirements**

Functional requirements must be traced back to business requirements or features to prevent a misunderstanding of a customer's needs.

IIBA®, *BABOK® Guide* V2.0, 2009, 5–6, 67–68

79. **d.**   **Any combination of these techniques may be suitable**

To keep the group members engaged and to encourage them to contribute both in the group and one-on-one, the facilitator should use a variety of elicitation techniques.

IIBA®, *BABOK® Guide* V2.0, 2009, 157–158, 198–199

Brûlé, Glenn, *Business Analysis Terms: A Working Glossary*, 2009, 48, 118

80. **d.**   **Verify Requirements**

Verification of transition requirements are done to ensure that quality standards are effectively practiced in the capturing and documenting of transition requirements.

IIBA®, *BABOK® Guide* V2.0, 2009, 114, 132

81. **a.**   **Data flow diagram**

Data flow diagrams (DFDs) play a role in assessing organizational readiness by providing insight into current and future proposed states for how information will be managed within the newly proposed solution. DFDs consider such things as interactions with external systems and how data will be stored, captured, and moved from external to internal systems (if external systems are part of the solution) and within internal systems.

IIBA®, *BABOK® Guide* V2.0, 2009, 129, 162

82. **c.**   **A solution approach**

When defining solution scope, an understanding of solution approach can help a business analyst determine how the proposed solution and its capabilities might be delivered to ensure the most efficient means of implementation.

IIBA®, *BABOK® Guide* V2.0, 2009, 93

83. **b.** **Closed-ended question**

    This example of a closed-ended question will yield a yes or a no response. A mix of open-ended and closed-ended questions will allow for a wider variety of data collected, but they may not prove to be insightful or helpful when trying to identify additional stakeholders.

    IIBA®, *BABOK® Guide* V2.0, 2009, 179

84. **c.** **Business Analysis Planning and Monitoring**

    When stakeholders, elicitation activities, and effort are determined, so too can the tools be selected that are appropriate to accomplish the tasks. This particular task is addressed during the management of business analysis performance activities.

    IIBA®, *BABOK® Guide* V2.0, 2009, 49

85. **a.** **Process modeling**

    Process models may be best in depicting a series of activities, interdependent activities, and activities within an activity. The depiction of processes is most likely to be captured in a hierarchical format until a visible output is produced.

    IIBA®, *BABOK® Guide* V2.0, 2009, 106–107

86. **a.** **Data flow diagram**

    A DFD uses data collected from a context diagram to depict how information is received and delivered in a system.

    IIBA®, *BABOK® Guide* V2.0, 2009, 161

87. **c.** **Transition of data from one format to another**

    In a project where data conversion (from business to user) is required, a business analyst will want to ensure that the overall business needs are met and that there is minimal disruption to the business. These types of requirements are referred to by the *BABOK®* as Transition requirements and are typically addressed during

    IIBA®, *BABOK® Guide* V2.0, 2009, 6, 131

88. **b.** **The scope of the system being modeled**

    The rectangle or boundary used in use case diagramming is optional. When the boundary is used, a title is placed either at the top inside or bottom inside of the boundary. The boundary depicts the scope of the system, subsystem, or a business area being represented.

    IIBA®, *BABOK® Guide* V2.0, 2009, 111, 204

89. **c.** **Active/visible observation**

Active or visible observation or user task analysis is an alternative technique in which a business analyst might ask a user to participate in an exercise that simulates how he or she interacts with a system. The exercise allows a BA to document the processes and ask questions about the activities based on the user's experience in carefully crafted scenarios.

IIBA®, *BABOK® Guide* V2.0, 2009, 187

90. **d.** **When he or she is satisfied with how the communication plan is developed**

When a business analyst creates a communication plan, he or she must consider delivery methods, target audiences, how information will be received and stored, and the objectives for communicating the requirements. All of these outputs are considered during the Business Analysis Planning and Monitoring efforts, specifically during the Plan Business Analysis Communication activities.

IIBA®, *BABOK® Guide* V2.0, 2009, 37

91. **a.** **The complexity of the project**

The more complex a project is, then the greater the tendency there is toward a high number of requirements. The greater the number of requirements, then the higher the risk and the number of specialized resources. All these considerations combined may make the project unfeasible.

IIBA®, *BABOK® Guide* V2.0, 2009, 94–96

92. **b.** **Use the stakeholders' own terminology**

By using stakeholder terminology, you can avoid any misunderstandings that may prevent you from understanding the real business issues.

IIBA®, *BABOK® Guide* V2.0, 2009, 178

93. **c.** **Ensure that requirements have referable points to related solution artifacts and business requirements**

All requirements must demonstrate an intrinsic relationship to business and solution requirements, other artifacts, and solution components.

IIBA®, *BABOK® Guide* V2.0, 2009, 68

94. **c.** **Requirements structure**

The output produced after requirements have been organized is referred to as requirements structure. The requirements structure essentially serves as a "directory" of requirements to ensure all project team members are aware of the location of requirements and that all requirements and sets of requirements are in compliance with the overall scope of a solution.

IIBA®, *BABOK® Guide* V2.0, 2009, 108

95. **b.** **The project manager and business analyst were assigned "A" for requirements management.**

    Only one person should be designated as the decision maker or person accountable on a project for any given activity. In this case, the BA should be the sole person accountable for "requirements management."

    IIBA®, *BABOK® Guide* V2.0, 2009, 29

96. **b.** **Nonfunctional requirements**

    Requirements that do not directly relate to the behavior or functionality of the solution are often referred to as non-functional requirements. Non-functional requirements often describe the qualities a system must possess including ease of use, ease of navigation, etc.

    IIBA®, *BABOK® Guide* V2.0, 2009, 6

97. **a.** **Availability**

    If customers are only available for certain periods of time, then a plan-driven approach is probably most appropriate versus customer availability. Throughout the development of the solution, a change-driven approach may be in alignment with development needs.

    IIBA®, *BABOK® Guide* V2.0, 2009, 23, 192

98. **b.** **Profiles**

    Profiles, user classes, or roles can serve as input for the development of organizational models, process models, or even use cases.

    IIBA®, *BABOK® Guide* V2.0, 2009, 105

99. **c.** **Solution [constructed]**

    A solution can only be validated if it actually exists. It may or may not be physically operational within the sponsoring organization.

    IIBA®, *BABOK® Guide* V2.0, 2009, 134

100. **b.** **Solution scope**

    Solution scope is a required input into the planning and preparation of Elicitation activities, as it provides a business analyst with the context for the type of information, specifically business requirements, that will be necessary to elicit from stakeholders.

    IIBA®, *BABOK® Guide* V2.0, 2009, 54

101. **c.** **Systematic**

It is a generalization, but implementers very often are systematic in their approach to delivering solutions. Therefore, to appeal to their communication style, a business analyst should present requirements using bulleted lists and very clearly defined workflow models, such as swim lane diagrams and data flow diagrams.

IIBA®, *BABOK® Guide* V2.0, 2009, 117, 150

102. **c.** **Organizational process assets**

Organizational process assets are required as an input for the execution of stakeholder analysis activities.

IIBA®, *BABOK® Guide* V2.0, 2009, 24

103. **c.** **Functional decomposition**

Functional decomposition is a modeling technique for breaking an organizational unit into a finite group of associated parts where requirements may be represented for each group of parts.

IIBA®, *BABOK® Guide* V2.0, 2009, 106

104. **d.** **Problem resolution**

It is unlikely that a stakeholder will need to sign off on every aspect of the requirements activity. However, signing off on problem resolutions and the tracking of problems as they relate to or have an impact on solution scope are likely to require signatory authority.

IIBA®, *BABOK® Guide* V2.0, 2009, 51

105. **c.** **Stakeholder profiles**

Stakeholder profiles, including a RACI chart, stakeholder matrix or onion diagram, will provide insight into what is most important to the stakeholders and will help to determine the content that a business analyst needs to deliver during his or her presentation.

IIBA®, *BABOK® Guide* V2.0, 2009, 73–75

106. **b.** **Traceability**

Traceability is an activity that, depending on organization governance, requires a business analyst to demonstrate the linkage of one requirement to another and its interdependencies. This mapping further validates requirements and ensures that functionality in the design solution is not missed.

IIBA®, *BABOK® Guide* V2.0, 2009, 67–68

107. **b.**   **Tree diagram**

Goals are text-based requirements that can be easily decomposed to their lowest level of detail by using a tree diagram. In the *BABOK®* tree diagrams are cited as an element of functional decomposition.

IIBA®, *BABOK® Guide* V2.0, 2009, 83–85, 175

108. **b.**   **Eliciting requirements**

Elicitation is the term that refers to defining requirements. It means "to draw forth or bring out."

IIBA®, *BABOK® Guide* V2.0, 2009, 53

109. **b.**   **Business requirements**

Business requirements—the highest level of requirement that a business analyst seeks to develop—address such topics as goals, objectives, and measurements of success. Business requirements evolve from activities related to defining the business need and serve as a "requirement" to support all other Enterprise Analysis activities.

IIBA®, *BABOK® Guide* V2.0, 2009, 81–82

110. **a.**   **Objectives and audience**

Before doing anything else—including creating content—a business analyst must be 100 percent clear on the overall objective of his or her presentation and whom it will target. From there, explicit content will follow.

IIBA®, *BABOK® Guide* V2.0, 2009, 79

111. **c.**   **Individual who is affected by the project's outcome**

A stakeholder is an individual or group of individuals who are affected by or have influence over a project's outcome. Stakeholders include but are not limited to the following: sponsors, customers, end users, and external users. They are the primary source for requirements.

IIBA®, *BABOK® Guide* V2.0, 2009, 10, 232

112. **b.**   **Stakeholder concerns**

Stakeholder concerns are developed during Elicitation activities. They are issues identified by a business analyst that considers assumptions, constraints, risks, and any other information that may have a positive or negative impact on the desired deliverables.

IIBA®, *BABOK® Guide* V2.0, 2009, 61, 113

113. **d.** **Storyboarding**

Storyboarding is referred to as a type of prototyping technique in the *BABOK®*. To create storyboards, business analysts use common office tools to depict visually, step by step, how a user might interact with a system.

IIBA®, *BABOK® Guide* V2.0, 2009, 197

114. **d.** **Evolutionary prototype**

The evolutionary prototype allows a project team to incrementally refine requirements based on stakeholder feedback so that a system evolves its capabilities and software code until a working product is completely developed.

IIBA®, *BABOK® Guide* V2.0, 2009, 196–197

115. **a.** **Qualitative, quantitative**

Business goals are qualitative statements that identify business needs and opportunities. As business goals are decomposed into a more descriptive language and quantified, they become objectives. Objectives, according to the *BABOK®*, are statements that follow the pneumonic SMART—specific, measurable, achievable, relevant, and time-bound.

IIBA®, *BABOK® Guide* V2.0, 2009, 83–84

116. **c.** **Top-down costing**

Top-down costing is a high-level technique used to estimate a project based on very little information and is typically done at the beginning of a project to establish a high-level view of potential costs, referred to as a rough order of magnitude or analogous estimation.

IIBA®, *BABOK® Guide* V2.0, 2009, 170

117. **b.** **False**

Formal sign-off of requirements may be done electronically, verbally, or with a physical signature.

IIBA®, *BABOK® Guide* V2.0, 2009, 67

118. **b.** **Organizational process assets**

It is likely that organizational process assets will provide some insight and guidance on the types of tools, guidelines, templates, and supporting documentation necessary to deliver a formal review of requirements.

IIBA®, *BABOK® Guide* V2.0, 2009, 66

119. **a.** **All In**

All In is an approach to the timeboxing/budgeting technique that requires a business analyst to assign requirements for prioritization based on assignment of requirements according to their assigned duration and cost, and removal of those requirements that are outside the scope of both budget and time constraints. All Out is a process of adding requirements until both budget and time limitations are reached. The Selective approach seeks to evaluate requirements with assigned costs and time constraints until both are satisfied.

IIBA®, *BABOK® Guide* V2.0, 2009, 102

120. **d.** **Stakeholder analysis**

It is during stakeholder analysis activities where groups of stakeholders that share common business needs, goals and objectives, roles, responsibilities, and expected participation at certain intervals during the development of the solutions are identified.

IIBA®, *BABOK® Guide* V2.0, 2009, 24

121. **a.** **Backwards traceability**

Backwards traceability is often referred to as a derivation or the demonstration of traceability from where a requirement originated.

IIBA®, *BABOK® Guide* V2.0, 2009, 68

122. **a.** **The evaluation of solution performance**

The intention of evaluating solution performance is to ensure that the solution is performing as prescribed post-implementation. This includes its use or lack of use by those affected by the solution and evaluating the degree of adopting such things that include, but are not limited to, policies, procedures, and business rules.

IIBA®, *BABOK® Guide* V2.0, 2009, 137

123. **b.** **Focus groups**

Focus groups are an elicitation technique intended to capture qualitative data, in the form of reaction, ideas, and attitudes of a group, for a solution that may be in the process of being understood, designed, or developed.

IIBA®, *BABOK® Guide* V2.0, 2009, 129, 172

124. **a.** **Stakeholder requirements**

COTS-based solutions often target a very specific group or groups of stakeholders with multiple versions of their offerings. Consider this example: Microsoft® operating systems and application suites typically have three to four target audiences: home, office, enterprise, and/or school-related versions. Each addresses different stakeholder requirements and specifications.

IIBA®, *BABOK® Guide* V2.0, 2009, 5

125. **b.** **During Requirements Analysis**

Requirements Analysis is the sequence of activities that would likely follow the elicitation of requirements according to the *BABOK® Guide* V2.0.

IIBA®, *BABOK® Guide* V2.0, 2009, 53–54

126. **b.** **Prototyping**

Prototypes are intended to provide the user a snapshot of the potential system and to elicit feedback about his or her experience. Screen shots and report layouts are a couple of tools that a prototype may offer.

IIBA®, *BABOK® Guide* V2.0, 2009, 196

127. **a.** **Requirements [approved]**

Requirements agreed to and signed by all respective stakeholders is an output necessary to drive forward any subsequent business analysis activities.

IIBA®, *BABOK® Guide* V2.0, 2009, 67

128. **c.** **Fishbone diagram**

A fishbone diagram may also be referred to as an Ishikawa diagram or a cause-and-effect diagram. It may be used as a result of the validation of a solution when defects have been found so that the source of a defect may be identified and resolved accordingly.

IIBA®, *BABOK® Guide* V2.0, 2009, 136, 203

129. **c.** **Stakeholder requirement**

Stakeholder requirements describe the needs of stakeholders and how they will interact with a proposed solution. Needs are further decomposed and analyzed through requirements analysis and elicitation techniques.

IIBA®, *BABOK® Guide* V2.0, 2009, 5

130. c. Quality of service requirements

Quality of service requirements or nonfunctional requirements are considered constraints and, as such, often do not have any direct effect on the functionality of the system. Environmental requirements, interface requirements, safety, and quality requirements are all categories into which nonfunctional requirements fit.

IIBA®, *BABOK® Guide* V2.0, 2009, 6

131. c. High-level description of the AS-IS and/or TO-BE models

The domain model can be used to describe the current and desired future state of the enterprise. It is used by the business analyst and stakeholders to ensure that they have an accurate understanding of the current state of the enterprise and to verify that stakeholders have a unified understanding of the proposed solution. It is generally considered to be a top-level data flow diagram used to define the scope and boundaries of a solution.

IIBA®, *BABOK® Guide* V2.0, 2009, 93, 206

132. a. Customers pay for the product and users interact with it

Simply put, customers (who can be grouped as internal or external customers, as well as other categories) will ultimately accept or pay for a product and reap the business benefit. Users will interact with a system either directly or indirectly and are more focused on the product's functionality. This is best depicted through the use of an onion diagram.

IIBA®, *BABOK® Guide* V2.0, 2009, 29-30

133. d. The type of information that you will present must appeal to a very specific audience

A homogeneous audience is made up of a group of stakeholders who all share common interests. For example, you may be asked to tailor your findings to the interests of the implementers who will likely want to know the success criteria for the project as well as any specification.

IIBA®, *BABOK® Guide* V2.0, 2009, 173

134. a. Developing a requirements communication plan

Developing a requirements communication plan will ensure that efforts, identified stakeholders, and the types of communication to be used are necessary to support collaboration with other projects that depend on the output of your project.

IIBA®, *BABOK® Guide* V2.0, 2009, 37

135. **b.** **Context diagram**

A context diagram provides enough information about a particular system and how it might interact with other internal or external systems.

IIBA®, *BABOK® Guide* V2.0, 2009, 162, 206–207

136. **d.** **Stakeholders' willingness to come to a consensus**

Bringing stakeholders to consensus on anything, from a glossary of terms to business rules and definition of the AS-IS and TO-BE state, is critical to ensuring a solution's feasibility and the delivery of goods and services that meet the overall business needs. Time frame, budget, and complexity of the project should have been determined during Enterprise Analysis activities. Stakeholder lists, roles and responsibilities are used as input for the planning of elicitation activities

IIBA®, *BABOK® Guide* V2.0, 2009, 54

137. **d.** **A means by which consensus will be reached**

A joint application design session or a requirements workshop must include a process by which a facilitator may bring a group to consensus. This process may include multivoting or delegation, negotiation, and other methods.

IIBA®, *BABOK® Guide* V2.0, 2009, 55, 198–199

138. **a.** **Requirement attributes**

A functional requirement and its attributes are in the example statement. Priority, ownership, and status are all cited in this attribute. A business analyst would likely document requirements attributes in a table format.

IIBA®, *BABOK® Guide* V2.0, 2009, 44–45

139. **a.** **A requirements package**

Requirements packages are delivered to targeted audiences. This specificity requires that their contents be carefully considered.

IIBA®, *BABOK® Guide* V2.0, 2009, 72

140. **b.** **Project costs**

Project costs are likely to evolve out of solution scope and are later refined during the Requirements Planning and Management activities.

IIBA®, *BABOK® Guide* V2.0, 2009, 93

141. **a.** **Document analysis**

Document analysis is an elicitation technique a business analyst would employ to understand the current state of an existing system or to compare one system with another or with solutions that share similar qualities.

IIBA®, *BABOK® Guide* V2.0, 2009, 53, 169

142. **d.** **What deliverables will be produced and when**

Depending on what solution development life cycle is used, a business analyst can determine the types of teams, deliverables, and times at which deliverables will be produced. An organization's solution development life cycle is likely to dictate the type of approach the development of requirements would take—change or plan driven.

IIBA®, *BABOK® Guide* V2.0, 2009, 18

143. **c.** **Decomposed business functions**

It is likely that Paul started decomposing the business units by creating a context diagram and then further decomposed them by major activities within those business units. Context diagrams have been identified by the *BABOK®* as a type of scope modeling.

IIBA®, *BABOK® Guide* V2.0, 2009, 93, 207

144. **a.** **Solution approach**

Solution approach is used as a general guideline to help a business analyst and stakeholders to consider options for implementation of a proposed solution. This information will likely guide the development of solution scope.

IIBA®, *BABOK® Guide* V2.0, 2009, 93

145. **a.** **Purpose and deadline**

By providing an explanation and deadline to complete the questionnaire, you will receive more accurate data and will achieve a better response rate.

IIBA®, *BABOK® Guide* V2.0, 2009, 214

146. **c.** **Organizational change**

Transition requirements consider organizational change and the impact that will be realized by the people affected either directly or indirectly by the solution. New skills, new resources, and new job functions may all be proposed recommendations where transition requirements are concerned.

IIBA®, *BABOK® Guide* V2.0, 2009, 133

147. **c.** **Software requirements specification (SRS)**

A software requirements specification (SRS) document describes its implementers' specifications or behaviors required for a system to satisfy a stakeholder's needs.

IIBA®, *BABOK® Guide* V2.0, 2009, 75–76

148. **c.** **Can only be developed after the solution has been defined**

Transition requirements are unique in that they only can be defined after a solution has been defined. They are also considered temporary requirements as their lifespan is only as long as it takes to implement the proposed solution. After implementation, the requirements are no longer useful or relevant.

IIBA®, *BABOK® Guide* V2.0, 2009, 131

149. **b.** **Process model**

Process models (and, specifically in this question, flowcharts) may be used to identify current and future state changes to existing activities and the magnitude of changes that they may impose on stakeholders and the business.

IIBA®, *BABOK® Guide* V2.0, 2009, 129, 193

150. **b.** **Five**

The *BABOK® Guide* V2.0 identifies five requirement types: business requirements, stakeholder requirements, functional requirements, non-functional requirements, and transition requirements.

IIBA®, *BABOK® Guide* V2.0, 2009, 5–6

APPENDIX

STUDY MATRIX

OVERVIEW

The *Business Analysis Body of Knowledge (BABOK® Guide)* version 2.0 serves as the foundation for the International Institute of Business Analysis (IIBA®) Certified Business Analysis Professional™ (CBAP®) certification examination. *BABOK® Guide* V2.0 and other texts cited in the References section serve as the foundation for our two 150-question practice tests. Note that a great deal of the references used in the development of the exams here are also cited in the bibliography of the *BABOK® Guide* V2.0.

The distribution of our two practice tests is as follows:

I	Business Analysis Planning and Monitoring	19.33% or 29 questions
II	Elicitation	14% or 21 questions
III	Requirements Management and Communication	16% or 24 questions
IV	Enterprise Analysis	15.33% or 23 questions
V	Requirements Analysis	19.33% or 29 questions
VI	Solution Assessment and Validation	16% or 24 questions
		150 questions

The matrixes for both practice tests are included following this Appendix and identify each practice test question according to its performance knowledge area for the relevant practice test.

The matrixes are designed to help you to—

❖ Assess your strengths and weaknesses in each of the performance knowledge areas

❖ Identify those areas in which you need additional study before you take the CBAP® exam

Here is an easy way to use the matrix:

Step 1 Circle all the questions that you missed on the practice test in Column 1.

Step 2 For each circled question, note the corresponding knowledge area in Column 2.

Step 3 To determine whether any patterns emerge indicating weak areas, tally the information that you obtained from the matrix.

Step 4 To ensure that you have a good understanding of the knowledge and skills required to perform the major tasks that are included in each of the knowledge areas, we strongly suggest that you use *BABOK® Guide* V2.0 for study purposes. This is available online at IIBA's website: **www.theiiba.org**.

The last column in the matrix is provided for your notes.

STUDY MATRIX—PRACTICE TEST 1

Practice Test Question Number	Knowledge Area	Study Notes
1	Requirements Management and Communication	
2	Solution Assessment and Validation	
3	Enterprise Analysis	
4	Requirements Analysis	
5	Business Analysis Planning and Monitoring	
6	Business Analysis Planning and Monitoring	
7	Business Analysis Planning and Monitoring	
8	General	
9	Requirements Analysis	
10	Requirements Management and Communication	
11	Requirements Analysis	
12	Business Analysis Planning and Monitoring	
13	General	
14	Business Analysis Planning and Monitoring	
15	Requirements Management and Communication	

Practice Test Question Number	Knowledge Area	Study Notes
16	Elicitation	
17	Business Analysis Planning and Monitoring	
18	Solution Assessment and Validation	
19	Requirements Analysis	
20	Requirements Analysis	
21	Elicitation	
22	Business Analysis Planning and Monitoring	
23	Requirements Analysis	
24	Requirements Analysis	
25	General	
26	Solution Assessment and Validation	
27	Business Analysis Planning and Monitoring	
28	Business Analysis Planning and Monitoring	
29	Elicitation	
30	Elicitation	
31	Elicitation	

Practice Test Question Number	Knowledge Area	Study Notes
32	Requirements Management and Communication	
33	General	
34	Solution Assessment and Validation	
35	Requirements Analysis	
36	Business Analysis Planning and Monitoring	
37	Elicitation	
38	Solution Assessment and Validation	
39	Requirements Analysis	
40	Enterprise Analysis	
41	Business Analysis Planning and Monitoring	
42	General	
43	Elicitation	
44	Requirements Management and Communication	
45	General	
46	General	
47	Business Analysis Planning and Monitoring	

Practice Test Question Number	Knowledge Area	Study Notes
48	Requirements Analysis	
49	Enterprise Analysis	
50	Elicitation	
51	Elicitation	
52	Requirements Management and Communication	
53	Enterprise Analysis	
54	Requirements Management and Communication	
55	Business Analysis Planning and Monitoring	
56	Business Analysis Planning and Monitoring	
57	General	
58	Elicitation	
59	Enterprise Analysis	
60	Requirements Analysis	
61	Business Analysis Planning and Monitoring	
62	Solution Assessment and Validation	
63	Elicitation	

Practice Test Question Number	Knowledge Area	Study Notes
64	Business Analysis Planning and Monitoring	
65	Requirements Analysis	
66	Solution Assessment and Validation	
67	Requirements Management and Communication	
68	General	
69	General	
70	Solution Assessment and Validation	
71	Business Analysis Planning and Monitoring	
72	Requirements Analysis	
73	Solution Assessment and Validation	
74	Elicitation	
75	Business Analysis Planning and Monitoring	
76	Elicitation	
77	General	
78	Business Analysis Planning and Monitoring	
79	Elicitation	

Practice Test Question Number	Knowledge Area	Study Notes
80	Business Analysis Planning and Monitoring	
81	Solution Assessment and Validation	
82	Requirements Management and Communication	
83	Enterprise Analysis	
84	Enterprise Analysis	
85	Requirements Management and Communication	
86	General	
87	Requirements Management and Communication	
88	General	
89	Requirements Analysis	
90	Enterprise Analysis	
91	Elicitation	
92	Enterprise Analysis	
93	Requirements Management and Communication	
94	Requirements Analysis	
95	Enterprise Analysis	

Practice Test Question Number	Knowledge Area	Study Notes
96	Requirements Analysis	
97	Requirements Management and Communication	
98	Requirements Management and Communication	
99	General	
100	Business Analysis Planning and Monitoring	
101	General	
102	Business Analysis Planning and Monitoring	
103	Solution Assessment and Validation	
104	Business Analysis Planning and Monitoring	
105	Business Analysis Planning and Monitoring	
106	Elicitation	
107	Enterprise Analysis	
108	Requirements Analysis	
109	Requirements Management and Communication	
110	General	
111	Business Analysis Planning and Monitoring	

Practice Test Question Number	Knowledge Area	Study Notes
112	Requirements Analysis	
113	General	
114	General	
115	Requirements Analysis	
116	Business Analysis Planning and Monitoring	
117	Business Analysis Planning and Monitoring	
118	Requirements Analysis	
119	Business Analysis Planning and Monitoring	
120	Business Analysis Planning and Monitoring	
121	Requirements Management and Communication	
122	Requirements Analysis	
123	Requirements Management and Communication	
124	Business Analysis Planning and Monitoring	
125	Business Analysis Planning and Monitoring	
126	Elicitation	
127	Requirements Management and Communication	

Practice Test Question Number	Knowledge Area	Study Notes
128	Solution Assessment and Validation	
129	Requirements Management and Communication	
130	Elicitation	
131	Elicitation	
132	General	
133	Requirements Management and Communication	
134	Enterprise Analysis	
135	Requirements Analysis	
136	Requirements Analysis	
137	Elicitation	
138	Enterprise Analysis	
139	Elicitation	
140	Requirements Analysis	
141	Business Analysis Planning and Monitoring	
142	Enterprise Analysis	
143	Requirements Analysis	

Practice Test Question Number	Knowledge Area	Study Notes
144	Elicitation	
145	Business Analysis Planning and Monitoring	
146	Solution Assessment and Validation	
147	Requirements Analysis	
148	Solution Assessment and Validation	
149	Business Analysis Planning and Monitoring	
150	Requirements Analysis	

Study Matrix—Practice Test 2

Practice Test Question Number	Knowledge Area	Study Notes
1	Requirements Analysis	
2	Requirements Analysis	
3	Elicitation	
4	Solution Assessment and Validation	
5	Business Analysis Planning and Monitoring	
6	Enterprise Analysis	
7	General	
8	Elicitation	
9	Solution Assessment and Validation	
10	Requirements Management and Communication	
11	Requirements Analysis	
12	Business Analysis Planning and Monitoring	
13	Business Analysis Planning and Monitoring	
14	Requirements Management and Communication	
15	General	

Practice Test Question Number	Knowledge Area	Study Notes
16	Business Analysis Planning and Monitoring	
17	Business Analysis Planning and Monitoring	
18	Business Analysis Planning and Monitoring	
19	Elicitation	
20	Business Analysis Planning and Monitoring	
21	General	
22	Business Analysis Planning and Monitoring	
23	Enterprise Analysis	
24	Elicitation	
25	Requirements Analysis	
26	Requirements Analysis	
27	Business Analysis Planning and Monitoring	
28	Requirements Analysis	
29	Elicitation	
30	Enterprise Analysis	
31	Business Analysis Planning and Monitoring	

Practice Test Question Number	Knowledge Area	Study Notes
32	Requirements Management and Communication	
33	Business Analysis Planning and Monitoring	
34	Solution Assessment and Validation	
35	Requirements Analysis	
36	Business Analysis Planning and Monitoring	
37	Solution Assessment and Validation	
38	Requirements Analysis	
39	Elicitation	
40	Business Analysis Planning and Monitoring	
41	General	
42	Business Analysis Planning and Monitoring	
43	General	
44	Requirements Management and Communication	
45	Solution Assessment and Validation	
46	Enterprise Analysis	
47	Requirements Management and Communication	

Practice Test Question Number	Knowledge Area	Study Notes
48	Requirements Analysis	
49	Enterprise Analysis	
50	Requirements Management and Communication	
51	Solution Assessment and Validation	
52	General	
53	Enterprise Analysis	
54	Requirements Analysis	
55	Elicitation	
56	Business Analysis Planning and Monitoring	
57	General	
58	Requirements Analysis	
59	Business Analysis Planning and Monitoring	
60	Business Analysis Planning and Monitoring	
61	Elicitation	
62	Requirements Analysis	
63	Elicitation	

Practice Test Question Number	Knowledge Area	Study Notes
64	Business Analysis Planning and Monitoring	
65	Requirements Management and Communication	
66	Solution Assessment and Validation	
67	Requirements Analysis	
68	Requirements Management and Communication	
69	Elicitation	
70	General	
71	Requirements Management and Communication	
72	Elicitation	
74	Elicitation	
74	Requirements Analysis	
75	Requirements Management and Communication	
76	Requirements Management and Communication	
77	Enterprise Analysis	
78	Requirements Management and Communication	
79	Elicitation	

Practice Test Question Number	Knowledge Area	Study Notes
80	Requirements Analysis	
81	Solution Assessment and Validation	
82	Enterprise Analysis	
83	Elicitation	
84	Business Analysis Planning and Monitoring	
85	Requirements Analysis	
86	General	
87	Solution Assessment and Validation	
88	Requirements Analysis	
89	Elicitation	
90	Business Analysis Planning and Monitoring	
91	Enterprise Analysis	
92	Elicitation	
93	Requirements Management and Communication	
94	Requirements Analysis	
95	Business Analysis Planning and Monitoring	

Practice Test Question Number	Knowledge Area	Study Notes
96	General	
97	Business Analysis Planning and Monitoring	
98	Requirements Analysis	
99	Solution Assessment and Validation	
100	Elicitation	
101	Requirements Analysis	
102	Business Analysis Planning and Monitoring	
103	Requirements Analysis	
104	Elicitation	
105	Business Analysis Planning and Monitoring	
106	Requirements Management and Communication	
107	Enterprise Analysis	
108	Elicitation	
109	Enterprise Analysis	
110	Requirements Management and Communication	
111	General	

Practice Test Question Number	Knowledge Area	Study Notes
112	Elicitation	
113	Elicitation	
114	Elicitation	
115	Enterprise Analysis	
116	General	
117	Requirements Management and Communication	
118	Requirements Management and Communication	
119	Requirements Analysis	
120	Business Analysis Planning and Monitoring	
121	Requirements Management and Communication	
122	Solution Assessment and Validation	
123	Solution Assessment and Validation	
124	General	
125	Elicitation	
126	Elicitation	
127	Requirements Management and Communication	

Practice Test Question Number	Knowledge Area	Study Notes
128	Solution Assessment and Validation	
129	General	
130	General	
131	Enterprise Analysis	
132	Business Analysis Planning and Monitoring	
133	Elicitation	
134	Requirements Management and Communication	
135	Enterprise Analysis	
136	Elicitation	
137	Elicitation	
138	Business Analysis Planning and Monitoring	
139	Requirements Management and Communication	
140	Enterprise Analysis	
141	Elicitation	
142	Business Analysis Planning and Monitoring	
143	Enterprise Analysis	

Practice Test Question Number	Knowledge Area	Study Notes
144	Enterprise Analysis	
145	Elicitation	
146	Solution Assessment and Validation	
147	Requirements Management and Communication	
148	Solution Assessment and Validation	
149	Solution Assessment and Validation	
150	General	

REFERENCES

Ambler, Scott W. *The Elements of UML™ 2.0 Style*. New York: Cambridge University Press, 2005.

Brûlé, Glenn. *Business Analysis Terms: A Working Glossary*. Arlington, VA: ESI International, 2009.

International Institute of Business Analysis (IIBA®). *Business Analysis Body of Knowledge® (BABOK® Guide)*. Version 2.0. Toronto: International Institute of Business Analysis, 2009.

_____. *Certified Business Analysis Professional® (CBAP®) Handbook*. Toronto: International Institute of Business Analysis, 2008.

Ward, J. LeRoy. *Dictionary of Project Management Terms*. 3rd ed. Arlington, VA: ESI International, 2008.

Also From ESI International

Business Analysis Terms: A Working Glossary

First edition. 2009. 220 pages. $29.95

Glenn R. Brûlé, CBAP, CSM

Over the past few decades, business analysis has steadily developed into a widely recognized global discipline. Now, more than ever, business analysts must communicate clearly and unambiguously, choosing words that need no further interpretation. This convenient reference will help you and your team establish a common business analysis language that conveys universally understood meaning and context. It contains more than 1,600 definitions, phrases, and acronyms used in day-to-day business analysis that are essential to today's business analyst.

Risk Management: Concepts and Guidance

Fourth edition. 2010. 448 pages. $58.95.

Carl L. Pritchard, PMP

Gain a higher-level perspective on risk management. This fourth edition contains 35 tool-packed chapters focusing on a systematic approach to risk management. It highlights specific techniques to enhance organizational risk identification, assessment, and management.

PMP® Exam: Practice Test and Study Guide

Eighth edition. 2009. 400 pages. $44.95.

J. LeRoy Ward, PMP, PgMP and Ginger Levin, D.P.A., PMP, PgMP

This rigorous study guide provides 40 multiple-choice questions in each of the nine knowledge areas and the professional and social responsibility domain plus a composite 200-question practice test intended to simulate the PMP® certification exam. All answers are fully referenced and keyed to the five project management process groups. Also included is a bibliography and a study matrix to help you to focus on specific areas.

DICTIONARY OF PROJECT MANAGEMENT TERMS

Also available in Kindle format!

Third edition. 2008. 512 pages. $39.95.

J. LeRoy Ward, PMP, PgMP

Now in its third edition, this practical, pocket-sized book is more than 200 pages longer and includes 1,400 more terms than its last edition. The *Dictionary of Project Management Terms* contains 3,400 key terms, words, and phrases used in the day-to-day practice of project management. Along with traditional project management terms, it includes broader business terms to help seasoned managers and their successors navigate more easily the ubiquitous language of project-speak. You will find that the *Dictionary of Project Management Terms* provides you with a distinct advantage on every project you face.

THE COMPLETE PROJECT MANAGEMENT OFFICE HANDBOOK

Second edition. 2007. 752 pages. $89.99.

Gerard M. Hill, PMP

This handbook offers a structured approach for developing critical project management capabilities through project management office (PMO) functionality. It describes 20 PMO functions that are crucial to defining and developing an effective approach to project oversight, control, and support.

PMP® EXAM ONLINE PRACTICE TEST

$39.95.

This 200-question, Web-based practice test precisely follows the PMI® PMP® exam blueprint. You will answer the same number of questions in each of the *PMBOK® Guide* process areas as on the actual exam, including the professional responsibility domain. And the questions are just like the ones that you will see on the real exam. After logging in, you are given exactly four hours to take the exam, and the results are automatically scored, telling you the number of right and wrong answers in each of the process areas tested. Don't use the real exam as your first "practice" test. Rather, reduce your anxiety and let ESI help you succeed. Together with our other proven PMP® exam study tools, this Web-based practice test will greatly increase your chances of passing the PMP® exam.

THE PORTABLE PMP® EXAM PREP: CONVERSATIONS ON PASSING THE PMP® EXAM

Three volumes, nine CDs. Fourth edition. $109.95.

Carl L. Pritchard, PMP and J. LeRoy Ward, PMP, PgMP

This three-volume set of nine CDs addresses the nine areas of the project management body of knowledge and professional responsibility, and includes a bonus session on test-taking tips. Ward and Pritchard's informative, engaging style is easy to listen to, plus you can take the CDs anywhere you go.

PMP® Exam Challenge!

Fifth edition. 2009. 614 pages. $48.95.

J. LeRoy Ward, PMP, PgMP and Ginger Levin, D.P.A., PMP, PgMP

This easy-to-use, flashcard-format book lets you quiz yourself on all nine of the project management knowledge areas, as well as the professional and social responsibility domain. Each of the 600 questions includes references to the five project management process groups on the PMP® certification exam.

The Project Management Drill Book: A Self-Study Guide

2003. 197 pages. $54.95.

Carl L. Pritchard, PMP

Gear up for the PMP® certification exam! Learn project management one drill at a time. ESI's *Project Management Drill Book* provides a provocative way to challenge you with hundreds of project management practice drills. From earned value to expected value, from precedence diagrams to decision trees and from the WBS to professional responsibility, this data-packed volume builds your understanding of the language and confidence in the practice of project management. Multiple-choice, fill-in-the-blank, and true-or-false drills deepen your understanding of available project management tools and how to use them effectively.

ESI's Real-Time Source™

ESI's Real-Time Source™ provides quick and easy access to ESI's project management and business analysis concepts, tools, templates, and terms. With dynamic search functionality and a comprehensive glossary of terms, ESI's Real-Time Source enables you to find exactly what you need, including just-in-time project resources, phrases and keywords, templates and tools, *PMBOK® Guide* and *BABOK® Guide* knowledge areas, and key content from many of ESI's project management and business analysis courses.

ESI's Real-Time Source is available through individual annual subscriptions or corporate licensing subscriptions based on the number of users. To learn more, visit **www.esi-intl.com/source**.

Precedence Diagramming: Successful Scheduling in a Team Environment

Second edition. 2002. 62 pages. $25.00.

Carl Pritchard, PMP

The biggest challenge in project management is bringing order to the sheer volume of competing priorities. By using precedence diagrams, project managers can clearly identify the sequence and interdependence of critical activities, clarify work processes and solidify team member roles and buy-in.

This concise overview teaches you how to construct and interpret precedence diagrams—the most common model used in software programs—and apply them to strengthen team commitment and project success.

Individual and Organizational Assessments

Whether you're focusing on individual capabilities, or measuring the knowledge and skills of your organization as a whole, ESI has assessment services to help you identify strengths and areas that need improvement.

Individual Assessments

By assessing individual competencies for each employee, you can more effectively target your training efforts, set pre- and post-course benchmarks to measure success and determine areas in which training reinforcement is necessary.

Our **appraisal products** provide a snapshot of your team's grasp of best-in-class methods and techniques. This ensures that your employees are receiving the training they need and that you're getting the most from your training dollars.

ESI can also help you assess employee competency beyond technical knowledge. Our **360-degree evaluation** measures project manager's hard and soft skills and provides detailed reports of their effectiveness in these key categories:

❖ Organizational and industry acumen

❖ Process expertise

❖ Customer focus

❖ Team leadership, communications and effectiveness

Organizational Assessments

ESI's **organizational maturity assessments** help assess the maturity and capability of your organization and provide recommendations on how to improve efficiency and effectiveness. By assessing organizational performance, you can ensure that you have the systems and processes in place to efficiently complete your projects on time and on budget while also identifying obstacles in the way of success.

With ESI's data-driven assessment models, you can—

❖ Analyze your project managers' performance within your organization

❖ Baseline project management capability

❖ Identify organizational executive-level involvement

❖ Develop short- and long-term improvement strategies

In addition to conducting organizational maturity assessments, ESI has a proven track record in conducting **Level 3 Training Assessments**, which can help you gain insight into how much of your employees' new knowledge is being applied back on the job after their training is complete. You'll be able to evaluate the value of your investment and identify the key catalysts for success and the key obstacles that often lead to below-par results.

For more information about ESI's individual and organizational assessments, please call **+1 (877)766-3337** or **+1 (703) 558-4445** or email **totalsolutions@esi-intl.com.**

COMPLIMENTARY RESOURCES FROM ESI

ESI offers a number of useful, free tools and resources covering essential topics such as:

- ❖ Managing Projects and Programs
- ❖ Building Business Analysis Competencies
- ❖ Developing Critical "Soft Skills"
- ❖ Applying Earned Value Management

WHITE PAPERS, INDUSTRY REPORTS, AND ESI VIEWPOINTS

What are the top challenges, trends and issues affecting you and your organization? From saving troubled projects to mitigating the unique risks in outsourcing to navigating acquisition reform, ESI provides expert analysis of these and many other topics. ESI's white papers, industry reports and ViewPoints bring the perspective of nearly 30 years of experience working with best-in-class global companies and most U.S. government agencies, plus our industry-leading subject matter experts. Download one today at **www.esi-intl.com/resources**.

PODCASTS

Download ESI podcasts to your MP3 player for free and listen to them in the office, at the gym, on a plane or anywhere else in the world. Project managers and business analysts who listen to these podcasts are eligible for Self Directed Learning (SDL) PDUs from the Project Management Institute (PMI®). Visit **www.esi-intl.com/podcast** today.

WEBINARS

Watch on-demand presentations online from top industry experts on the issues you deal with daily on the job. Project managers, business analysts, contract managers and program managers will find these online seminars valuable to their professional development. ESI's library of on-demand webinars are available any time you want, as often as you want. Download a webinar today at **www.esi-intl.com/webinar**.

ESI HORIZONS NEWSLETTER

ESI Horizons is a free, monthly newsletter focusing on issues, processes and challenges in project management and business analysis. As a subscriber, you'll receive an e-mail notification each month when the newest issue is live. You'll also have access to the Horizons archives, where you can view past articles. Subscribe today!

Americas: **www.esi-intl.com/horizons** EMEA: **www.esi-emea.com** Asia: **www.esi-intl.com.sg**